Staatsverständnisse | Understanding the State

edited by
Rüdiger Voigt

Volume 146

Günther Grewendorf [ed.]

Chomsky on State
and Democracy

 **Nomos**

The Deutsche Nationalbibliothek lists this publication in the
Deutsche Nationalbibliografie; detailed bibliographic data
are available on the Internet at http://dnb.d-nb.de

ISBN   978-3-8487-7757-0 (Print)
        978-3-7489-2377-0 (ePDF)

British Library Cataloguing-in-Publication Data
A catalogue record for this book is available from the British Library.

ISBN   978-3-8487-7757-0 (Print)
        978-3-7489-2377-0 (ePDF)

Library of Congress Cataloging-in-Publication Data
Grewendorf, Günther
Chomsky on State and Democracy
Günther Grewendorf (ed.)
236 pp.
Includes bibliographic references.

ISBN   978-3-8487-7757-0 (Print)
        978-3-7489-2377-0 (ePDF)

Onlineversion
Nomos eLibrary

1st Edition 2021
© Nomos Verlagsgesellschaft, Baden-Baden, Germany 2021. Overall responsibility
for Manufacturing (printing and production) lies with Nomos Verlagsgesellschaft mbH
& Co. KG.

Editorial

Das Staatsverständnis hat sich im Laufe der Jahrhunderte immer wieder grundlegend gewandelt. Wir sind Zeugen einer Entwicklung, an deren Ende die Auflösung der uns bekannten Form des territorial definierten Nationalstaates zu stehen scheint. Denn die Globalisierung führt nicht nur zu ökonomischen und technischen Veränderungen, sondern sie hat vor allem auch Auswirkungen auf die Staatlichkeit. Ob die „Entgrenzung der Staatenwelt" jemals zu einem Weltstaat führen wird, ist allerdings zweifelhaft. Umso interessanter sind die Theorien früherer und heutiger Staatsdenker, deren Modelle und Theorien, aber auch Utopien, uns Einblick in den Prozess der Entstehung und des Wandels von Staatsverständnissen geben.

Auf die Staatsideen von Platon und Aristoteles, auf denen alle Überlegungen über den Staat basieren, wird unter dem Leitthema „Wiederaneignung der Klassiker" immer wieder zurückzukommen sein. Der Schwerpunkt der in der Reihe *Staatsverständnisse* veröffentlichten Arbeiten liegt allerdings auf den neuzeitlichen Ideen vom Staat. Dieses Spektrum reicht von dem Altmeister *Niccolò Machiavelli*, der wie kein Anderer den engen Zusammenhang zwischen Staatstheorie und Staatspraxis verkörpert, über *Thomas Hobbes*, den Vater des Leviathan, bis hin zu *Karl Marx*, den sicher einflussreichsten Staatsdenker der Neuzeit, und schließlich zu den zeitgenössischen Staatstheoretikern.

Nicht nur die Verfälschung der Marxschen Ideen zu einer marxistischen Ideologie, die einen repressiven Staatsapparat rechtfertigen sollte, macht deutlich, dass Theorie und Praxis des Staates nicht auf Dauer voneinander zu trennen sind. Auch die Verstrickung Carl Schmitts in die nationalsozialistischen Machenschaften, die heute sein Bild als führender Staatsdenker seiner Epoche trüben, weisen in diese Richtung. Auf eine Analyse moderner Staatspraxis kann daher in diesem Zusammenhang nicht verzichtet werden.

Was ergibt sich daraus für ein zeitgemäßes Verständnis des Staates im Sinne einer modernen Staatswissenschaft? Die Reihe *Staatsverständnisse* richtet sich mit dieser Fragestellung nicht nur an (politische) Philosophen und Philosophinnen, sondern auch an Geistes- und Sozialwissenschaftler bzw. -wissenschaftlerinnen. In den Beiträgen wird daher zum einen der Anschluss an den allgemeinen Diskurs hergestellt, zum anderen werden die wissenschaftlichen Erkenntnisse in klarer und aussagekräftiger Sprache – mit dem Mut zur Pointierung – vorgetragen. Auf diese Weise wird der Leser/die Leserin direkt mit dem Problem konfrontiert, den Staat zu verstehen.

Prof. Dr. Rüdiger Voigt

Editorial – Understanding the State

Throughout the course of history, our understanding of the state has fundamentally changed time and again. It appears as though we are witnessing a development which will culminate in the dissolution of the territorially defined nation state as we know it, for globalisation is not only leading to changes in the economy and technology, but also, and above all, affects statehood. It is doubtful, however, whether the erosion of borders worldwide will lead to a global state, but what is perhaps of greater interest are the ideas of state theorists, whose models, theories and utopias offer us an insight into how different understandings of the state have emerged and changed, processes which neither began with globalisation, nor will end with it.

When researchers concentrate on reappropriating traditional ideas about the state, it is inevitable that they will continuously return to those of Plato and Aristotle, upon which all reflections on the state are based. However, the works published in this series focus on more contemporary ideas about the state, whose spectrum ranges from those of the doyen *Niccolò Machiavelli*, who embodies the close connection between the theory and practice of the state more than any other thinker, to those of *Thomas Hobbes*, the creator of Leviathan, those of *Karl Marx*, who is without doubt the most influential modern state theorist, those of the Weimar state theorists *Carl Schmitt, Hans Kelsen* and *Hermann Heller*, and finally to those of contemporary theorists.

Not only does the corruption of Marx's ideas into a Marxist ideology intended to justify a repressive state underline the fact that state theory and practice cannot be permanently regarded as two separate entities, but so does Carl Schmitt's involvement in the manipulation conducted by the National Socialists, which today tarnishes his image as the leading state theorist of his era. Therefore, we cannot forego analysing modern state practice.

How does all this enable modern political science to develop a contemporary understanding of the state? This series of publications does not only address this question to (political) philosophers, but also, and above all, students of humanities and social sciences. The works it contains therefore acquaint the reader with the general debate, on the one hand, and present their research findings clearly and informatively, not to mention incisively and bluntly, on the other. In this way, the reader is ushered directly into the problem of understanding the state.

Prof. Dr. Rüdiger Voigt

Acknowledgment

I would like to thank Ron Orders and Audrey Battersby for help and encouragement, and Christie Brown for allowing me to use an image of her wonderful sculpture on the front cover.

Inhaltsverzeichnis

Introduction

Human Nature and the Emergence of Social Institutions

The Relation of the Individual to the State and the Gist of Anarchism

Human Rights and the Notion of Freedom

State Power and Resistance

Introduction

Günther Grewendorf

Interview with Noam Chomsky on State and Democracy

(1)

Günther Grewendorf:
Your linguistic research led to revolutionary views on the nature of language, the properties of the human mind, and the uniqueness of human nature. Although you are rather cautious when it comes to the question of whether there is a connection between your linguistic studies and your political analyses, you do not completely deny that your political views on the notion of freedom, the role of the state and the function of democracy are closely related to your insights into the essence of human nature.In what way is your notion of state and democracy inspired by your linguistic ideas?

Noam Chomsky:
It's hard to disentangle. My general ideas on socioeconomic issues trace back to early childhood. I didn't start thinking seriously about linguistics until college, and soon began to regard my own developing ideas as a kind of private hobby. After a few years I began to find the hobby more interesting than prevailing conceptions. It's hard to miss the fact that ordinary language use is fundamentally creative in ways that go far beyond the standard notions of habit and analogy that were prevalent among linguists, let alone the behaviorist doctrines that were virtual dogma in the Cambridge environment that I entered in 1951. At that point the two domains – socioeconomic-political, linguistic-philosophical – began to intermingle, but I had no conscious awareness of interaction beyond that. Connections became more salient as I began to learn more about the history of these ideas, also a private hobby.

(2)

Günther Grewendorf:
In one of the "Barsamian Interviews" of 1988 (edited by Carlos Otero) you describe the state system as a "very artificial system" imposed on societies by force and economic and hegemonial interests and being unrelated to human needs. But you add that we "shouldn't expect it to be permanent". As an alternative you advocate an anarchistic concept of the state in the sense of Bakunin's theory of state. Do you see

any tendency in the history of the world that artificial and autocratic states come to an end and are replaced by egalitarian social organisations of free human beings which allow the individuals to develop their creative potentials?

Noam Chomsky:

Seems to me a matter of more or less, not yes or no. It goes too far to say that states are "unrelated to human needs." There has been a slow and uneven transition over time, not without regression, to social and political systems more influenced by popular pressures for more freedom and democracy. The ideal that you describe is approached in some social arrangements, but sporadically.

(3)

Günther Grewendorf:

Turning to the current situation and the role of the state in times of a worldwide catastrophe like the corona crisis. Despite numerous warnings the majority of states were not prepared for a pandemic like this. Instead of guaranteeing the health of the citizens by increasing the capacities of hospitals and intensive care units, providing medical infrastructure and health care systems, the state has strengthened the economy, supported the needs of corporations, lowered the costs of labor, encouraged globalized outsourcing of essential medical products like medicine, masks, respirators and protective suits. Now we find ourselves in the middle of an overwhelming catastrophe and have to face the failure of the state to take care of the health of the citizens instead of the profit of corporations. But given this situation it emerges that only the state is capable of handling and overcoming a crisis of such a scale. Do you think that on the basis of the conception of state that you propagate it will be possible for the state to take the measures required to manage (and to avoid) crises of this kind?

Noam Chomsky:

In state capitalist societies like ours, we cannot expect private powers to undertake the task of serving the public interest, surely not in the neoliberal period governed by the dictum that it is the duty of the corporation to maximize the wealth of (overwhelmingly rich) shareholders and management. With occasional exceptions, mostly for reputational reasons, they seek profit and market share. The only other institution with resources and large-scale planning options is the state. And states reacted differently to the information provided by China, where scientists within weeks of appearance of clusters of symptoms had identified the virus, sequenced the genome, and provided the information to the world. States in Asia and Oceania reacted quickly and have the situation pretty much under control. Others varied. The US has been a catastrophe.

What would happen in differently organized societies with informed publics and more direct popular participation in decision-making and regional and global integration? We cannot speak with confidence, but I don't see any reason why performance should not be superior, certainly superior to the states with the worst records.

(4)

Günther Grewendorf:
It is certainly true that without health there will be no economy. But it is also true that without the economy there will be no health. Accordingly we can observe that among the free human beings living in Western democracies, there seem to be two interest groups: people who defend their right not to lose their job, and people who defend their right not to lose their life. Do you think that without the regulating power of an "artificial" state system, solidarity between those who are resilient and those who are vulnerable is possible and can make this choice obsolete?
Noam Chomsky:
I'd prefer to put the point a little differently. I suppose that everyone would like to keep their jobs and to stay alive, and there are differing individual assessments as to how to deal with the quandary. The state system that has been constructed over the years affects this choice in many ways. To take a current case, the US government provides some unemployment insurance, limited by the standards of comparable countries, but some. That provides a measure of support for a decision not to risk life by returning to work under unsafe conditions. Employers prefer to have control over this decision, so generally oppose extending the insurance, which is running out. Working people prefer to have enough support to make the decision themselves. Accordingly, Republicans, which are by now hardly more than an agency of great wealth and business power, want to kill the support system. One of their most influential figures – by their standards, one of the more – is Senator Lindsay Graham, who has just said that it will be extended over his dead body. The Democrats, particularly under the impact of the popular movements inspired in large part by Bernie Sanders, are more committed to the rights of working people.

The issue doesn't seem to me a matter of the regulating power of the state, but rather whose interests are deemed worthy of protection by state authorities: business profits or people's lives. Class war, to put it in classic terms. This is of course simplification, overlooking many important qualifications, but it seems to me an appropriate way to look at the matter.

This discussion presupposes that state capitalist institutions remain intact, even if not in their brutal neoliberal form. Under different socioeconomic arrangements the questions would be posed in very different ways.

(5)

Günther Grewendorf:
When society is threatened by economic or medical crises the citizens call for help from the state because in such situations they no longer rely on the market, they rely on the state. But catastrophes have often been exploited as opportunities for the state to suspend democratic principles and basic civil rights. As we can see from many crises in the past, the citizens are used to accepting the protective measures of the state as the justification for restrictions of their democratic rights. In the corona crisis the majority of the people approve the suspension of specific civil rights and accept measures such as confinement, social distancing and tracking systems, provided that the decisions made by the state are necessary to guarantee their health and are only valid for a limited period. In the interview mentioned above you call the view that "the state is your master" "a fascist conception of the state". Would you allow the state the temporary suspension of certain civil rights in a situation like the corona crisis?

Noam Chomsky:
I'm a little uncomfortable about the way the question is framed. We do not, of course, live in Tudor England or Stalinist Russia. In state capitalist democracies the state is not an independent entity hovering over us. It is an arena of contending forces. To first approximation, sufficient for the specific question at hand, we can think of the main contending forces as capital and labour. The high tech quasi-monopolies, the huge financial sector, and other major segments of capitalist autocracy would like to maximize their control over the population. The state they largely dominate has similar interests. The working population – almost everyone – is rightly suspicious of according them such control. The process has been underway for some time – what Shoshana Zuboff has called "surveillance capitalism," which seeks to extend capitalist control beyond land, resources, labour to life quite generally. The coming "internet of things" provides means to extend the process. Just about everything we do send huge amounts of data to high tech, car manufacturers, state authorities, and far more. There are already experiments with implanting chips in workers in order to control them in ways that go far beyond Taylorism. Without chips, such practices already are implemented in fiercely controlled work environments like Amazon warehouses. Some sectors of power are surely entranced by the Chinese social credit system of surveillance and control. Tech companies are already proposing means for exploiting the pandemic controls to the post-virus world. Capital is relentless in pursuit of power, profit, domination, and the state authorities that are closely linked to private capital have similar ends.

But there are contending forces, as throughout modern history. Take the United States. The country was founded in a ferment of contending forces. The major schol-

arly work on the Constitutional Convention is entitled "The Framers' Coup" (Michael Klarman), namely the elite coup against the democratic aspirations of the mass of the population. But popular struggle went on, with many successes and intermittent regression. And does right now, including on the critical issues you raise.

Günther Grewendorf

Chomsky's Concept of Human Nature and the Role of the State System

Noam Chomsky's linguistic research has led to revolutionary insights into the nature of language, the nature of the human mind and thus into the uniqueness of human nature. Nevertheless, it is not his achievements in cognitive science that has made him known to the public but rather his political analyses and activities. Although Chomsky himself is rather cautious on the question of whether there is a connection between his linguistic research and his political analyses, it is undeniable that his concept of human nature and his view on the innate creativity of language and mind has an influence on his political opinions. Although there is no necessary connection between his linguistic research and his political commitments, the connections are nevertheless salient and derive from the freedom-centered view of human nature.

> "a social theory should be grounded on some concept of human needs and human rights, and in turn, on the human nature that must be presupposed in any serious account of the origin and character of these needs and rights." (Chomsky 1976: 195)

Since human beings can only develop their creative potentials if they can have a life without coercion and repressive authority, a "need for freedom is at the core of human nature" (Chomsky 1988: 386). This freedom-centered concept of human nature is at the root of Chomsky's political views on the notion of freedom, the role of the state and the function of democracy. So it is the essence of human nature which is incompatible with structures of power and domination. This Cartesian idea correlates with the vision of man in nature defended by Jean Jacques Rousseau, according to which the principles of natural law can be derived from the properties of human nature.

A similar implication, which is crucial for Chomsky's view on the state, can be found in the work of Wilhelm von Humboldt, one of the founders of classical liberalism. Chomsky points out that Humboldt's notion of human nature is essential for his ideas about the role of the state. Like Chomsky, Humboldt derives his critique of the authoritarian state from a specific concept of human nature:

> "I have felt myself animated throughout with a sense of the deepest respect for the inherent dignity of human nature, and for freedom, which alone befits that dignity." (quoted from Chomsky 1970: 148).

"Whatever does not spring from a man's free choice, or is only the result of instruction and guidance, does not enter into his very being, but remains alien to his true nature" (ibid. pl. 150)

These are the ideas on which Humboldt grounds his view of the role of the state, which tends to "make man an instrument to serve its arbitrary ends, overlooking his individual purposes" but which should only be allowed "the most minimal forms of state intervention in personal or social life" and "is not to meddle in anything which does not refer exclusively to security".

So Chomsky takes Humboldt to be a " forceful advocate of libertarian values " (ibid. p.148) who considers the state as a social organization for free individuals in which the latter can develop their potentials, interests and energies in a free and creative way. Nevertheless Humboldt agrees that state intervention in social life is legitimate if "freedom would destroy the very conditions without which not only freedom but even existence itself would be inconceivable" (ibid. p. 151). According to Chomsky, Humboldt expresses a classical liberal doctrine and is no primitive individualist in the style of Rousseau, but "looks forward to a community of free association without coercion by the state or other authoritarian institutions". Chomsky takes Humboldt's idea of a society in which freely constituted bonds replace the fetters of autocratic institutions as an "anarchist vision that is appropriate, perhaps, to the next stage of industrial society" and thus makes Humboldt a predecessor of libertarian socialism.

Chomsky has called himself "some kind of anarchist" (1988: 744): "My personal visions are fairly traditional anarchist ones, with origins in the Enlightenment and classical liberalism." (Chomsky 1996: 71). When he speaks of "classical liberalism" he means the ideas that were swept away by state capitalist autocracy but

"survived (or were re-invented) in various forms in the culture of resistance to the new forms of oppression, serving as an animating vision for popular struggles that have considerably expanded the scope of freedom, justice, and rights." (ibid. p.73)

Neil Smith (1999: 186f) points out that Chomsky is not an anarchist in the sense that he favors a state of lawlessness and disorder: "Anarchy as a social philosophy has never meant 'chaos' - in fact, anarchists have typically believed in a highly organized society, just one that's organized democratically from below." (Chomsky 2003: 199)

Chomsky is an anarchist in the tradition of Humboldt, Bakunin and Rudolf Rocker and his anarchism is to be understood as a system of political ideas that is characterized by a vision of human society free of coercion, oppression and concentration of power. Anarchism in this sense basically means democratic control of one's "productive life" (McGilvray 1999: 197):

"According to this anarchist vision, any structure of hierarchy and authority carries a heavy burden of justification, whether it involves personal relations or a larger social order. If it cannot bear that burden - sometimes it can - then it is illegitimate and should be dismantled." (Chomsky 1996: 73)

For Chomsky, the state system is a very "artificial system" that represents a transitory historical phase:

"In its modern form it developed in Europe, and you can see how artificial it is by just looking at European history for the last hundreds of years, a history of massacre, violence, terror, destruction, most of which has to do with trying to impose a state system on a society to which it has very little relation." (Chomsky 1988: 745)

The formation of states outside of Europe (Africa, India, Asia etc.) is basically a result of colonialization. Their boundaries

"cut across all kinds of communities and interests and they bring people together who have nothing to do with each other. The result is constant warfare and struggle and oppression and so on. Furthermore, within each of these artificial systems, imposed usually by force, you have some kind of usually very sharply skewed distribution of power internally. The concentration of power inside usually takes over the state for its own good. It suppresses other people, suppresses people outside, etc. So we're stuck with this state system, for a while, at least. But we shouldn't expect it to be permanent." (ibid.)

On the contrary, Chomsky considers the state system as a "lethal system" and claims that the only reason why stability in Europe was established after the world wars was "because the next step was going to destroy everything, given the level of weaponry":

"That's the nature of the state system. It's going to lead to more and more destruction. Maybe there will be a way to abort it now, because the next step is to kill everything, but maybe not, in which case we will kill everything. From every point of view that state system looks artificial in the sense that it's unrelated to human needs and imposed by certain interests and power distribution." (ibid.)

Nevertheless, Chomsky accepts state power as a transitory phenomenon if it serves to provide welfare, health care, and security and protects the citizens from illegitimate private structures of coercion such as domination by business for private profit as well as private control of banking, land and industry:

"My short-term goals are to defend and even strengthen elements of state authority which, though illegitimate in fundamental ways, are critically necessary right now to impede the dedicated efforts to 'roll back' the progress that has been achieved in extending democracy and human rights." (Chomsky 1996: 73; see also Chomsky 2003: 344)

Although anarchist ideas have not led to a worldwide political movement, they have not been without any influence on political thinking. They continue to be effective in populist protests against abuse of state power and the excesses of the new "predatory capitalism" of modern globalization. Since "free enterprise" only exists in close cooperation with that "archaic structure called the state" (Otero 1994: 356), for Chomsky a true libertarian is an adversary of state power.

From this brief survey of the main characteristics of Chomsky's social theory, the main topics of this volume can be derived:

- Human nature and the emergence of social institutions
- The relation of the individual to the state and the gist of anarchism
- Human rights and the notion of freedom
- Power and resistance

In what follows I will assign the contributions to these topics and give a brief summary of their content.

Human Nature and the Emergence of Social Institutions

Using evidence from language acquisition Roeper's paper *Connecting Cognitive Science, Species Self-Knowledge, and Maladaptive Institutions* advocates the view that children show a universalist perspective on the world and thus have a notion of community that is associated with conceptions of equality and rudiments of other political categories such as the notion of cooperation. Roeper shows that the child acquires such notions without any explicit instruction and at a surprisingly young age. He then concludes that these notions have innate psychological roots.

The view that the ingredients for social relations are innate is at variance with the Piagetian claim that children are "egocentric" and self-interested and only see things from their own point of view. The inevitability of institutional failures is due to the fact that every social system or action has unintended and unanticipated consequences. These consequences should not lead us to deny the necessity of social organization but, Roeper argues, the creativity of social self-knowledge will help us to keep those consequences under control. However, the creativity of social self-knowledge, as every kind of creativity, needs freedom to evolve.

The Relation of the Individual to the State and the Gist of Anarchism

Rai's contribution *Anarchism, Government and the State* proceeds from Chomsky's claim that the need for freedom is rooted in the properties of human nature. Any form of authority or domination is therefore essentially illegitimate unless it is justified on independent grounds. In the first part of his contribution Rai describes communal forms of self-organization and self-government such as the *zanjera* irrigation communities of the Philippines, the socialization of factories in the Italian *biennio rosso* period of 1919-1920 and the collectivization of industry and commerce in Barcelona in the thirties. He takes these movements as an example of the grassroots democratic institutions that Chomsky has in mind when he favors an anarchist model of the state.

In the second part of his paper Rai deals with Chomsky's view that in capitalist societies of the western world representative democracy is limited to the political sphere and does not affect the economic sphere, where private power exerts an enormous influence on the state without being subject to public democratic control.

Rai then discusses the distinction between state and democracy and shows that Chomsky uses at least three definitions of the concept of 'the state'. According to his preferred definition in the sense of his 'state-corporate nexus', the state and the major capitalist corporates are part of the same system of decision-making power in which state power is invoked to protect the corporations from destructive developments of the market, to secure resources and to guarantee private privilege and profit. Political decisions are thus influenced by investment decisions, and those who hold the wealth of society (the capital and its distribution) determine the conditions of life for everyone in society. Chomsky considers that kind of concentration of power as deeply undemocratic and advocates the view that state institutions should first be reformed in order to provide concrete solutions to the fundamental problems of our society (environment, welfare, education, quality of life, peace etc.) and should ultimately be replaced with a 'libertarian socialist' system.

According to Bošković' paper *On the (Im)practicality of the State: Why do I have to have a Country?* Chomsky favors a stateless society but emphasizes in many places that this situation can only be considered a long-term goal. Bošković argues that citizens are in many ways owned by the state, as can be seen from eminent domain and military draft, and describes the individual's servitude to the state as the inclination to belong to a larger group and to measure themselves by the achievements of that larger group. Although it is in the long-term interest of anarchism to undermine this phenomenon of belonging to a state, anarchists like Chomsky still advocate a pragmatically-motivated anarchism in the sense that they recommend supporting the state in a transitional period in order to achieve a freer and more just society that comes closer to anarchist ideals.

Schiffmann in his paper *The Soft-Spoken Anarchist: Chomsky, Populism, and the Question of "From Here to There"* analyzes the specific nature of Chomsky's notion of anarchism in the sense of a struggle for a free and just society and the liberation of people from oppression, the goal of anarchist principles being the development of autonomous individuals and collective self-determination. Schiffmann relates Chomsky's variant of anarchism to other crucial topics of his political work such as the manipulating role of the media ("manufacturing consent"), creativity as a crucial trait of human nature and the responsibility of intellectuals.

Human Rights and the Notion of Freedom

Domination by totalitarian structures in our economic lives has a great effect on the general character of the culture. Against the background of a brief history of liberalism, Uriagereka shows in his contribution *Culture as a Human Right - within the National State Framework* that the idea of culture as a human right emerged at the end of the 20th century as a result of a better understanding of culture as a crucial ingredient of human nature. He takes Chomsky's notion of freedom, according to which freedom is what we create, as a cultural notion of freedom (in the sense of Roosevelt's "four freedoms") and discusses the problem of freedom with respect to the rights of minorities, the "nation-building" process and the relationship between nationality, culture and state.

According to Bricmont's *Freedom of Speech, Chomsky and France*, Chomsky considers freedom of speech as a fundamental principle in a democratic society since it is a prerequisite for the citizens of a state to get the information that crucially affects their social, political, and religious life. Most people agree that there must be limits and exceptions to this principle but the crucial question is what those limits are and how they can be justified. The distinction between disapproving of what somebody says and defending his right to say it played an important role in the so-called Chomsky-Faurisson affair. The paper by Jean Bricmont deals with these questions and in particular discusses the situation of freedom of speech in France.

State Power and Resistance

In order to reconstruct Chomsky's view of terrorism, Meggle in his paper *Chomsky on Terrorism* proceeds from an explication of the basic concepts that are related to the notion of terrorism. The first and fundamental question that he tries to answer is "What is terrorism?" or, more specifically, "When is an action a terroristic one?". Meggle defines a descriptive aspect of terrorism according to which terroristic acts are "acts of (attempts of) achieving one's ends by means of violence-induced strong intimidation" (Universal Definition of Terrorism). He then shows that not only Chomsky uses this simple descriptive notion in his thinking about terrorism, it is more or less also suggested by the Pentagon and the British government. For Chomsky there is an evaluative aspect of this definition which holds that terroristic acts are to be morally condemned, and this aspect has to be extended by a Principle of Universality according to which the same standards we apply to others have to apply to ourselves. According to Meggle's reconstruction, Chomsky's critique of terrorism is based on the rigorous application of these three components: the Universal Terrorism-Definition, the moral evaluation of terrorism, and the moral Principle of Universality.

Against the background of these components, Chomsky's crucial verdict is given as follows: "Most of our common condemnations of terrorism are blatant offences against the Principle of Universality". In other words, Chomsky takes most of those condemnations to be based on Double Standards: terroristic acts can only be performed by others ("operative definition of terrorism"). As Meggle shows, Chomsky illustrates his verdict with numerous examples, ranging from the War Crime Trial at Nuremberg and the atomic bombing of Hiroshima and Nagasaki over the Yugoslavia vs. NATO-Tribunal to the wars in Asia, South and Central America, Africa, the Middle East, and Southern Arabia (Yemen). It doesn't come as a surprise that the US were involved in most of these examples since it is mostly the powerful who are exempt from being accused of terrorism. Since the media usually take sides with the powerful and keep people ignorant about the difference between the universal and the operative definition of terrorism, Chomsky recommends, as Meggle demonstrates, to take a clear and unbiased look at the facts and to find out whether the Principle of Universality is sincerely accepted.

In his paper *The Chomsky Approach: Considering the Limits on State Action* Barsky discusses Chomsky's opinion on popular uprisings and shows that according to him, popular movements which focus on short-term achievements such as the reform of police practices will not lead to fundamental changes of a society unless they pursue a long-term perspective that aims at a world free of the power structures which create repression, injustice and racist exclusion. He then elaborates on Chomsky's approach to resisting arbitrary authority and bringing about a legitimized social organization which is free of oppression, social inequality and racist conflicts.

Bibliography

Chomsky, Noam, 1970: Language and freedom. In: Peck, James, (ed.), 1970: The Chomsky Reader, New York, p.139-155.

Chomsky, Noam, 1976: Equality: language development, human intelligence, and social organization. In: Peck, James, (ed.) 1987: The Chomsky Reader, New York, p.183-202.

Chomsky, Noam, 1988: Language and politics. ed. by Carlos Otero.

Chomsky, Noam, 1996: Powers and prospects. Boston.

Chomsky, Noam, 2003: Understanding power. London.

Grewendorf, Günther, 2006: Noam Chomsky. München.

McGilvray, James, 1999: Chomsky. Language, mind, and politics. Cambridge.

Otero, Carlos P., 1994: Introduction to Chomsky's social theory. In: Otero, Carlos (ed.), 1994: Noam Chomsky. Critical assessments, vol. III, London/New York, p.347-372.

Rai, Milan, 1995: Chomsky's politics. London.

Smith, Neil, 1999: Chomsky: Ideas and ideals. Cambridge.

Human Nature and the Emergence of Social Institutions

Tom Roeper

Connecting Cognitive Science, Species Self-Knowledge, and Maladaptive Institutions

1.0 Anarchist Background

"It's not human nature that is the problem, it is institutions" Noam Chomsky has remarked several times in talks (MIT Press interview). We will explore what that comment may mean. It is a commonplace to assert that every political philosophy has an implicit (or explicit) vision of human nature. Are our institutions not in fact and intentionally reflections of human nature – of the human beings who created them?

Anarchism – from many angles – asserts the impossibility of an adequate State, hence adequate institutions, because, from one perspective, the nature of individuality is such that we do not share the same goals – we really are all different. So every institution will elicit strong resistance from those whose interests it fails to include.

This is anarchism as the ultimate libertarian individualism. And yet elsewhere in anarchist thought there are strong commitments to community, to the quest for consensus, and mutual aid in spontaneous forms of organization – like those that surrounded public outpourings of generosity after the 911 attacks, or those manifested in the Occupy Wall St movement in New York and throughout the USA, or the Black Lives Matter movement. Nonetheless, terrible problems remain. Why do societies find it difficult to let go of policies the majority dislikes – to acheive gun control when 90% of the population wants it?

Other strands of anarchism highlight workers' rights, ownership of the means of production, and an important insight that we must rid ourselves of "obsolete institutions". Here the idea is that institutions themselves are wedded to the circumstances in which they arise and they easily become a negative force when they no longer fit the population and people they are designed to govern, but leave behind powerful administrative structures.

Let us first look at some traditional anarchist views and then ask how a modern view of Cognitive Science and the biology from which it must spring can lead us to a different vision that begins to explain (somewhat) why we are the way we are and why we inevitably create the quandries and new sorts of calamities from which we suffer. In a book on child grammar (Prism of Grammar (2007)) I entitled a chapter "Who are we?" and recent work by Chomsky has a similar title What kind of creatures are we? Both titles aim to acknowledge that fundamental aspects of human nature remain a mystery which we do not even know how to think about, and which apparently rational methods, such as vast domains of "social science" fail to grasp or acknowledge. Our answer – which reflects anarchism – is built around the question of how to see that creativity and the exercise of Free Will[1]should be the core of human dignity. Cognitive Science can offer us a model of ourselves which holds the promise of making this vision more explicit. Nevertheless our formulations below remain inadequate and under-articulated as well.

1. 1 Anarchist Perspectives on Individuals
Early views go back to Rousseau and his vision of man in nature. Bakunin and Marx also ruminated about where human nature fits into their view of society. Another early advocate is William Godwin who presents the classic anarchist argument that authority is against nature and that social evils exist because men are not free to act according to reason. Godwin also sketches out a decentralized society composed of small autonomous communities, or parishes. Within these communities, democratic political procedures would be dispensed with as far as possible, because, according to Godwin," they encourage a majoritarian tyranny and dilute individual responsibility."[2]

Marx himself, particularly in his early work, criticizes "the traditional conception of human nature as a species which incarnates itself in each individual, instead arguing that human nature is formed by the totality of social relations [https://en.wikipedia.org/wiki/Social_relations]. Thus, the whole of human nature is not understood, as in classical idealist philosophy, as permanent and universal: the *species-being* is always determined in a specific social and historical formation, with some aspects being biological."[3]

When Marx sought to integrate his vision of the human being into a community, he recognized a critical ambiguity:

> "[It is] ...a community to which these individuals belonged only as average individuals, only insofar as they lived within the conditions of existence of their class — a relationship in which they participated not as individuals but as members of a class. With the community of revolutionary proletarians, on the other hand, who take their conditions of existence [...] under their control, it is just the reverse; it is as individuals that the individuals participate in it. [...]"

Here again we have a sense that the uniqueness of individuals must be accommodated in an adequate theory of society.

---

1   See Why Free Will is real by Christian List (2019).
2   See his biography in Wikipedia.
3   *Theses on Feuerbach* (1845)

1.2 John Dewey had a positive view of human potential which he believed could naturally exist in a community that realized ethical ideals. For him "democracy is a form of moral and spiritual association "with personality as the first and final reality" with "the infinite and universal possibility within each person not for "mere self-assertion" an "individualism of freedom, of responsibilty, of initiative to and for the ethical ideal" – an optimistic view which presumed the harmony needed for a successful community and did not imagine the means of resolving conflicts. The goal is "securing and maintaining an ever-increasing release of the power of human nature in search of a freedom that is cooperative and cooperation that is voluntary"

Behind that vision of community was a view of the individual and *human thinking*:

> "human thinking is not a phenomenon which is radically outside of (or external to) the world it seeks to know; knowing is *not* a purely rational attempt to escape illusion in order to discover what is ultimately "real" or "true". Rather, human knowing is *among* the ways organisms with evolved capacities for thought and language cope with problems. Minds, then, are not passively observing the world; rather, they are actively adapting, experimenting, and innovating; ideas and theories are not rational fulcrums to get us beyond culture, but rather function experimentally within culture and are evaluated on situated, pragmatic bases. Knowing is not the mortal's exercise of a "divine spark", either; for while knowing (or *inquiry*, to use Dewey's term) includes calculative or rational elements, it is ultimately informed by the body and emotions of the animal using it to cope." (from Stanford Encyclopedia of Philosophy)

This view adumbrates the current interest in body language and "embodied cognition" (Wilson and Golonka (2013) that captures the fact that our whole body responds to our mental state even when it is largely unconscious. We blush, tremble, blink or turn away from situations, words, or possibilities whose content is abstract, like the mere sight of someone with whom we have disagreed. This illustrates that the whole body can incorporate subtle aspects of mind.

While the notion of creativity and infinite potential is clearly present here, there is no effort to actually specify a mechanism of thought or social adaptation.

1.3 Paul Goodman ruminated for years on the question of what the ideal form of community would be for individuals who each have a unique perspective and generate unique goals. He finally arrived at the view that anarchist philosophy succeeded ideally only in fact-to-face communities. It required real specific interactions among people to achieve an adequate community. Colin Ward (a community organizer) commented: "Paul Goodman brought a new invigorating stream into American anarchism, simply through his insistence that in all the problems of daily life we are faced with the possibility of choice between authoritarian and libertarian solutions . ."

What is noticeable in various anarchist works is the precision of many negative concepts (hierarchy, paternalism, authoritarianism, dictatorship, autocracy, organizational rigidity) and the vagueness of positive visions. Consider the American declaration of independence which champions "life, liberty, and the pursuit of happiness" or the anarchist doctrine of "free association among people" or Dewey's vision of an " ever-increasing release of the power of human nature in search of a freedom". These are obviously noble and laudable goals but why are they so broad and imprecise? Why should what is essential and important to us be so difficult to formulate? Why does the word "freedom" itself seem negatively defined – it means "not bound" by anything?

2.0 Background to Modern Cognitive Science

Human Nature is the most challenging scientific quarry ever pursued. Science has always sought principles and abstractions. Many of the abstractions lay in the recognition of patterns. The great insight of modern Cognitive Science, which emerged from Russell's philosophical ruminations on what it means for a set to contain itself and then Chomsky's work on developing algorithms that would generate unbounded grammars. shows that we can specify forms of creativity as precise mechanisms formulated as mathematical rules. The further claim is that our mind uses these algorithms to generate unique sentences with unique meanings in milliseconds. In a word, these algorithms are psychologically real and serve as the foundation of modern linguistics and cognitive science.

The physicist Steven Weinberg has articulated a similar view:

"I do think that we will have an understanding of behavior...in the path laid out by Galileo and Newton: the discovery of increasingly comprehensive mathematical laws"

And Paul Churchland in his presidential address to the American Philosophical Society shares this vision of mental representations:

"Suppose also the internal character of each of the representational spaces is not fixed by some prior decree, either divine or genetic, but is slowly shaped or sculpted by...extended experience... So we begin by expanding the number of representational spaces, into the hundreds and thousands... And we reach out to include motor cognition and practical skills, along with perceptual apprehensions and theoretical judgment, as equal partners in our account of human knowledge."

2.1 Humanism and Social Science

On the other hand, we have no shortage of humanistic claims about self-discovery, self-actualization, self-fulfillment, and governmental goals like "life, liberty, and the pursuit of happiness". They are inspiring but quintessentially opaque. The scientific question "what is a human being?" is a descendant of the 19th century search for the "life force" which was eventually abandoned in favor of the highly illuminating but reductionist exploration of microbiology. Yet the core question remains and part of the answer ordinary intuition tells us – has something to do with whatever constitutes "human dignity".

What we have come to call "social science" offers seemingly endless further reductionist accounts that seek to explain us to ourselves. They seek to explain human behavior in terms of known subsystems. They usually lead to "the goal of an organism is reproduction" or "the satisfaction of urges and desires" or 'achieving dominance" in a world governed by self-interest and competition. Or the purpose of life is a fight to survive over others with the same goal. Many of these "scientific" approaches are enshrined in capitalist thinking. They also make crude connections with mechanistic claims about biology and observeable phenomena of how we pursue food and reproduction.

Typical approaches to governmental institutions either entail reductionist views of human nature as well, or they once again enshrine ill-formulated humanistic goals like "freedom", "the rights of man", or visions of "rationality" (scientific marxism) as the basis of governmental organization and a justificiation for governmental power.

2.2 Democracy

The dominant tradition in the 20th century has been a vision that governments should be "democratic" as the ideal with the actual form of organization quite variable but usually linked to some form of voting. Nonetheless, the level of complexity of modern life has now led large forces, popular and coercive, to claim that the problems generated in modern society make that ideal of democracy impracticable, such as the current Chinese communist doctrine which is explicitly authoritarian.

What the future holds is impossible to know. So we should do our best to understand why institutions generate policies and programs that are both enriching of society and individuals and very threatening at once.

One question is what new dimensions of humanity emerge with technology? The internet has created a new constellation of potential human relationships – and difficulties of course: how important is face-to-face interaction compared to email? Does "the internet diminish us" as Chomsky (pc) once suggested.

Chomsky has been a primary force in the modern field of Cognitive Science through the development of generative grammar, its most advanced example. He has also offered social commentary on current politics from a broadly anarchist perspective. We shall try to draw some connections between them. Basic questions remain very much alive: Why do we not understand the implications of institutions we create? Could the failure of institutions be inevitable? And are we capable of learning from failures with some legitimate optimism?

Our approach may offer insight, but no ready solutions for how to reform institutions. Nevertheless if we can identify one crucial missing ingredient, the social computational power of mind – like Mendel's postulation of an invisible gene – it might help us see where we can envision a viable future.

3.0 Cognitive Science and Recursive Rules

Cognitive Science evolved in close association with theories and mathematical formulations that enabled computer software to develop. Chomsky's formulation of Generative Grammar is the first and leading example of how creativity can be captured by a well-defined and finite system. The stunning claim was that these structures were psychologically real and a mental attribute. One example is the use of Phrase-structure-rules to generate a form of Category-recursion that is potentially infinite. It uses finite rules to generate an infinite output. Here is an example that involves potentially infinite prepositional phrases (arrow => = rewrite as, and parentheses = optionality):

1) Nounphrase or NP => Noun (Prepositional Phrase) (or PP)
    PP => Preposition (NP)

The re-appearance of NP inside PP allows it to cycle infinitely. These two rules generate the infinite loop that can produce (2):

2) the dog next to the cat next to the horse next to the alligator...

The rules work beautifully and operate in any language despite variations in word-order and auxiliary operations of case-assignment, intonation assignment, and the substantial challenge of associating a compositional semantics with the syntax. Chomsky claimed these abilities were innate and language acquisition has shown that 2yr old children exhibit virtually every one of the most sophisticated abilities we have, as we shall provide some examples of.

3.1 Children's Exhibition of Innateness

An example of generative complexity lies in our capacity to project other minds, attribute propositions to them, and embed those propositions again in syntax with recursive sentences like the nounphrases above. Two-year olds can treat themselves as having two minds as when one says (2.11 years):

3) "I thought I was lost" (from Childes)

implying that she is not now lost and can recognize both her current mind and an earlier one.

A 5yr old is explicit that her thought and reality are at odds:

4) "when we went lookin(g) for it , we thought it was upstairs but found out that it wasn't"

Or a 6yr old who said:

5) "so she knew that I thought she thought that Easter was only three days and I told her Easter was one day"

This child uses embedded clauses to represent independent mental states of herself and others utilizing a form of semantic composition that, in philosophical parlance, integrates three Possible Worlds, one in each clause, into a complex social thought. To be more specific think (I thought) takes an opaque (uncertain truth) complement which has another opaque complement (she thought) all of which is inside a "factive" complement (she knew).

The factive complement must refer to an independently true proposition, but interestingly, the true proposition contains an indeterminate opaque one. The compositional mechanics of this syntax-semantics interface has not been theoretically stated thus far. These complex embeddings are so natural for adults that we do not immediately recognize how amazing it is that a child could command them with no instruction.

The self-reflective capacities of a child is transparently clear in an utterance like:

6) 6yr old: " My mind is very angry, and so am I"

Or locutions from a 4yr old like:

7) "I thought I forgot"

which entails a previous (forgotten) state of mind that refers to a proposition in a still earlier state of mind when it was not forgotten.

These are both sophisticated syntactic and social embeddings built upon the same edifice.

3.2 Beyond Grammar: the Structure of Emotions

Now let us take some steps beyond grammar. Are our emotions generated in the same manner? Are the complex social relations that we not only experience but create woven from the same combinatorial powers that enable language to carry a precise intricacy? We generate not only unique sentences with unique meanings, but unique emotions never before experienced (like perhaps the emotion we have about holding an election within a pandemic).

If we listen to conversations we find endless complex relations described much like the "Easter" discussion, as in this artificial one:

8) "because he felt if she felt bad about him then he would feel unsure about her sister who feels that they are a perfect couple."

Where we find feelings that are generated within a web of other feelings that presuppose the existence of other ones. The architecture looks like the same kind of generative mechanism could be behind it and if so, then the feelings in fact entail propositions with logical properties. All of this says that not only grammar but the structure of emotions can be embedded and such emotional structures are available in nursery school. Moreover they can be composed, expressed, and understood in milliseconds.

The claim is that these capacities are not only available to what one can call "slow thought"[4] where complex rumination occurs, but it is also part of a mechanical mental system for generating complex objects in milliseconds. Another case: physical activity entails the same dimensions of creativity. For a basketball player to plan moves that involve feinting, dodging, and throwing in one complex motion is much like the complex emotions we just alluded to.

3.3 Social Creativity

Now we can take a further step. If human beings are capable of linguistic and emotional creativity, then social creativity is the next obvious mental projection which humans can project where we embed social relations inside of each other:

9) [town [school [class [friends]]]]

and we can project emotions that systematically build up our perspectives by embedding them inside of each other. This is a crude picture, but it entails pivotal connections that we use to construct emotions, attitudes, and plans, again with self-embedded structures:

---

4   Kahneman (2011) for an economic view, see also Roeper (2007) for a linguistic perspective.

10) [Situation 1 [Situation 2 [Situation 3]]]
   [Situation1: Individuals – emotional connection- organization
   [Situation2: Individuals – emotional connection- organization
   [Situation 3: Individuals – emotional connection- organization]]]

And we may have emotional algorithms that can create a composite – a version of semantic compositionality – that can combine these emotions in a logical and transparent way that enables us to generate propositions with cause and effect logic. We formulate sentences that mirror the emotional pattern of situations like:

11) the students reacted negatively to the half-hearted teacher's directions which were a reflection of poorly thought out new school policies created to fit overcrowded conditions created by local government reactions to restrictive budget policies.

And we can generate an emotion to cover the complexity: "the situation was disheartening".

Computation across complex kinship relations are known to be unusually complex from numerous anthropological studies. Cultural patterns and norms presumably vary in much the same way, for instance, the structure of caste systems must be taught to children in order for people to calculate how policies work. Although they have arisen through complex historical circumstances, they contribute to a unified conception that are the basis for further social thought: programs, policies, and systematic political thinking, and familiar organizational charts. In many respects the charts resemble complex sentences with units, subunits, and defined interactions.

Thus we have government bodies, with committees and subcommittees and the defined transmission of modified information (reports from the chairman) from one level to another, much like a question word is fed from one clause to another [what did this committee say their subcommittee claimed the expert said__]. Members of those bodies can, because they have a social imagination "think" in terms of these units and subunits helped by a thought-syntax similar to question sentences. Nonetheless, of course many arrangements are not captured by hierarchical structures. How does our social imagination work? Are there limits on social creativity?

How well do we compute the impact of a new idea upwards, downwards, and sideways or in terms of discontinuous social units?

Although preferred metaphors for social organization have often been biological over the centuries – we hear about the "branches" of government – modern science has turned to the mechanical models which physics introduced (the Chicago "political machine").

Our hypothesis is that our social imagination – whatever its ingredients – has algorithmic computational powers like the rest of our mind. We are capable of projecting unique social relations across unique dimensions. One might observe that Zoom meetings held with participants around the world are generating unusual new social patterns in our minds which dictate both words and actions. Why is remote teaching a challenge? It is because it calls for subtle configurations of social relations, different for nursery schools and nursing homes, that we do not yet know the best ways to "think" in.

4.0 Independent Evidence of Universal Perspectives and Awareness of Community in Children

Does the structure of language reveal our biases toward community? The deepest reflections of mental attitudes lie in automatic assumptions – particularly those embedded invisibly in our behavior.

A powerful example lies in the interpretation of unpronounced subjects of infinitives, Children as young as 1.9 years use infinitives ("to have") linked to ("Mom") the subject of going:

12) "mom going to have tea"

These invisible subjects vary systematically, but they always include a more abstract option with, I argue, a community connection. It has never been observed before, to my knowledge, to have political implications. In technical terms the invisible subject is called Pro-arb, which means an "arbitrary pronoun", but the term may hide an important reality about how we think not just for ourselves but for and about everyone in the details of life. Consider these sentences which entail a Universal perspective on action and therefore entail the capacity to view the world through a generic notion of (for) *everybody*:

13) a. it is good to get exercise [= good [PRO-arb to get exercise]
    b. it is easy to ride a bike
    c. it is unwise to ignore the weather forecast

PRO-arb has a systematic interpretation is as a universal generic reference: anyone or everyone. It is evidence of an automatic innate political bias to conceptualize situations from a universalist perspective. It seems to presuppose an egalitarian posture because it entails a typical, generic human being. If that is true, then Everyman famous in Medieval literature, is a concept available to all human beings, even 2yr olds, without explicit instruction (and minimal inference from situations).

Note that it is not totally open, it refers to Humans:

14) a. it is not good to eat dog food

Obviously this is not true if the subject were a dog. And we can overtly modify it:
  b. it is only good for dogs to eat dogfood
Or it can be modified to a subgroup:
  c. it is good for children to go to bed early
although it can involve even more abstract expletives as in:
  d. it is going to rain.
Again it is found among 2yr old children who use adjectives like "easy" or "hard" with implied complements that have a universalist PRO-arb subject even before they command the syntax of infinitives which vary from language to language. "easy" shows up with 1.7 yr olds and often with 2yr olds:

15) 2.1 "easy"
    2.5 "that is easy"
    2.8 "because it's easy"
    2.9 "it's not quite easy"

It seems to contain a hidden complement: easy/hard to do, which means exactly easy for anybody to do.[5] And the infinitival complement can be present too at the age of 2yrs:

16) 2.5 "that's hard to do"
    2.5 "it's hard to open"
    2.7 "hard to get in"
    2.8 "hard to take it out"

Or in this conversation:

17) Adult: he couldn't take it apart
    Child: Why? It's hard to take apart?

This universalist perspective is the exact opposite of the Piagetian claim that children are "egocentric" and only see things from their own point of view. Studies of all kinds of empathy from 2yr olds suggest the opposite as well.[6]

---

5 See C.Chomsky (1969) for original experimental evidence and Roeper (2016) for experimental evidence on PRO-arb readings in anti-pragmatic environmentst. ("is it easy to eat the tops of trees? "yes, if you are a giraffe").
6 see https://psychcentral.com/lib/how-children-develop-empathy/.

4.1 Overt Universal Quantifiers

It should be no surprise that children easily acquire overt words like everybody or with their own creativity "all-body", or "nobody" and "anybody" Again the term is compatible with the notion that there is a proto-sense of community entailed.

18) 2.10 that scares everybody
    2.2 I want show allbody...everybody my puppy
    2.2 everybody don't like the fan
    2.5 everybody can't hit me.
    3.5 and everybody can do it too

Nobody:

19) 1.10 "nobody"
    1.1.11 "and get diapers for nobody"

    2.4 nobody take my cheese away
    2;10 nobody's gonna get the blocks.

    2.8 "so nobody can get in"
    2.10 "not for nobody go in"

20) Anybody:
    2.10 "not let anybody in this house
    2.0 "anybody can put it away"
    3.0 "anybody didn't do it"

The variety of terms suggests that the child has easy access to both inclusive (everybody) and exclusive (nobody) terms where the child or a group can be not included, but no one else:

21) 2.5 "nobody can eat our food, but ourselves"

This remark from a 4yr old (Roeper diary, Maria Roeper) clearly alludes to universality:

22) "I love everybody, even that I don't know"

The rudiments of political conceptions can be found in very early grammars. And to hammer home a claim that runs against popular thinking born in academic work: these utterances are clearly not governed by ego-centricity, but more than that. They involve social and ethical reasoning from a general point of view. Another clearly universal case:

23) " everybody sleeps at night"

4.2 Fair

And social words that contain complex egalitarian judgements also exist, entailed in terms like "fair" again found with 2yr olds, which may seem elementary but any philosophical examination immediately reveals that they entail a complex interaction of morality and aesthetic proportion.

24) 2.6 "it's not fair"
    2.8 "not fair"
    3.3 "that's not fair"
    3.6 "that's not fair"

    4.9 "that wouldn't be fair if only girls had diarrhea"
    4.6 "it's not fair to boys"
    4.8 "next time I'm gonna make it fair"
    4.8 "I'm just trying to be fair"

While what lies behind a term like "fair" remains a topic of vigorous philosophical and legal debate, its core meaning is instantly recognized because, we argue, it is a part of innate knowledge of social relations that may be as easily connected to concepts as the equally complex word "mama" (although it is true that "fair" is much more common over the age of 3, which is still younger than many people think children have such notions).

4.3 Referential Systems and Cooperation

The intricacies of syntax and semantics with pronouns provide a substantial challenge for children. They can misunderstand him as himself and himself as him. But a more interesting error which was discovered in work by Green (2008) and (Gulzow (2011) in experiments with children and their bias toward symmetrical readings of reciprocals. It is found with empty objects in English:

25) the boys are fighting or pushing

where they receive an implicit "each other" interpretation. In many languages like German a simple reflexive, like sich, can also be a reciprocal. In experiments in English and German, we found that even unambiguous reflexives (they kissed themselves) were interpreted reciprocally (they kissed each other) for a number of verbs like:

26) wash, shave, hug, kiss

that is: they hugged, they hugged each other, and they hugged themselves or in German sie umarmen sich selbst, were all interpreted with a strong bias toward the reciprocal reading among children, but not adults, who differentiated the meanings. That reciprocal bias exists for adults for a verb like kiss: it is possible, but odd to say he kissed himself. The opposite bias exists for wash: they washed themselves is naturally interpreted distributively (each washes himself).

In both English and German experiments we found errors were all in the direction of taking a reflexive [themselves, sich selbst] as a reciprocal, with little effect for lexical bias:

27) English:
    26 children, 3- 5, 13 adult controls.
    Age Group 1 3;0 through 3;11.
    Age Group 2 4;0 through 4;11.
    Age Group 3 5;0 through 5;11

only 22% of three-year-olds chose the reflexive picture for verbs *shave, dress,* and *wash*, *hug, kiss* when given both alternatives and instead they preferred reciprocal over reflexive readings. Thus they took picture A over B for they kissed, washed or hugged themselves (Gulzow (2011):

A   *B*

HUG

wash

The bias was always toward the reciprocal reading (A) and not the self-referential reading (B). The so-called reciprocal is most often really a joint reading or it is called a symmetrical reading (Gleitman and Partee (UMass talk)). We prefer the "joint" description because it fits the claim that a notion of cooperation, critical to anarchist theory, has innate psychological roots.

4.4 Collective Reading

There is a similar bias toward the collective and away from distributive readings for children. If you ask them to "circle all the turtles" in a picture of turtles, they will at first put a circle around the whole group, not the individuals. And in general the word all is one of the first acquired as in "allgone" in English and "alle" in German.

In sum from a variety of perspectives we have seen that social attitudes are built into language vocabulary (everybody, fair) but also formal structures, (Arbitrary PRO control) and reciprocals in a way that suggests innate social biases and not intricate concept learning.

What this indicates is that it is arguable that the ingredients for egalitarian social philosophy are inborn and natural. They are compatible with early Marxist views but not with his claims about "historical materialism" which veers away from a cooperative vision with innate roots.

While modern psychology has extensively defended the notion that children are ego-centric and self-interested much like a capitalist view of human nature would expect, a close look at the language of 2yr olds has shown that the acquisition of concepts that are oriented toward community and equality are available without explicit instruction at a surprisingly young age.

This optimistic view of human nature does not deny other biological capacities that run in the opposite direction and produce conflict: self-defense and hoarding of resources. Most of civilization suggests that the impulse toward egalitarian principles is the stronger one.

It may be that it is precisely in the intricacy of complex institutions that unfairness seems to have a much too secure haven. Then they become a threat to us. This situation is, to invoke a common metaphor, why we say "watch out for the small print" in contracts. It is there that less generous and less egalitarian goals find a home.

5.0 Biological Background: the Missing Dimension

We have argued, essentially, that all rapid computation must have a mechanical basis like the generation of sentences. It is not only sentences and their meanings, organization of physical activity, but also our emotions and conceptualization of our social environment that participate in virtually instantaneous computations through generative rules. These are all essentially innate.[7]

Modern biology – working from its reductionist perspective – has a view of evolution which dominates the field (as far as a non-specialist can tell). The idea is that mutation is random – although this is mathematically dubious – and each new organism succeeds if it fits into some unoccupied environmental niche in nature. Unanswered in this perspective is why evolution persistently creates ever more complex creatures with new and unusual powers. Consider now a radically different perspective which runs absolutely against the survival-of-the-fittest doctrine and the ethic that goes with it. We argue that the Cognitive Science perspective that promotes well-defined algorithms of creativity also entails the notion of expanding environments via generative processes. That extension includes the projection of new Possible Worlds in the mind – and its consequences – like the existence of virtual worlds through the creative capacity of computers. We need to see these steps as logical consequences of an enriched theory of evolution.

We argue that biology follows principles like those in physics and has goals that are not reductionist. We suggest that simple observation is compatible with the view that the goal of evolution and the persistent mutation toward greater complexity is:

7 See M. Hauser and J. Watumull (2017) who consider a theory of a Universal Generative Faculty in a similar vein to apply to all thought. If there are domain-specific constraints on the formulation, for instance of Category-recursion, then it can explain why many properties of recursion are not found in animal languages.

28) Freedom from the environment.

In other words, organisms evolve with ever-greater powers of motion to:

29) Escape their environments

No doubt determined scientists can redefine "environment" to capture this observation as if 29) means "compatible with environment". Nevertheless the intuition that we are not bound by our environment should be clear.

This is the opposite of the claim that organisms mutate in order to fit a small "niche" in their environments, hopefully safe from the aggression of other organisms. We think that freedom should be the pivotal concept here – not environment nor the role of other creatures.

There are hints of this perspective in political discourse. Lyndon Johnson in his graduation speech in Swartthmore College (1964) said that "the truth is, far from crushing the individual, government at its best, liberates him from the enslaving forces of his environment".

One biological story after another suggests that organisms evolve to be free of environmental constraint. Ambulatory fish migrated onshore and occupied the earth. Dinosaurs turned into birds, evolved wings and the capacity to fly, which means to fly from their nests to anywhere. Monkeys jump from tree to tree.

Overt biological evidence exists as well – neurologists can explain everything about motion but the voluntary aspect – what enables us to decide to do something. This has been pointed out by two MIT neurologists Bizzi and Adjemian (2015) who observe that they can explain every detail about how one moves a finger – what is co-ordinated, how electrical impulses carry instructions from the brain, but one ingredient remains a mystery: the "voluntary" part, the *decision* to lift a finger. The fact that it is exercised in milliseconds means that we must ultimately assimilate the voluntary (Free Will) part to biology in a mechanical system. The idea that free will is present in microseconds means that it belongs to the realm of "fast thought" in the terms of Kahneman. Slow thought – how to decide who to marry or where to go on vacation – is another free will mystery, which our approach might also eventually address, but it is not done in milliseconds. We intuitively prize our free will and hold the belief that it is essential to our notion of responsibility and the core of human dignity.

From that perspective, occupying a "niche" in traditional biology misses the essence of what organisms are up to, while the exercise of Free will is the key to human dignity and those concepts like "self-fulfillment". Christian List argues in a compatible vein [(Harvard 2019)] that a supersystem allows personal Agency to play a role when selecting between alternatives and that agency is real and not an illusional epiphenomenon of a deterministic body. He extends a traditional philosophical perspective which we intend to push a step further.

In sum, we suggest that our biology has purposes, a teleology which includes: the pursuit of freedom. This statement lacks the mechanical precision, which would be desireable, but it still lies within the realm of mechanical creativity championed by Cognitive Science. We can make a further claim about teleology: Freedom is a path to Knowledge.

5.1 Species-Identity and Creative Freedom

We can now ask a further question: how does this affect humans and perhaps animals as a species?

We have argued above that organisms have a self-conception which includes the society of which they are a part – so evident, for instance, in the organization of ant colonies. And we claimed that it was present in the earliest uses of grammatical devices like PRO-arb for the unspoken subjects of infinitives that can assume the role of anyone or perhaps everyone.

Once again, the fact that we can exercise Free-Will in micro-seconds means that there must be an explanation at the mechanical level. Let us suppose that it is not quite so mysterious: it is another version of the recursive system that generates sentences, but now at a level up, which is in part what computational theory is about. It is, to seek a new metaphor, what automatic programming or meta-programming is like which is the theory that allows a program to generate new programs by treating a program as just another object in a generative system. It is not in principle a system of a different kind, although we might be wrong here.

Thus we can generate new theories of ourselves by taking whatever system we have generated as an object of the same kind. Grammars generate a set of sentences and a higher system that then generates a set of grammars in the same way, and a yet higher human system that can imagine these systems. This is probably wrong, and certainly too simple, but it may not disturb the further edifice I would like to build over it.

If we invent a new system which generates outputs, like a system of voting that generates a set of representatives, we then generate a set of consequences many of which are unanticipated. The representatives have their own motives and dynamics beyond those of the voters. It is in the nature of generative systems that we have only an abstract sense of what they can generate but not a reliable system to see their consequences when they encounter a novel environment. That is, we can generate sentences of unbounded length which therefore have unique meanings whose character we do not know in advance.

These generative outputs interact with a world – an environment – which we do not understand perfectly. They will generate unanticipated consequences (For instance, like the fear over Y2K that made many people afraid that innocuous dates in the programs of many systems would fail in the year 2000 and many dependent systems, like airplane flights, would then crash). Thus we claim that the consequence of creativity is:

30) Every system or action engenders unanticipated consequences

We can then recalibrate our goals as we see the output of our actions, including their unanticipated implications and consequences. We are aware that we necessarily do not understand the implications, the full consequences, of our actions, because they are an inherently unanticipateable side-product of an infinite system.

5.2 Unintended Consequences as Species Education

Our societies are built around interpersonal actions which carry both carefully conceived intentions and an awareness – because we are dealing with other minds that have the same freedom – that we cannot anticipate consequences beyond a limited degree. If we give a birthday gift, we calculate that it will surprise and gratify the recipient, but we must wait and see how another free person reacts in order to know. And the interpersonal event, the moment of discovery of the unknown consequence, gives "meaning" to the experience. All of our actions – the result of a higher-order Free Will – has this mystery and then discovery as part of its purpose. In effect, every act is an experiment leading to new knowledge.

This is formulated in humanistic language, but a real scientific claim is being made. Actions have unanticipated consequences that teach us about the free variables in the machine – teach us about ourselves. From this perspective the teleology of life is self-knowledge.

Life then consists of small experiments, delivering new knowledge, via actions designed by Free Will, with both intended and instructive unintended consequences.

In sum, every action is a source of self-enlightenment about who we are individually. Now we propose an extension that is part of the biological teleology:

31) Every action reveals who we are as a species.

So we, quite sensibly, learn about the power of any system by seeing what it does. Can this get us from the domain of individual freedom to a point where we can address the emergence of new institutions? The ancient adage "know thyself" may contain not only wise advice but an implicit engine of both individual and social growth, that is, collective experience provides a form of Species-self-knowledge which is gratifying to know.

Now in effect we argue that Creativity is a source of Explanation: self-realization leads to self-knowledge which leads to species-self-knowledge.

Unanticipated implications are then a form of explanation of the system that generates the implications. Consequences are explanations of the greater power of free organisms in miniature. Actions provide explanatory insights into human nature that constitute forms of collective self-discovery.

We see self-knowledge itself as a goal for a society. At the material level, if we generate new environments, as Climate Change has begun to do, we will always need the Creativity to cope materially with the consequences of our actions. We have succeeded in going to the moon, climbing mountains, and socially integrating other cultures, or failing to do so, creating plastics for ever-new purposes. And we generate utterly unanticipated consequences: oceans full of plastic waste, turtles with plastic straws in their noses, and pollution from almost every handy invention that endangers us and our children. There are many paths to self-destruction (like nuclear weapons) but while unanticipated consequences are inevitable, neither our success nor failure to surmount them is inevitable. The fault is not in human nature, nor are our imperfect institutions at fault for being inevitably inadequate.

Over time new systems reveal undeniable improvements in social welfare and organization of material existence – which became the focal point that Marx pursued.

Traditional anarchism argues that:

32) (1) individual diversity means that there is no ideal system for everyone.
   (2) that each new system may apply to a specific set of historical circumstances, and therefore over time becomes obsolete and therefore requires a new system.

The argument here is that new forms of social organization are independently successful or failures not simply in terms of their efficacy for particular situations, but for the sense of community success that they create as a result of their originality. Consider sports. A new pass play in football that leads to a winning game is independently gratifying even if the game could have been won with old pass plays. Or elections: The introduction of rank-ordered voting may not change the outcome of many elections, but it is a gratifying success because it seems to be a superior form of democracy, an example of "a more perfect union" as it says in the US constitution.

The computer revolution and the existence of virtual worlds both enrich and diminish our experiences – compared to the face-to-face world that Goodman advocated. Computers, via social media, offer a source of new forms of human organization and communication, as well as profound dangers, which are not automatically positive or negative. The fact that a programmer can imagine the positive effects on society of his program provides a knowledge-based source of satisfaction which now motivates thousands of programmers. The individual is in effect partaking of a collective experience, and the scientist who discovers a new vaccine does the same, so species-knowledge can profoundly penetrate and fulfill our personal experience. We are each other. The introduction of a new level of social self-knowledge for society – in our view an expression of biological teleology, is a much richer and humane goal than traditional notions of reproduction or self-preservation.

5.3 The Inevitability of Institutional Failures

Now let us return to the question of why institutions so often fail us. The serious downside of these ruminations is that new forms of social organization will always outpace our capacity to understand their unintended consequences. There is a doctrine that that we are a "failed mutation" because the species may self-destruct from unanticipated or poorly anticipated consequences, like much of what has happened during the Coronavirus pandemic.

While our minds operate in milliseconds, our social constructs rarely do. The speed of our inventions, planes and computers, quickly create consequences which cannot be democratically absorbed and evaluated. Much of what we value highly calls for rumination or "slow thought" which in turn must be shared through discussion in order to achieve mutually sought and cooperative goals. The speed of technology is, in a sense, inherently anti-democratic.

Can we grasp this consequence of our creativity and reverse it so that there is room for the evolution of a culture that does not take precipitous action? It is definitely possible that we can succeed and certainly possible that we can fail. A recent call for a law that would prevent any president from launching a nuclear weapon alone – without consent from other societal representatives – is an obvious move in this direction. It is a form of unilateral disarmament because it would mean that if weapons were already launched against a society, it could not react quickly. Countries that have renounced nuclear weapons experience a form of societal self-knowledge that other countries do not have.

The failure to grasp or anticipate the consequences of creativity are true for animals as well as humans. That notion follows from the fact that the environments in which creativity occurs are never fully knowable in advance. An animal that is caught by a trap has the same experience of an unknown territory as we do by our invention of nuclear weapons. Animals perform experiments as well, deciding if other animals (like humans) are trustworthy or should be avoided. Such experimentation, and then knowledge, is part of the animals' teleology.

It entails some form of Free Will as well.

Many have also pointed to the fact that the earth will not last forever. That is not a fault of humans and our efforts to seek other civilizations in the universe show our efforts toward surmounting those dangers. Others have placed their faith in the astonishing "innovation" modern economies have exhibited – and yet there is nothing inevitable about their continued success either.

6.0 The State

The State is a conglomerate of institutions and the source of enforcement power. Therefore it is an institution of a different order – one toward which we must be wary and imagine methods to protect ourselves. Typically states are either overpowerful or immobilized by the gridlock of opposing forces.

Here is where the anarchist approach to freedom of association and movement becomes important. Either liveable compromises or independent communities must be sought. The notion that our societies will be dominated by neutral spaces is unlikely.

Personal liberty can be obtained in many ways and often is. Once again, it is the creative power of algorithmic thinking in the social sphere which may allow hitherto unimagined forms of organization which provide both solutions and the psychological satisfaction of social creativity. These formulations, like many in this essay, remain vague and unsatisfying because there is no deeper formula for a peaceful and prosperous society. Marx's sensible goal of a rational theory of society seems attractive, but with human creativity always producing more unintended consequences, it is both unrealistic and undesireable.

The perspective we have advocated here – a view of human nature that includes awareness of society and community from the earliest years in children's lives – and accepts that our fundamental mental creativity has consequences we cannot easily control, should be seen as a reality and not a criticism.

Instead of expanding current institutions, we are in the process of creating a galaxy of new informal institutions which exhibit gargantuan new powers in the form of online communities, online monitoring, and even new financial organizations (bitcoin). These as well have both positive and malevolent capacities.

What is a possible goal of this evolution? It is that we establish a community of institutions that voluntarily work toward co-operative action, To do that we will have to fire up our institutional imaginations, not deny the necessity of organization, as some who are often called "anarchists" from a rightwing perspective are tempted to do.

If we can prevent environmental catastrophe, then a culture for a community of institutions can evolve through our extraordinary new communicative capacities. The UN is a first example of this kind of effort since it largely organizes but does not really control its members. It is rare that one encounters someone in favor of a complete "world government" with absolute enforcement powers. At a macro-level the UN experience demonstrates that voluntary cooperation must be the goal of a community of institutions.

It is clear that one-man-one vote democracy cannot work on a global scale. We cannot have an election for president of the UN with 6 billion voters speaking several thousand languages. Nonetheless intermediate forms of democracy are very possible. The current UN is an experiment with many failures as well as successes. Its overpowerful Security Council is perhaps a lesson in how not to organize a community of institutions.

The Black Lives Matter movement has spontaneous leaders, but not elected ones. Will it work? It is an experiment whose consequences we must still appraise.

6.1 Conclusion

In sum we have argued that all organisms have a teleology. It is a teleology that leads to increased complexity and mutations that allow Free Will and seek freedom from the immediate environment. This freedom then creates the opportunity for mental, social, and physical creativity, using the kinds of mechanical algorithms that are the heart of Cognitive Science. Such creativity can apply to its own output – often called recursive operations. Systems with infinite generative capacity inevitably generate unanticipated consequences, good and bad, which both instruct us about ourselves as a species and lead to new systems.

A constant effort to create new social organizations provides not only self-knowledge for individuals but a kind of social self-knowledge for societies which is independently fulfilling for individuals and communities. And it creates dangers that we are confronted with every day via unintended consequences. Yet it is even more dangerous if the world community loses faith that there can be an eventual world order that has room for everyone to prosper.

Acknowledgements: thanks to Noam Chomsky for laying the groundwork in both Cognitive Science and social commentary for this easay, and for relevant personal communication over the years. And to Günther Grewendorf for providing a forum where the larger social implications of Cognitive Science are welcome.

Also: Manfred Bierwisch Jill devilliers, Bart Hollebrandse,Wolfram Hinzen, Steven Pinker, among many, many others all provided stimulating perspectives, although they might not recognize any connecctions in the text..

There are other real sources in my education, family history, and career as a cognitive scientist doing linguistics and language acquisition.

These include my grandparents (Max Bondy) and great-uncle (Curt Bondy) who were leaders of the Jugendbewegung in Germany in the 1920's (a part of the Socialist Party Jungsozialisten). They created impressive democratic communities (Schule Marienau, Gross-Breesen, Windsor Mountain School, and the Roeper School). Their progressive educational philosophy contained the seeds of this approach to Cognitive Science, where individuality, Free Will, and systematic unconscious computation have a basis in sophisticated views of the human mind.

They and other institutions like them prove that communities that follow the essence of these principles can and do exist.

Bibliography

CHILDES (Child Language Data Exchange System) ed. Brian MacWhinney, 1990 Carnegie-Mellon, https://childes.talkbank.org/

Chomsky, Carol, 1969: The acquisition of Syntax from 5 to 10, MIT Press

Chomsky, Noam, 2019: MIT Press interview "On Language and Humanity: In Conversation With Noam Chomsky", https://thereader.mitpress.mit.edu/noam-chomsky-interview/

Chomsky, Noam, 2016: What kind of Creatures are we? Columbia University Press, New York

Dewey, John, 2000: entree in Stanford Encyclopedia of Philosophy (1995) Wikipedia

Hauser, Marc and Jeffrey *Watumull*, 2017: The Universal Generative Faculty: The source of our expressive power in language, mathematics, morality, and music, Journal of Neurolinguistics 43, DOI: 10.1016/j.jneuroling.2016.10.005

Gleitman, Lila and Barbara *Partee*, 2020: UMass talk on symmetrical predicates

Godwin, William, 2000: entree in Stanford Encyclopedia of Philosophy, Wikipedia [https://en.wikipedia.org/wiki/William_Godwin]

Goodman, Paul and Perceival *Goodman*, 1990: Communitas: Ways of Livelihood and Ways of Life. NY: Columbia University Press/Morningside.

Gulzow, Insa, 2011: ms. Acquisition of Reciprocals in German, Leibniz Institute (Berlin)

Green, Danny, 2008: Acquisition of Reciprocals in English, UMass Honors Thesis

Kahneman, Daniel, 2011: Thinking, Fast and Slow, Farrar, Strauss, and Giroux, Macmillan, New York

List, Christian, 2019: Why Free Will is real, Harvard University Press, Cambridge, Mass.

Marx, Karl, 1848: Theses on Feuerbach, Progress Publishers, Moscow, USSR.

Roeper, Tom, 2007: The Prism of Grammar, MIT Press, Cambridgee Mass.

Roeper, Tom, 2016: "Propositions carry implicit arguments with a general point of view" in Subjective meaning: Alternatives to relativism (2016) eds. Janneke van Wijnbergen-Huitink and Cecile Meier

Weinberg, Steven, 2001: The future of science and the universe, New York Review of Books 48, 18

Wilson, Andrew and Sabrina *Golonka,* 2013: "Embodied cognition is not what you think it is" Front. Psychol., 12 February 2013 | https://doi.org/10.3389/fpsyg.2013.00058

The Relation of the Individual to the State and the Gist of Anarchism

Milan Rai

Anarchism, Government and the State

1. Communal Forms of Self-Government

In general conversation, in journalism, and sometimes in academic research, 'the government' and 'the state' are often used as interchangeable terms. Noam Chomsky is one of those who believe that a useful and, in fact, important distinction can be drawn between the two concepts. However, Chomsky draws the lines between and around 'the government' and 'the state' in unusual ways. Chomsky is also unusual in being – with important qualifications, discussed below – for the abolition of both 'the government' and 'the state': an anarchist. Chomsky has made his anarchist commitments clear from his earliest writings, which expressed solidarity with the anarchist revolution in Spain during the 1936 – 1937 Civil War. Called an 'anarchist thinker' by a British journalist during a television interview, Chomsky suggested that he was, rather, 'a derivative fellow traveller' of the major anarchist thinkers – people such as Mikhail Bakunin (1814 – 1876) and Rudolf Rocker (1873 – 1958). (Chomsky 1981, p. 247) The label 'anarchism' has been used for a wide array of sometimes contradictory positions. We will examine below some aspects of Chomsky's approach to anarchism and libertarian socialism.

In Chomsky's view, all genuine political positions are rooted in 'some implicit concept of human nature, as biological given'. (Chomsky 1988a, p. 385) If we are opposed to slavery, for example, 'it is because we think that slavery is inconsistent with fundamental human rights, which are rooted in the nature of humans, which demand that they be free and not owned by others.' We oppose slavery because it is 'an interference with the essential human nature, an essential human right to be free and under one's own control'. (Chomsky 1988a, p. 597) Chomsky traces this freedom-centred view of human nature back to the Enlightenment and to such founders of classical liberalism as Wilhelm von Humboldt (1767 – 1835). Humboldt wrote in 1792:

> 'The true end of Man, or that which is prescribed by the eternal and immutable dictates of reason, and not suggested by vague and transient desires, is the highest and most harmonious development of his powers to a complete and consistent whole. Freedom is the first and indispensable condition which the possibility of such a development presupposes; but there is besides another essential – intimately connected with freedom, it is true – a variety of situations.' (Chomsky 1973, p. 177)

Humboldt argued that 'nothing promotes this ripeness for freedom so much as freedom itself'. To think otherwise, Humboldt suggested, is to misunderstand human nature and to wish 'to make men into machines'. (Chomsky 1973, pp. 177, 178) The position that one becomes capable of freedom only by exercising freedom was also taken by Immanuel Kant (1724 – 1804). Kant made this argument while defending the French Revolution during the terror, as Chomsky points out. (Chomsky 2005 [1970], p. 39)

If a need for freedom is at the core of human nature, it follows that 'any form of authority or domination is... an infringement, and is therefore essentially illegitimate.' (Chomsky 1988a, p. 386) Chomsky argues that it is the responsibility of those who exercise power to show that it is legitimate in some way. The burden of proof does not lie on others to show that power is illegitimate: 'It's illegitimate by assumption, if it's a relation of authority among human beings which places some above others.' If it cannot be shown to be legitimate, the structure of power should be dismantled. In rare circumstances, authority can be justified, Chomsky concedes: 'So to take a homely example, if I'm walking down the street with my four-year-old granddaughter, and she starts to run into the street, and I grab her arm and pull her back, that's an exercise of power and authority, but I can give a justification for it, and it's obvious what the justification would be.' (Kreisler 2002) Authority tends to justify itself by analogy to that kind of situation, protecting those who are incapable of protecting themselves, or restraining those who are incapable of restraining themselves. (See Humboldt and Kant, above.)

A classic formulation of the authoritarian position was put forward by US ecologist Garrett Hardin (1915 – 2003), and summarised in his influential and misleading phrase, 'the tragedy of the commons'. (Hardin 1968) In Hardin's view, unless there is either private ownership or state control, valuable resources will always be exploited to the point of disaster. In a thought-experiment, Hardin gave as an example a field held as common property by a community, and used for cattle to graze on. Hardin argued that such a pasture would soon have too many cows on it and overgrazing would destroy this resource for everyone. Hardin declared that the economic benefit to an individual herder of adding another cow to her or his herd would outweigh the damage done to the pasture. The extra benefit would go solely to the herder. The extra damage would be shared by all the herders. Rational herders would inevitably keep adding to their herds until the pasture was destroyed. 'Freedom in a commons brings ruin to all', Hardin stated. Common property is disastrous.

One of many faults in Hardin's analysis was that he did not consider the history of actual commons. This omission was rectified by Nobel-prize-winning economist Elinor Ostrom (1933 – 2012) in her magisterial work, *Governing the Commons: The Evolution of Institutions for Collective Action.* (Ostrom 1990)

Ostrom details a number of successful common property systems from around the world, including the *zanjera* irrigation communities of the Philippines. The *zanjera*s have existed since at least 1630. That is when they were first written about by Catholic priests who were part of the Spanish colonial occupation of the archipelago. '*Zanjeras* have been established both by landowning farmers wanting to construct common irrigation works and by individuals organizing themselves so as to acquire land,' writes Ostrom. (Ostrom 1990, p. 82)

In a *zanjera*, a group of irrigators draw up their own rules, choose their own officials, and construct, maintain and guard their own dams and canals. The *zanjera* does not simply regulate how much water can be taken by each individual member, it builds the infrastructure that brings water to the members' fields.

For example, there might be a piece of land that is not very productive because it has no access to irrigation water. The owner of the land could form a *zanjera* with a group of tenant farmers. Together, all the members of the *zanjera* could build a dam upstream on the nearest river and dig canals to bring water to the previously-unirrigated land.

Each member of the *zanjera* would then gain 'the right to the produce from a defined portion of the newly-irrigated land', Ostrom writes. She goes on:

'This type of contract – called a *biang ti daga* or a "sharing of the land" – allows the landowner to retain ownership. Use rights are extended to the *zanjera* dependent on continued maintenance of the irrigation system.' (Ostrom 1990, p. 82)

Each member of the *zanjera* has a single share (*atar*), which carries with it the right to farm a proportionate share of the land controlled by the *zanjera*. Usually, according to Ostrom, the land held by the *zanjera* is divided into three or more large sections, and each farmer is given a plot in each section. Every member will have a plot near the head of the system, where the irrigation water enters the land, and every member will have a plot in the least-advantageous area, in the tail of the system, which is the last to get irrigation water. Ostrom points out that this enables a fair sharing of scarcity in years when there is not enough rainfall – the *zanjera* can decide not to irrigate the bottom section of land, impacting all sharers equally. People who serve as officials in the *zanjera* may be given a parcel of land at the tail end of the system as payment. Ostrom notes that this gives an incentive for those in leadership positions to make sure water gets to the tail end of the system.

The *atar* (share) also defines the labour commitment and materials that the *atar*-holder must supply at the time of construction. There are fines for not showing up for *zanjera* work periods.

Ostrom illustrates the working of the system with the example of a *zanjera* federation on the northwestern tip of Luzon Island. (Ostrom 1990, pp. 83 – 88) Originally, there were a lot of individual *zanjera*s which operated independently, taking water from the Bacarra-Vintar River. However, the river changed course over time, cutting some *zanjera*s off. The groups began banding together during the nineteenth century and by the 1950s nine *zanjera*s were in the Bacarra-Vintar federation. In 1980, there were 431 individuals owning shares (or parts of shares) in one or more of the nine *zanjera*s.

The federation draws water from the river by building (and maintaining) a 100-metre-long brush dam – a relatively crude traditional technology – across the river. In the Philippines, a brush dam uses small tree branches (brushwood), poles, bamboo and stones to make a semi-permeable barrier to hold and to divert river water.

When leading members of the Bacarra-Vintar *zanjera* federation decide it is time to rebuild or repair the dam, each *zanjera* must supply workers and a share of the construction materials needed for the week. The width of the river is divided into sections, proportional to the size of the work teams and the difficulty of the terrain.

The work of maintaining the main canal coming off the river is divided in a similar way. The smaller offshoot canals are maintained by each *zanjera* separately.

For her information on the Bacarra-Vintar *zanjera* federation, Ostrom relied on the work of Filipino development economist Robert Y Siy. (Siy 1982) Siy acknowledges that the allocation of water between the nine *zanjera*s is not as efficient as it could be, but that it is seen as fair by members. Ostrom comments: 'when external experts, working without the participation of the irrigators, have designed systems with the primary aim of achieving technical efficiency, they frequently have failed to achieve either the hoped-for technical efficiency or the level of organized action required to allocate water in a regular fashion or to maintain the physical system itself'. (Ostrom 1990, p. 88)

For hundreds of years, the *zanjera* system has provided an effective method of constructing vital infrastructure and irrigating land for agriculture. It has also been a stable grassroots democratic institution enabling poor farmers to govern themselves without the intervention of external authority. It has also enabled them to gain sustained access to land without needing to build up a store of money in advance.

What the *zanjera* system shows is that communal forms of self-government can be effective, enduring and egalitarian without needing participants to all become completely unselfish altruists. Community-defined standards of fairness, community-agreed institutional checks and balances, and an interlocking system of incentives and sanctions decided on by participants themselves, have produced effective grassroots governance.

All this has happened without private property in the dams or canal systems (or the water itself) – or external regulation by governmental authorities.

If we go back to Hardin, he wrote: 'The only kind of coercion I recommend is mutual coercion, mutually agreed upon by the majority of the people affected.' What Hardin failed to see was that holding productive resources as common property has been successful in many cases, and that effective self-government in relation to such resources has often been based on 'mutual coercion, mutually agreed on by the people affected'. (Hardin 1968)

Exploring the *zanjera* system in such detail, in an essay on Chomsky's ideas, may give the misleading impression that Chomsky subscribes to a rural, small-scale, agrarian vision of a desirable society. This is the kind of anarchism associated with one of the major anarchist thinkers, Peter Kropotkin (1842 – 1921).[1]

To the contrary, Chomsky has repeatedly and vehemently rejected the idea that anarchist ideas belong to the pre-industrial phase of human society. He once explained in an interview:

> 'I think that industrialization and the advance of technology raise possibilities for self-management over a broad scale that simply didn't exist in an earlier period. And that in fact this is precisely the rational mode for an advanced and complex industrial society, one in which workers can very well become masters of their own immediate affairs, that is, in direction and control of the [work]shop, but also can be in a position to make the major substantive decisions concerning the structure of the economy, concerning social institutions, concerning planning regionally and beyond. At present, institutions do not permit them to have control over the requisite information, and the relevant training to understand these matters.' (Chomsky 1981, pp. 248 – 249)

Earlier, Chomsky wrote: 'What is far more important [than anarchist and libertarian socialist thinking and writing about direct workers' control of industry] is that these ideas have been realized in spontaneous revolutionary action, for example in Germany and Italy after World War I and in Spain (not only in the agricultural countryside, but also in industrial Barcelona) in 1936.' (Chomsky 1973, p. 162)

In Italy, during the *biennio rosso* ('two red years') of 1919 – 1920, hundreds of factories were occupied and continued producing goods under the control of workers' representatives. In Turin, the most militant area, control was exercised by elected factory councils. Elsewhere, power was often held by the traditional and generally reformist *Camere del Lavoro* ('Chambers of Labour'), originally founded as labour exchanges. (Sipriano 1975 [1964], p. 84) For almost the whole of September 1920, for example, over 400,000 metalworkers occupied all the metallurgical factories in north-western Italy. (Sipriano 1975 [1964], p. 60) In Turin, the factory councils were 'the disciplined core of this whole complex of activity in workers' management', with sub-sections for 'provisioning, subsidies, kitchens, internal discipline, defence, propaganda' and so on. (Sipriano 1975 [1964], p. 118) Workers in other industries also occupied their places of work, including an oxygen plant and the Michelin tyre factory in Turin – by 13 September, 150,000 workers were occu-

---

1   Chomsky 'rarely' mentions Kropotkin, Paul Marshall notes in his 'Noam Chomsky's anarchism', *Our Generation* Vol. 22 Nos. 1&2 Fall 1990 – Spring 1991, p. 11. Marshall adds in a footnote: 'This does not mean that Chomsky finds little of value in Kropotkin. He believes that Kropotkin's Mutual Aid was "perhaps the first major contribution to sociobiology" (*The Chomsky Reader*, p. 21).'

pying their plants in the Turin area. (Williams 1975, p. 247) In Turin, among other forms of workers' power, there were 'communist kitchens' (not Communist Party kitchens, as the party did not exist in Italy until January 1921) supplied by the Turin Co-operative Alliance. There was also an alternative workers' currency (five-lira vouchers issued by the local *Camera del Lavoro* and honoured by the union of small shopkeepers). (Williams 1975, p. 248)

In Spain, there was a wave of collectivisation of agriculture during the 1936 – 1937 Spanish Revolution, but Chomsky is most interested in Barcelona, which had been a leading industrial city since the mid-nineteenth century. (It was known as 'the Manchester of the South'.)

In an early essay, 'Objectivity and Liberal Scholarship', Chomsky noted: 'The success of collectivization of industry and commerce in Barcelona impressed even highly unsympathetic observers such as Franz Borkenau.' Borkenau, an Austrian ex-Communist, was extremely hostile to anarchism. According to diary notes he later published as a book, Borkenau visited a collectivised factory in Barcelona on 8 August 1936. (Borkenau 2016 [1937]) This was just three weeks after a revolutionary upsurge had stopped a military coup in Barcelona and two weeks after the end of a general strike in the city.

Borkenau reported that the bus company's repair workshop, under the control of the anarchist CNT union, seemed to 'run as smoothly as if nothing had happened'. The new management of the factory had been elected by the workers in the factory – 'but in fact it seemed to be the old factory committee of the CNT [ordinary workers, in other words], which was an established authority among the men long before the civil war'. Borkenau emphasised: 'one must not forget that this firm has lost its whole managing staff'. He noted: 'These Catalan workers have actually started their management with the introduction of cuts in expenditure, and there is nothing they are more proud of.'

In the weeks since the socialisation (not 'nationalisation') of the factory, the workers had repaired two buses, finished one which had been under construction, and built a completely new bus, which Borkenau saw. The new bus, the workers said, had been manufactured in five days, 'against an average of seven days under the previous management'. Borkenau concluded:

> But if it would be hasty to generalize from the very favourable impression made by this particular factory, one fact remains: it is an extraordinary achievement for a group of workers to take over a factory, under however favourable conditions, and within a few days to make it run with complete regularity. It bears brilliant witness to the general standard of efficiency of the Catalan worker and to the organizing capacities of the Barcelona trade unions.

There were different reasons for workers taking over control of factories. According to one count, of the 34 metalworking and automobile firms taken over by workers in

Barcelona in August and September 1936, over a quarter (nine) were socialised because the employers had vanished. In another quarter of the cases (eight), the employer is said to have voluntarily 'gifted' the enterprise to the workers. (Mintz 2013 [1970], p. 73) (There must be doubt as to how voluntary this 'gifting' actually was.) According to two Spanish sources, when owners and managers who had fled in July 1936 returned to Barcelona after Franco's victory in early 1939, they expressed surprise that their businesses were in such good condition. (Seidman 1982, p. 433 n. 79) US historian Michael Seidman comments:

> 'The working-class militants had even improved the backward industries which they had inherited from a bourgeoisie which was weak both politically and economically. The unions and factory councils had often rationalized, standardized, and modernized production under trying circumstances. They bought new machinery, improved working conditions, built schools, and tried to eliminate a number of the most glaring inequalities.' (Seidman 1982, p. 429)

Seidman describes the usual course of events:

> 'Militants from the CNT, quite often with the collaboration of members of the Communist-oriented UGT (Unión General de Trabajadores), took charge of the abandoned factories. Many firms, especially those with over a hundred workers, were collectivized. The collectives, as they were called, were ruled by a factory council, usually composed of both CNT and UGT militants elected by the workers of the firm. Many other factories and workshops, particularly those which had less than fifty workers and whose owners remained in Barcelona to work during the Revolution, were managed jointly by the owner and a control committee of CNT and UGT militants.' (Seidman 1982, p. 416)

Seidman points out that both CNT and UGT militants wanted to bring together the scattered workforces of Barcelona's various industries into more efficient, effective units, and to promote standardisation, rationalisation and better health and safety conditions. In the textile industry, work done at home was abolished and workshops were set up with 'natural light and ventilation' (as well as 'experts' to direct the workers). (Seidman 1982, p. 418)

More testimony to the organising capacities of the Barcelona trade unions can be found in a collection of documents on collectivisation during the Spanish Revolution brought together by the French anarcho-syndicalist Gaston Leval (who took part in the revolution). (Leval 1975 [1971])

Leval records, for example, that almost all the 7,000 workers on the Barcelona tramways were members of the anarchist CNT union. According to Leval, the tramways, the most important means of transport in the city in 1936, were maintained by a company with its own repair workshops.

In the aftermath of the fighting in mid-July, in which buses and trams had often been used as barricades, seven workers were selected by the union to form an organising Syndicate or *Comité* which called together delegates from the electric power station and other departments: cables, repairs, traffic, conductors, stores, accounts and administration. 'All the engineers put themselves at the disposal of the Syndicate, including a former colonel whose active sympathy for the workers had resulted in his demotion from head of the traffic section and director of the Metro to a job in the archives section.' (Leval 1975 [1971] p. 246)

According to Leval, each section (power, cables, repairs and so on) had at its head 'an engineer nominated by agreement with the Syndicates, and a representative of the workers' – chosen at an assembly of all the non-engineering workers in the section. No engineer could take an important decision without consulting the local *Comité*, 'not only because he agreed that responsibility should be shared but also because often, where practical problems are involved, manual workers have the experience which technicians lack.' (Leval 1975 [1971] p. 247)

Just five days after the fighting in July, the organisation was operating 700 tram-cars instead of the usual 600. According to Leval, 'work had gone on night and day [without overtime pay] repairing and putting back into service a hundred tram-cars which had been discarded as being beyond repair.' The extra 100 tram-cars enabled the workers to stop using unpowered trailer-cars which had been responsible for accidents. (Leval 1975 [1971] pp. 246–247)

Many other improvements were made, including the introduction of a new safety and signalling system. The water, light and power company (now also under workers' self-management) was persuaded to move junction boxes out of the way to straighten tram routes, making the lines safer. (Leval 1975 [1971] p. 248)

Before the socialisation of the tramways, the company's workshops had only manufactured 2% of the material it used. By the end of 1936, according to Leval's information, the workshops were producing 98% of the material used by the organisation. (Leval 1975 [1971] p. 250)

There was a major effort to improve wages and to eliminate pay differentials in the company. Before socialisation, labourers in the tramways earned 8–9 pesetas a day; traffic controllers 10; lorry drivers, lathe operators and other skilled engineering workers 12. After socialisation, labourers received 15 pesetas a day, and skilled workers 16. A medical and home help service was set up which served not only workers but also their families, according to Leval. (Leval 1975 [1971] p. 252)

The number of passenger-journeys on Barcelona's trams is said to have increased by 50 million from 1936 to 1937, with over 233.6 million passenger journeys in the latter year. There was also a significant increase in passenger-miles, to 14.4 million. This was partly explained by the new policy of a flat fare of 0.20 pesetas per journey, rather than 0.10 to 0.40 pesetas based on distance. (Leval 1975 [1971] pp. 249–250)

According to Leval, the tramways subsidised other transport systems in Barcelona – giving 865,000 pesetas to the buses, for example. (Leval 1975 [1971] p. 251)

Borkenau reported that, when he reached Barcelona on 5 August 1936, 'Tramways and buses were running, water and light functioning' – all under workers' self-management, though he does not mention this. (Borkenau 2016 [1937])

Chomsky emphasises that these achievements were 'based on the patient work of many years of organization and education, one component of a long tradition of commitment and militancy.' After decades of struggle and planning, 'workers' organizations existed with the structure, the experience, and the understanding to undertake the task of social reconstruction when, with the Franco coup, the turmoil of early 1936 exploded into social revolution.' (Chomsky 1973, pp. 162, 163)

2. Government and the State

The seizure of power by workers at the shopfloor level – in Turin and even more so in Barcelona – and the creation of a grassroots industrial democracy answerable to the factory workforce in both cities were, Chomsky argues, attempts to fulfil the spirit of classical liberalism in a very different age.

Earlier, we saw that Humboldt, one of the founders of classical liberalism and a deep influence on John Stuart Mill, believed that freedom was an indispensable precondition for 'the highest and most harmonious development' of the individual's powers 'to a complete and consistent whole'.

Chomsky points out that Humboldt related this fundamental belief to work and exploitation. Humboldt wrote:

> '... man never regards what he possesses as so much his own, as what he does, and the labourer who tends the garden is perhaps in a truer sense its owner than the listless voluptuary who enjoys its fruits.... In view of this consideration, it seems as if all peasants and craftsmen might be elevated into artists, that is men who love their labour for its own sake, improve it by their own plastic genius and invented skill, and thereby cultivate their intellect, ennoble their character and exult and refine their pleasures. And so humanity would be ennobled by the very things which now, though beautiful in themselves, so often serve to degrade it. But, still, freedom is undoubtedly the indispensable condition without which even the pursuits most congenial to individual human nature can never succeed in producing such salutary influences. Whatever does not spring from a man's free choice, or is only the result of instruction and guidance, does not enter into his very being but remains alien to his true nature. He does not perform it with truly human energies, but merely with mechanical exactness.' (Chomsky 1973, p. 179)

And if a person acts in a purely mechanical way, reacting to external demands or instruction, rather than in ways determined by her own interests and energies and power, says Humboldt, 'we may admire what [s]he does, but we despise what [s]he is'. (Chomsky 1973, p. 179)

In many of the factories in Turin, and even more so in Barcelona, workers replaced the external, unaccountable authority of the owner and manager with forms of organisation and authority that they saw as legitimate, and which they felt were responsive and accountable to them. They were attempting to alter factory work from something degrading, mechanical and alien into something springing from their own free choice, which gave them an opportunity to apply their own 'plastic genius and invented skill', and in which they could give rein to their 'truly human energies'. ('Plastic' here relates to 'offering scope for creativity'.)

One of Chomsky's main objections to capitalist democracy as it is practised in the US and Britain, and other western nations, is that 'representative democracy is limited to the political sphere and in no serious way encroaches on the economic sphere.' (Chomsky, 1981, p. 246) Chomsky notes that 'the range of decisions that are in principle subject to public democratic control is quite narrow': 'it excludes in law and in principle the central institutions in any advanced industrial society, that is, the entire commercial, industrial, and financial system.' (Chomsky 2005 [1970], p. 47) Chomsky quotes John Dewey, who wrote in March 1931 that 'politics is the shadow cast on society by big business'. (Chomsky 2000, p. 208)

Furthermore, Chomsky points out:

> 'even within the narrow range of issues that are submitted in principle to democratic decision-making, the centers of private power exert an inordinately heavy influence in perfectly obvious ways, through control of the media, through control of political organizations, or by the simple and direct means of supplying the top personnel for the parliamentary system itself, as they obviously do. In Richard Barnet's recent study of the top four hundred decision makers in the postwar national security system, he finds that most "have come from executive suites and law offices within shouting distance of one another in fifteen city blocks in New York, Washington, Detroit, Chicago, and Boston." [Barnet 1969, p. 97] And every other study shows the same thing.' (Chomsky 2005 [1970], pp. 47 – 48) ,

As long as most people are forced to rent themselves on the market as ancillary tools, 'there are striking elements of coercion and oppression that make talk of democracy very limited, if even meaningful'. (Chomsky 1981, p. 246) Chomsky points out that domination by totalitarian structures in our economic lives has 'a great effect on the general character of the culture': it subtly induces 'an authoritarian cast of mind... in a very large mass of the population, which is subject to arbitrary decree from above'. (Chomsky 2005 [1970], pp. 46 – 47)

In the capitalist workplace, Chomsky observes, there are hierarchical structures 'of a kind that we would call fascist in the political domain'. (Chomsky 1988b p. 32) In an interview with *Business Today*, Chomsky stated:

'a corporation or an industry is, if we were to think of it in political terms, fascist; that is, it has tight control at the top and strict obedience has to be established at every level – there's a little bargaining, a little give and take, but the line of authority is perfectly straightforward. Just as I'm opposed to political fascism, I'm opposed to economic fascism. I think that until major institutions of society are under the popular control of participants and communities, it's pointless to talk about democracy.' (Chomsky 1988a, p. 162)

Corporations (in the US) 'are free from public control, except in the remote and indirect ways in which even a feudal nobility or a totalitarian dictatorship must be responsive to the public will'. (Chomsky 2005 [1970], p. 46)

In a talk in 1970, Chomsky argued that 'democracy is largely a sham when the industrial system is controlled by any form of autocratic elite, whether it's owners, managers, technocrats, a vanguard party, a state bureaucracy, or whatever.' (Chomsky 2005 [1970], p. 28) In 2000, he pointed to a fundamental choice, whether rights and freedoms and sovereignty belong to persons of flesh and blood, or only to small sectors of wealth and privilege, or even to 'abstract constructions like corporations, or capital, or states'. (In western law, a corporation is a 'legal person' separate from the human owners, managers and employees who are associated with it.) Chomsky pointed out:

'In the past century, the idea that such entities have special rights, over and above persons, has been very strongly advocated. The most prominent examples are Bolshevism, fascism, and private corporatism, which is a form of privatized tyranny.' (Chomsky 2000, p. 208)

The first two systems had collapsed, but the third continues to flourish 'under the banner TINA – There Is No Alternative' to the emerging system of state-corporate-managed trade.

We have finally come to 'the state' and to the distinction between 'the state' and 'the government'. There has been some confusion on this question, and disagreement over whether these two entities are in fact distinct. In a recent survey of the debate, US geographer Edward Heath Robinson urges political geographers to use the abstract definition of 'the state' that operates in international law. In this perspective, states are nonphysical legal persons with four characteristics: they control a permanent population and a defined territory and they possess both 'a government' and the 'capacity to enter into relations with other states'. In contrast, Heath Robinson frames his definition of 'a government' using Weber's concept of 'the form of human community that (successfully) lays claim to the *monopoly of legitimate physical violence* within a particular territory'. (Heath Robinson 2013, p. 561) In this view, the government is the tangible representative of the intangible state; it is a group of human agents authorised to coerce others in the name of the (non-physical) state.

At another point on the political spectrum, British sociologist Ralph Miliband drew the distinction between 'the state' and 'the government' quite differently in *The State in Capitalist Society*. For Miliband, the government is the 'political executive', the group of ministers who hold national office. The state system, on the other hand, is made up of 'the government [ministers], the administration [the bureaucracy], the military and the police, the judicial branch, sub-central government and parliamentary assemblies'. Outside the state system, for Miliband, is the wider 'political system' including political parties and pressure groups, and also non-political but influential institutions such as 'giant corporations, Churches, the mass media, etc.' (Miliband 1969, p. 54)

Miliband was primarily interested in the relationship of the state, as he defined it, to 'the economically dominant class' in society. The question, in his view is:

> 'whether this dominant class... exercises a much greater degree of power and influence than any other class; whether it exercises [a] decisive degree of political power; whether its ownership and control of crucially important areas of economic life also insures its control of the means of political decision-making in the particular political environment of advanced capitalism.' (Miliband, 1969, p. 48)

Miliband was at pains to state that it 'cannot be assumed, in the political conditions which are typical of advanced capitalism' that the state is simply the 'agent' of the economically dominant class. (Miliband 1969, p. 54)

For Chomsky, as far as I can see, it is not exactly that this proposition can be assumed, it is just overwhelmingly likely to be true from first principles. In any nation-state, Chomsky seems to believe, dominant sections of society will become part of the ruling state system: 'when you move to state power you get organized systems of violence and coercion and the people who have real power are going to take them over because they need them and want them.' (Chomsky 1988a, p. 744) 'Governments [meaning "states"] are serving certain interests, whatever the interest of some domestic power is. It would be just the merest accident if that happened to have a morally favourable quality to it.' (Chomsky 1988a, p. 744)

We can find Chomsky using at least three definitions of 'the state'. We have already seen Chomsky invoking an 'abstract construction' definition of the state, where the state is an idea. We find something similar in Chomsky's withering phrase 'the Holy State', referring to a nation-state that is worshipped by an intellectual – it can do no wrong. (Chomsky 1985, p. 178) Usually this is the intellectual's own home country, but sometimes a foreign state is favoured.

A more common usage of 'the state' in Chomsky's writings is more concrete and rather conventional. It refers to physically-existing government-connected institutions (staffed by flesh-and-blood 'natural persons'). This usage refers to something very similar to Miliband's list of institutions above. Thus, Chomsky said once that the state 'does have its own independent interests' (independent of the economically dominant class). For example, it is true there is 'a partially independent managerial system' in the Pentagon structure, 'which simply has tremendous assets at its disposal.' (Chomsky 1988a, p. 185)

However, it turns out that Chomsky's preferred concept of 'the state' is rather more unconventional, what we might call an expanded definition. Chomsky wrote in *Turning the Tide*:

> 'We might make a distinction between the state and the government, where the state is a system of institutions, including private institutions, that set conditions for public policy, which are relatively stable, changing slowly if at all. These constitute the actual nexus of decision-making power in the society, including investment and political decisions, setting the framework within which public policy can be discussed and is determined.' (Chomsky 1985, p. 230)

In contrast, for Chomsky, 'the government' is merely 'whatever groups happen to control the political system, one component of the state system, at a particular moment.' (Chomsky 1985, p. 230)

Thus it is perfectly possible for the mainstream media to be 'critical of the government while they remain obedient to the state'. (Chomsky 1985, p. 230)

In Chomsky's expanded definition, 'the state' includes the institutions listed by Miliband: government ministers, the civil service and government agencies, the military, intelligence services and the police, the judiciary, local government and parliamentary assemblies. However, it also includes corporations, major (private) financial institutions as well as 'a few law firms that cater primarily to corporate interests and thus represent the broad interests of owners and managers rather than some parochial interest'. (Chomsky 1987, p. 117) Chomsky has also referred to a wider 'tightly linked network of planning and social control' in the US that includes foundations and universities. (Chomsky 1981, p. 62)

So when Chomsky refers to the 'state-corporate nexus' in western societies (Chomsky 1989, p. 149; Chomsky 1993, p. 99), he is using the term 'the state' in a conventional Miliband-style way, but his phrase summarises the expanded definition of the state. The words 'state-corporate nexus' do not simply mean that the state and major capitalist firms are deeply connected in western societies. Chomsky means that they have become part of the same system of concentrated power that determines the conditions of life for everyone in society: 'the actual nexus of decision-making power in the society, including investment and political decisions'. (Chomsky 1985, p. 230)

In *Year 501*, Chomsky surveyed decades of scholarship documenting the crucial importance of the 'visible hand' of the state in the industrial development of Japan and South Korea, as well as China and Germany – and the United States and Britain. (Chomsky 1993, pp. 101 – 104; 9 – 17) The work of the 'visible hand' included planning and co-ordination of production, marketing and R&D. In more recent times, Chomsky has referred, for example, to Mariana Mazzucato's revelation that every technology that makes the iPhone so 'smart' was funded by the US government: the internet (a DARPA military research project); GPS navigation (developed for the US Navy); touch-screen display technology (made for the US Air Force); and the iPhone's voice-activated assistant, Siri (DARPA again). (Mazzucato 2018) According to the *Financial Times*, there is something in the world of finance known as the 'Chomsky trade': 'Mr Chomsky once pointed out that, if you want to know what's worth investing in, look at what US federal research funding organisations such as the National Institutes of Health (NIH) and the Defence Advanced Research Projects Agency (Darpa) are investing in today, and then go long 30 years.' (Blyth 2017)

Chomsky quotes development economist Lance Taylor on the importance of state-supported 'import substitution' to industrialisation:

'In the long run, there are no laissez-faire transitions to modern economic growth. The state has always intervened to create a capitalist class, and then it has to regulate the capitalist class, and then the state has to worry about being taken over by the capitalist class, but the state has always been there.' (Chomsky 1993, p. 104)

Chomsky adds:

'Furthermore, state power has regularly been invoked by investors and entrepreneurs to protect them from destructive market forces, to secure resources, markets, and opportunities for investment, and in general to safeguard and extend their profits and power.' (Chomsky 1993, p. 104)

Chomsky observes that, by the 1930s, 'faith that capitalism might be viable had virtually disappeared, as the advanced countries moved towards one or another form of state-integrated economic system.' (Chomsky 1993, p. 104) 'Capitalism' since the 1930s has meant state-supported/state-integrated/state-enforced capitalism. It has not meant the unregulated Wild West free market that (according to mainstream economic theory) is supposed to automatically correct itself and magically bring about the best outcomes for society through the aggressively self-seeking behaviour of individuals. Instead, we have a 'state-corporate nexus' – a state that has expanded to include corporations as crucial decision-makers and power centres.

Chomsky remarks: 'business has long had a love-hate relation to the state: it wants a strong state to serve its needs, a state capable of intervening in domestic affairs and the international system; it wants a weak state that will not interfere with private privilege, but will enhance it.' Some ways that the state might be a problem could be 'to be a powerful competitor, interfering with the prerogatives of the businessman [or woman] or organizing popular forces that might act in the parliamentary arena or elsewhere to counter business dominance of the society.' (Chomsky 1987, p. 118)

Of course, not all corporations have the same interests: 'the ruling class itself has internal conflicts.' Chomsky remarks: 'Those elements of the ruling class that have a particular interest in one or another sphere of governmental activity will probably tend to dominate them. What they do may be in conflict with class interests of others, but the others do not care that much; it's not a major thing with them, so they let it go.' (Chomsky 1988a, p. 184) While there are sometimes serious conflicts, 'it seems not unfair to speak of the state executive [government] as simply a branch of the ruling class which is governing this particular centralized structure.' (Chomsky 1988a, p. 185)

What does Chomsky mean when he talks about corporations having a decisive say in 'setting the framework within which public policy can be discussed and is determined'? He referred to 'the actual nexus of decision-making power in the society, including investment and political decisions'. Investment decisions, Chomsky explains, 'have to do with what is produced, how it is produced, what work is done, how production and profits are distributed and to whom, how the conditions of work are managed and controlled, and so on.' (Chomsky 1987, p. 115) These decisions are taken, ultimately, by investors, those who hold the concentrated wealth of society – capital. Chomsky observes:

'In a capitalist democracy, the primary concern of everyone must be to ensure that the wealthy are satisfied; all else is secondary. Unless the wants of investors are satisfied, there is no production, no work, no resources available for welfare, in short, no possibility of survival.... Only to the extent that the demands of the wealthy – those who control investment decisions – are satisfied can the population at large hope for a decent existence in their role as servants of private power, who rent themselves to those who own and manage the private economy.' (Chomsky 1987, p. 116)

This concentration of power has been reinforced by the financial liberalisation imposed on the world economy since the early 1970s: 'As well understood by international economists, these measures create a "virtual Senate" of investors and lenders who can exercise "veto power" over government decisions by threat of capital flight, attacks on currency, and other means.' (Chomsky 2006, p. 219) If rich people (investors and lenders) don't like the policies a government is carrying out, they can move their money out of the country concerned, bringing the economy to its knees for lack of investment – or they can crash the value of the currency by selling it, creating unbearable political pressure. During the Bretton Woods era (roughly 1945–1973), rules put in place by the US and Britain restricted the movement of capital, financial speculation and attacks on currencies. Chomsky writes:

'The effect was to allow a form of "embedded liberalism," as it is sometimes called, in which social democratic policies could be pursued. The outcome is often termed the "golden age" of capitalism (more accurately, state capitalism), with unprecedented economic growth that was also egalitarian, and enactment of significant welfare-state measures to benefit the general population. All of this has been reversed in the neoliberal period.' (Chomsky 2006, p. 219)

There are many beneficial reforms that can take place within a state capitalist structure – some have been implemented and then reversed. There is a wide range of state capitalist models, ranging from the United States to, say, Sweden.

Chomsky once suggested that it was possible that, 'if it were not for external pressures', the ruling class in a country like Sweden could theoretically give up its privileges voluntarily. The 'deterioration in control and self-confidence' of the ruling class could reach a point where it had no effective defence 'either physical or moral' against the surrender of its power. Chomsky stressed the importance of moral defences: 'they have to convince themselves that what they're doing is right.' (Chomsky 1988a, p. 191) I should make clear that Chomsky has never believed that this could actually occur in a single small country like Sweden. He believes that such a transformation would be snuffed out by military or other forms of intervention from outside. In his view, a transition from capitalism to libertarian socialism (however achieved) would be at major risk of being crushed by military attack even if it took place simultaneously in Western Europe as a whole. On the other hand, if there was a social revolution in the United States, Chomsky observes, 'it's hard to imagine that there would be any credible enemy from the outside that could threaten that social revolution – we wouldn't be attacked by Mexico or Cuba, let's say'. (Chomsky 1981, p. 252)

Going back to the issue of range, there are many possible models of state capitalism, some of them much more humane and sustainable than, say, the United States in its current form. However, in Chomsky's view, all of them are marked by the fundamental democratic deficit that 'representative democracy is limited to the political sphere and in no serious way encroaches on the economic sphere.' This means that the range of decisions that are in principle subject to public democratic control 'excludes in law and in principle the central institutions in any advanced industrial society, that is, the entire commercial, industrial, and financial system.' These central institutions are fiercely anti-democratic, even totalitarian, in their internal structures, casting an authoritarian shadow over the non-work lives of their employees and in fact the entire culture, Chomsky suggests.

Furthermore, as Chomsky wrote in 1969:

'No one who gives a thought to the problems of contemporary society can fail to be aware of the social costs of consumption and production, the progressive destruction of the environment, the utter irrationality of the utilization of contemporary technology, the inability of a system based on profit of growth-maximization to deal with needs that can only be expressed collectively, and the enormous bias this system imposes towards maximization of commodities for personal use in place of the general improvement in the quality of life.' (Chomsky 1981, p. 223)

These are consequences of organising society on the basis of state capitalism.

Chomsky's position is that authority must justify itself or be dismantled. He argues that the capitalist state cannot justify its fundamentally undemocratic authority. The state should therefore be abolished – including corporations, 'the private empires that govern most aspects of our lives with little pretense of public accountability and not even a gesture to democratic control.' (Chomsky 1982, p. 91)

Asked if 'government' was the problem, Chomsky once responded: 'No, concentration of power is.' If power was diffused, 'then some administrative authority could respond to the needs of a diffuse power and it would be much less destructive.' (Chomsky 1988a, p. 744) In the capitalist state, there is concentration of wealth and economic power in the hands of investors and the corporations they own and control. There is also concentration of violence and coercive power in the hands of government bureaucracies and police, intelligence, judicial and military forces. Both forms of concentrated power need to be undone and diffused in order for the organisation and administration of society to be less destructive and more democratic, in Chomsky's view.

One of the major qualifications we should recognise at this point is that Chomsky sees a vital need for some coercive aspects of the governmental state – at this point in history. This is because of the existential threat posed to humanity by the other side of the state-corporate nexus, including the corporate-induced climate crisis.

There is a phrase used by rural organisations in Brazil that has come to be associated with Chomsky: 'expanding the floor of the cage'. In this metaphor, state power is a cage which oppresses the people. Chomsky argues that popular movements are forced to both protect the cage (defend state programmes, policies and powers that are of human benefit) and expand the floor of the cage (increase democratic control over both the governmental state and over business):

> 'You have to protect the cage when it's under attack from even worse predators from outside, like private power. And you have to expand the floor of the cage, recognizing that it's a cage. These are all preliminaries to dismantling it.' (Chomsky 1997)

Chomsky argues that 'the immediate goal of even committed anarchists should be to defend some state institutions, while helping to pry them open to more meaningful public participation, and ultimately to dismantle them in a much more free society' (Chomsky 2002, p. 344). To be superficially 'revolutionary' by joining in the right-wing attack on the welfare state is, for Chomsky, actually to undermine the possibilities for social transformation.

Rather than focusing on a possible revolution in the future, Chomsky has urged radicals to focus on the steps available today that can improve lives and prevent harm, and create a powerful mass reform movement. This is the way to lay the basis for an even more powerful radical movement that may become capable of achieving libertarian socialism. This will mean developing an understanding of society and a vision of the future 'that is persuasive to a large majority of the population' and providing 'plausible, concrete solutions to the problems of our society'. The goals and structures of the movement must take shape through the active participation of most people in political struggle and social reconstruction. (Chomsky 1981, pp. 221 – 222, 230)

In the *zanjera* system of organising irrigation in the Philippines, we see administrative structures formed by, and under the control of – and acceptable to – the people whose lives are deeply affected by the *zanjera* administration. These administrative structures, which regulate access to vital productive resources (irrigation water and farming land), include some coercive and punitive elements (guards, fines and so on) as well as material incentives. These structures are not initiated, regulated or policed by an external legal system or government bureaucracy, and they are based on collective rather than individual property rights. There is, perhaps, something in such experiences that is hopeful, and supportive of Chomsky's politics.

Earlier, we glanced at Edward Heath Robinson's discussion of the state-government distinction. Heath Robinson notes in passing during this discussion that 'government is not necessarily the same as *governance*.' He observes that the term 'governance' can refer to the process of social and economic co-ordination, management and 'steering' – 'which does not need to involve a coercive organization at all'. He gives, as an example, cultural traditions that give special weight to the opinions of family or tribal elders in certain matters. Similar forms of steering 'can be present even in anarchy', Heath Robinson remarks. (Heath Robinson 2013, p. 562)

The *zanjera* system, and the many other examples of successful collective management of resources gathered by Elinor Ostrom, could be thought of as examples of governance without 'the government'. Ostrom's book, of course, is called *Governing the Commons*. It could be said to describe successful grassroots self-government without need for 'the government'.

Similarly, Barcelona during the Spanish Revolution produced many examples of effective grassroots industrial self-government – which had no need for 'the government', or externally-imposed managers, or owners.

Chomsky's belief in freedom – in a human 'instinct for freedom' – leads him to value certain strains of anarchism and left-wing Marxism, which together he describes as 'libertarian socialism'. (In the United States, Chomsky notes, the word 'libertarian' has right-wing meaning which is the opposite of 'libertarian socialism'.) In Chomsky's view, 'radical Marxism merges with anarchist currents' such as anarcho-syndicalism. He quotes approvingly, for example, from 'left-wing Marxist Anton Pannekoek, one of the outstanding left theorists of the council communist movement'. (Chomsky 1973, p. 161) Council communism rejects Leninist vanguardism, the supremacy of 'the Party', and the rule of the bureaucratic state. Instead, it upholds direct control of the shop floor and of industry as a whole by democratic workers' councils. This is very close to anarcho-syndicalism, which is equally devoted to direct democratic control of industry by the workers themselves, without intermediaries or externally-imposed managers.

Chomsky is reluctant to accept that workplaces need a specialised 'manager' class or centralised planning and control:

'In fact, it is difficult to see why the same technology that permits centralized decision-making might not also be adapted to free workers from stupefying labour and provide them directly with the information needed to make rational decisions democratically.' (Chomsky 1981, p. 240)

If specialised managers *are* needed because their skills are beyond the direct competence of the workforce, Chomsky argues that there is no reason why they should be answerable to private capital rather than the workforce and the community, whose lives are deeply affected by management decisions. (Chomsky 1981, p. 239) In a libertarian socialist society, those who are affected by decisions should have a decisive part in making them, not investors and owners:

'In any institution – factory, university, health center, or whatever – there are a variety of interests that ought to be represented in decision-making: the work force itself, the community in which it is located, users of its products or services, institutions that compete for the same resources. These interests should be directly represented in democratic structures that displace and eliminate private ownership of the means of production or resources, an anachronism with no legitimacy.' (Chomsky 1981, p. 240)

Ideally, for Chomsky, government should involve part-time rotating participation in the different levels of administration, alongside continuing work in the community or the workplace. (Chomsky 1981, pp. 250 – 251) He has also commended study of Michael Albert's work on participatory economics or 'parecon', which requires everyone to operate a 'balanced job complex'. This raises another barrier to the creation of a powerful elite, as every person would have roughly the same number of hours a week of empowering, confidence- and skill-building work, and the same number of hours of deadening routine work. (Albert 2004)

Bibliography

Albert, Michael, 2004: Parecon: Life After Capitalism. London.

Barnet, Richard J., 1969: The Economy of Death. New York.

Blyth, Mark, 2017: America tampers with the Chomsky trade at its peril: The government and taxpayers are the key investors in basic scientific research. In: Financial Times, 24 August.

Borkenau, Franz, 2016 [1937]: The Spanish Cockpit: An Eye-Witness Account of the Political and Social Conflicts of the Spanish Civil War. Hastings.

Chomsky, Noam,1973: For Reasons of State. London.

Chomsky, Noam, 1981: Radical Priorities. ed. by C.P. Otero, Montréal.

Chomsky, Noam, 1982: Towards a New Cold War: Essays on the Current Crisis and How We Got There. London.

Chomsky, Noam, 1985: Turning the Tide: US Intervention in Central America and the Struggle for Peace. London.

Chomsky, Noam, 1987: On Power and Ideology: The Managua Lectures. Boston.

Chomsky, Noam, 1988a: Language and Politics. Montréal.

Chomsky, Noam, 1988b: The Chomsky Reader. London.

Chomsky, Noam, 1989: Necessary Illusions: Thought Control in Democratic Societies. London.

Chomsky, Noam, 1993: Year 501: The Conquest Continues. Boston.

Chomsky, Noam, 1997: Expanding the Floor of the Cage: Noam Chomsky interviewed by David Barsamian. In: *Z Magazine*, April 1997. Web. http://www.chomsky.info/interviews/199704--.htm (accessed on 24 August 2014).

Chomsky, Noam, 2000: Rogue States: The Rule of Force in World Affairs. London.

Chomsky, Noam, 2002: Understanding Power: The Indispensable Chomsky. New York

Chomsky, Noam, 2005 [1970]: Government in The Future. New York.

Chomsky, Noam, 2006: Failed States: The Abuse of Power and the Assault on Democracy. New York.

Hardin, Garett, 1968: The Tragedy of the Commons. In: Science Vol. 162.

Heath Robinson, Edward, 2013: The Distinction Between State and Government. In: *Geography Compass* 7/8.

Kreisler, Harry, 2002: Anarchism and Power (part of 'Activism, Anarchism and Power: Conversation with Noam Chomsky, Linguist and Political Activist'). Institute of International Studies, University of California Berkeley, 22 March 2002, p.2 of 5, accessed on 8 March 2020.

Leval, Gaston, 1975 [1971]: Collectives in the Spanish Revolution. Translated by Vernon Richards. London.

Mazzucato, Mariana, 2018: The Entrepreneurial State: Debunking Public vs. Private Sector Myths. London.

Mintz, Frank, 2013 [1970]: Anarchism and Workers' Self-Management in Revolutionary Spain. Translated by Paul Sharkey. Edinburgh.

Ostrom, Elinor, 1990: Governing the Commons: The Evolution of Institutions for Collective Action.

Seidman, Michael, 1982: Work and Revolution: Workers' Control in Barcelona in the Spanish Civil War, 1936-38. In: Journal of Contemporary History Vol. 17, No. 3 (July 1982), pp. 409-433.

Sipriano, Paolo,1975 [1964]: The Occupation of the Factories: Italy 1920. Translated by Gwyn A. Williams. London.

Siy, Robert Y., 1982: Community Resource Management: Lessons from the Zanjera. Quezon City.

Williams, Gwyn A., 1975: Proletarian Order: Antonio Gramsci, Factory Councils and the Origins of Communism in Italy, 1911–1921. London.

Željko Bošković

On the (Im)practicality of the State: Why do I have to have a Country?

There are many well-articulated reasons to favor a stateless society. Chomsky departs from many anarchists in believing that such a society is more likely to be achieved through a long, drawn out process that slowly erodes the machinery of the state rather than a single revolutionary moment. As a result, as Chomsky has emphasized in many places,[1] in the current political situation a stateless society can only be considered a long term goal. In the short run, the goal should actually be to strengthen the state in certain respects, namely, in the contexts where it helps achieve a freer and more just society—clear examples of this are providing a check on the power of large corporations and what has become a derogatory term on the right, the "welfare state"—which includes such horrible things as recognizing the right of every child, including those born to poor parents, to have food and get health care.[2] In a way, then, the state can be pragmatically used in the process of moving toward a more equitable stateless society. There is a conflict here between theory and what is practical, which is reflected in the long run vs short run opposition—the latter boils down to practical reasons. The conflict is only apparent however. Chomsky's political work is not an academic research exercise, in its heart is political (and economic, since the two are really inseparable) activism. There is pragmatism that comes with activism. This activism-motivated pragmatism is the reason why for Chomsky there is no contradiction, as there would be in a pure academic research exercise, between holding anarchist ideals, including stateless society, and using the state to achieve reforms that will lead to a more just society that is closer to anarchist ideals. There is also a reflection of Chomsky as a scientist here—if you are a scientist, say a physicist, you will use whatever methods you can to enlighten the issues you are investigating.[3] On a par with that, regarding his political work, Chomsky says:[4]

> "You should use whatever methods are available to you. There is no conflict between trying to overthrow the state and using the means that are provided in a partially democratic society, the means that have been developed through popular struggles over centuries. You should use them and try to go beyond, maybe destroy the institution. It is like the

---

1   See e.g. the following interview from March 11, 2010 (Reddit Blog) https://youtu.be/ke6YXjaZ 9HY and N. Chomsky, *On Anarchism*, The New Press, 2013.
2   See Chomsky 2013, p. 41.
3   In a mature scientific field like physics, there is no subfield or graduate classes devoted only to methodology, which reflects the general use-whatever-you-can methodological attitude.
4   N. Chomsky, *Chomsky on Anarchism*, ed. B. Pateman, AK Press, 2005; p. 239.

media. I am perfectly happy to write columns that are syndicated by the New York Times, which I do, and to write in Z Magazine."

The pragmatism that comes with activism, and the general use-whatever-methods-are-available-to-you scientific attitude are at the heart of Chomsky's political work —it cannot be properly understood without situating it in that context, which immediately dissolves what appear to be contradictions from the pure political-research-exercise point of view.[5]

While, for practical reasons, it is futile in the current political context to advocate for immediate overthrowing of the state and even advocating mere distancing from all state-related mechanisms can actually be damaging with respect to the issues noted above regarding the short run point, in spite of that, also for practical reasons and from the activist point of view, it is still important to keep talking about the absurdity of the concept of state, in fact in non-academic, simple, down to earth terms, in a way that would target issues that most people take for granted or do not even notice, the goal being to make the concept of a stateless society more palatable, more acceptable, to avoid its immediate dismissal as something crazy or impractically utopian, which would in turn at best confine it to an ivory tower research agenda. The practical aspect, which goes beyond the ivory tower research agenda, concerns the responsibility of the public intellectual, which has been the basis and the motivation of much of Chomsky's own work—it in fact lies at the root of his activism. It is addressed rather directly in *The Responsibility of Intellectuals*:[6]

---

5 Criticizing Chomsky's writing style, as Richard Kostelanetz does (when he calls it "surprisingly graceless" in his review of *Chomsky on Anarchism* published in *Social Anarchism; Baltimore* Issue 39, (2006): 39- 43, p. 40) or faulting him for not paying homage by failing to refer in a particular work (Chomsky's introduction to Daniel Guérin's *Anarchism* (1970)) to some members of the anarchist hall of fame, as George Woodcock does (as reported by Barry Bateman in Chomsky 2005 (p. 7)), also fails to appreciate the activist motivation behind Chomsky's political work. There is also a degree of jealousy in the anarchist elite club that even leads to statements along the lines that Chomsky's name will not be "central in histories of modern or American anarchism" (R. Kostelanetz, p. 42; R. Kostelanetz also dismisses Chomsky's linguistic work, something that would take years of careful studying to put one in a position to properly evaluate—one afternoon that R. Kostelanetz claimed to have spent with Chomsky in this context apparently sped up this process rather significantly). While I disagree with Kostelanetz's prediction, I strongly doubt that Chomsky would even care, given the driving force behind his political work. R. Kostelanetz also goes on to say (p. 41):
"Chomsky refuses to discriminate between those outlets that are large and those small and probably between those who pay him and those who do not. Nothing is envied more by writers whose prominence depend upon powerful publishers' publicists than fame that is self-earned, so to speak. If other political commentators ignore him, as too many do, one reason is their refusal to accept that such prominence could be realized without publicists or powerful publishers."
The above passage actually reflects the true motivation of Chomsky's political work, activism (which is rooted in the responsibility of the public intellectual discussed directly below), not seeking prominence, as is the case with most other political commentators.
6 Published in *The New York Review of Books*, February 23, 1967, in the context of discussion of a series of articles by Dwight Macdonald in *Politics* on the responsibility of peoples and the responsibility of intellectuals.

"It is the responsibility of intellectuals to speak the truth and to expose lies."

"When we consider the responsibility of intellectuals, our basic concern must be their role in the creation and analysis of ideology."

"Intellectuals are in a position to expose the lies of governments, to analyze actions according to their causes and motives and often hidden intentions."

Part of the responsibility of the public intellectual is to adopt an activist role in attempting to bring to the surface, to the conscious level, the latent biases we have, which were instilled into us by the machinery of the state and the authorities (and the class and political interests behind them). When it comes to the state itself, the two prong activist strategy of strengthening the state for the reasons noted above and keep talking about the absurdity of the concept of the state requires somewhat delicate balancing when both strategies are addressed together. Here, I will not do that, but will rather bluntly focus on the second, in particular, by taking the state vs the individual perspective within the broader issue of the relation of the individual to the state. This is an ambivalent perspective, with obvious arguments for strengthening the role of the state when it comes to providing broadly the social/health/education security net and checks on the power of large corporations (as part of the short run discussed above), but weakening it (even in the short run) when it comes to issues of personal freedom (where it does not infringe upon the rights of others—obviously there would be such infringement issues with the rights of a psychopathic serial killer to pursue their activities). I will here address the personal level (in the spirit of activism that permeates much of Chomsky's own work, which will also be reflected in the tone of this article), but from a somewhat different perspective from the one that is usually taken in discussions which concern the relation of the individual to the state, namely the perspective, often overlooked by those who belong to the "right" states in the sense discussed below, that equates the state and the individual, where the individual is in many respects measured like the state it belongs to. But before doing that, a more general note on the state and personal freedom is in order.

It concerns the concept of belonging to a state. In many respects the state curtails our rights, sometimes directly and sometimes indirectly. Illustrations abound. Regarding the latter, try for example going to the US with an Iranian passport. However, the rights of those who are stateless are even more curtailed—we really have no choice but to belong to a state.[7] We thus all have to belong to a state—this ownership by the state is in a way a remnant of slavery,[8] where the citizens are in many

---

7 United Nations High Commissioner for Refugees estimates that there are about 12 million stateless persons in the world. Official measures to prevent statelessness (like the 1961 United Nations Convention on the Reduction of Statelessness (which the US is not a signatory to) or the 1997 European Convention on Nationality) implicitly acknowledge that the rights of stateless persons are curtailed.

8 It is of course nowhere as bad as real slavery, hence the term "remnant" here (though "remnant" will often be dropped below for ease of exposition).

respects owned by the state, with the obvious implication that who owns the state[9] also owns us. The ownership can get rather extreme. Consider the concept of eminent domain, where the state is allowed to take private property for public purposes, with the state getting to determine what the valid public purpose is.[10] This actually extends to the most personal of all properties, namely ourselves. Military draft (henceforth draft) is the counterpart of eminent domain in this respect. With draft, the state gets to take you for public purposes, with the state determining what the valid public purpose is. With the Vietnam war, the valid public purpose was determined to be fighting in Vietnam. Just like with eminent domain, your body (in fact 2.2 million bodies in this case) was taken by the state; pursuing the valid public purpose defined by the state, it was transported to Vietnam (648,500 of them) and told to fight. There are those who resisted the enforcement of eminent domain in this respect, and refused to allow it, we all know what the consequences were (if you were not rich and/or politically connected of course; if you were rich, just like the property aspect of eminent domain, the person aspect of eminent domain did not really apply to you). The state really owns your property (eminent domain), and you (draft) too. Draft is just an extreme case of eminent domain, where you are the property that the state takes control of.[11]

---

9   An issue that Chomsky has discussed in many works (regarding the ownership of the state by large corporations, see e.g. E. Herman and N. Chomsky, *Manufacturing Consent: The Political Economy of the Mass Media,* Pantheon, 1988, and N. Chomsky, *Understanding Power: The Indispensable Chomsky,* The New Press, 2002), which I will not go into here.

10   The right of property in general is a separate issue that I will not go into here (see for example N. Chomsky, *For Reasons of State,* Pantheon, 1973 or https://www.youtube.com/watch?v=v9 OeYtubaek (an excerpt of a talk delivered at Harvard University, April 13, 1996, "Free Market Fantasies: Capitalism in the Real World"). While there certainly can be valid reasons behind eminent domain, it is worth noting that in the United States, the power of a state or the federal government to take private property for public use can be legislatively delegated to a third party, including corporations. Particularly instructive in this respect is the Supreme Court of the United States case Kelo vs City of New London (545 U.S. 469 (2005)), where eminent domain was used to transfer land from one private party to another private party for economic development in the absence of blight (in a way that would also benefit the Pfizer corporation).

11   As Chomsky puts it: "...people have the right to be free, and if there are constraints on that freedom then you've got to justify them." (N. Chomsky, *On Anarchism,* The New Press, 2013. p. 36; Chomsky in fact refers to this as the gist of anarchism) or "It's the responsibility of those who exercise power to show that somehow it's legitimate. It's not the responsibility of anyone else to show that it's illegitimate" (Chomsky, *On Anarchism,* The New Press, 2013, p. 88). This especially holds for calls for violence (i.e. going to war). If they can be legitimately justified, there won't be a need for a military draft (although under American law it was illegal for US citizens to join armed forces of other nations, many Americans volunteered for other nations' armed forces to fight the Nazis prior to America's entry into World War II in December 1941). It should be noted that although the United States Armed Forces moved to an all-volunteer military in 1973, the Selective Service System, which maintains information on those potentially subject to the military draft (interestingly, not limited to US citizens), is still in place (although there is a bill to repeal it, introduced on December 19, 2019; see https://www.congre ss.gov/bill/116th-congress/house-bill/5492). It should also be noted that both American anarchists and American libertarians, which are in many respects on the opposite side of the political/economic spectrum under the current mani-

Our ownership by the state extends to guilt by association. I was unfortunate to have the Yugoslavia passport during the Yugoslav wars in the 90s, when Yugoslavia was a pariah state. I don't have to go into any details regarding what travelling with that passport meant, it suffices to say that from the point of checking in at the airport, I was not allowed even to go to the toilet alone. Why was this happening to me? Because I was owned by a wrong state slave master. After I took the American passport, all that maltreatment stopped. Because now I had a right master. Many people find this kind of discrimination to be OK, especially those who belong to the right state masters, likely not an accident. (You were not a better person than me because you were an American, I did not become a better person when I got that passport. And please do not congratulate me on that—I did not win an Olympic medal or a Nobel prize; I did not achieve anything with that, except more freedom of movement). If I could not go to the toilet alone at the airport because of my race or my gender, everyone would scream about it, people at the airport likely would have complained. But since it was done to me because I had a wrong master (in the sense discussed above), that was basically fine—people are conditioned to accept this situation.

It is important to observe that the servitude to the state, which most of us in fact willingly subject ourselves to, does not come from "a natural inclination to servitude" that sophistic politicians and intellectuals talked about[12] but a natural inclination to belong to a larger group, which is in fact taken advantage of in this context. This natural inclination to belong to a larger group also includes judging oneself by the achievements of that larger group, which is in fact what this paper will be about. If we recognize this sense of belonging for what it really is, servitude (in fact, servitude to what the state represents—which is a class interest, large corporations interest (in modern times), or a more localized authoritarian interest (in authoritarian states)), getting rid of the state becomes part of the more general struggle for freedom, an undeniable human impulse.

This camouflage of servitude to the state as a sense of belonging to a larger group often leads to blind acceptance without thinking of situations that are clearly absurd. Consider for example the rather strong opposition in the US to the Iraq war before

---

festation of the latter in the United States, have opposed military draft, linking it to slavery and involuntary servitude. The former, including Emma Goldman, in fact challenged the draft in federal court on these grounds (i.e. Thirteenth Amendment's prohibition of slavery and involuntary servitude) in 1917. However, the Supreme Court upheld the constitutionality of the draft in the 1918 case *Arver v. United States*.

12 As noted in Rousseau's *Discourse on Inequality* (1755), discussed in Chomsky's *Language and Freedom* (*Proceedings of the University Freedom and Human Sciences Symposium*, Loyola University, Chicago, January 8–9, 1970, ed. by Thomas R. Gorman, also in *For Reasons of State,* Pantheon, 1973; N. Chomsky 2005, N. Chomsky 2013), which considers Rousseau's *Discourse on Inequality* "one of the earliest and most remarkable of the eighteenth-century investigations of freedom and servitude, ...in many ways a revolutionary tract" (p. 95 in Chomsky 2013).

the war started. Much of that opposition stopped once the war started, the often cited reason was that we have to support our troops. I don't understand what "our" means here (more precisely, I would understand it only to the extent that I personally knew any of them). What "our" is apparently intended to mean here is that whoever justifies ceasing the opposition to the Iraq war on these grounds ("we have to support our troops") and those troops are owned by the same master. If the action itself, going to war in Iraq, was deemed wrong before the war started, it did not suddenly become right. Wrong is wrong, whoever does it. If we oppose a different country going to a particular war, no one is going to stop opposing it once the war starts. It is very different when you and those who are actually going to the war are owned by the same state master. Most people accepted this without questioning, an incredible example of Pavlov-style state conditioning.

Suppose 5,000 miles from you there is a border, with John D. on your side of the border, and John E. on the other side of the border, and you don't know either of them at all. We are supposed to support John D. going to war with John E., even be ready to go to war for John D and against John E, although they are both strangers to us, and no matter what the reasons for all this are, just because we and John D are owned by the same state master? The sad fact is that we are not simply supposed to, most of us do accept this, without any questioning. (I should fight for the guy on "my" side of the border who I don't know against the other guy who I also don't know? How does that make any sense?) If I am against a particular war, I am supposed to stop being against it in order to support our troops? They are not *my troops in any normal and direct sense of "my". If they do something wrong, it is wrong, it is not right because they are "mine". (Now the state itself is in a different position here; those troops really are the state's, no apostrophe there.) Even many of those who are against death penalty accept this situation. No one should be able to force you to kill or hurt another human being. And if you are against death penalty, how can you accept this situation? Slaves were occasionally looked at as human beings, most of the time not. This is the case when the latter kicks in. You are not really killing human beings, just slaves owned by a different master (and your master told you to do that anyway; even the opposition to death penalty, where you yourself may be the executioner, can get suspended here).

As pointed out above, the natural inclination to belong to a larger group is taken advantage of in the context of accepting servitude to the state. This inclination to belong to a larger group also includes measuring oneself by the accomplishments of that larger group, where accomplishments of that larger group become your accomplishments. In this respect, guilt by association, discussed above, extends to smartness/dumbness by association. Absent proof to the contrary, you are as smart/dumb as your state master is deemed to be. There is a self-smartness syndrome that is particularly manifested and widespread in the states with a heightened sense of nationalism, like the US in fact. What constant recitation of the pledge of allegiance in schools, incessant singing of the American anthem at all kinds of events, constant bombardment with America is the greatest, the best.... slogans[13] leads to is the subconscious belief that the Americans are indeed smarter, better.... than others.[14] At least subconsciously, most Americans do view Americans as smarter than foreigners. I am not just talking here about the situations which all of us foreigners have experienced, where an American who has just met you speaks slower to you although it is pretty obvious that you can speak English quite fluently, the null hypothesis apparently being that as a foreigner you are dumb (which makes you feel like a performing seal; yeah, it is obvious that you have some intelligence, meaning that you can speak English; but you are still a seal), I am talking about a much less obvious level. Even in a field like linguistics, where there are many foreigners in the linguistics departments at American universities, and where the academics in general have been influenced more by Chomsky's political thinking, getting exposed to it more due to his prominence in linguistics itself, even in job situations where there are no visa issues, it is easier to get a top-level job if you are an American (by this I mean a "true" American) than if you are not. I am not accusing here job search committees of open discrimination. After all, most people on those job committees are self-proclaimed liberals who, if you would ask them, would find this kind of discrimination abhorrent, just the way they would find discrimination on the basis of gender, race, sexual orientation... abhorrent. Still, there are many respectable works demonstrating latent bias against for example women in academia. I am not aware of any works of that kind when it comes to foreigners. I am pretty sure what the result of such studies would be. The unspoken truth (unspoken when it comes to our American friends, we don't talk to them about this for obvious reasons) is that you have to be much better (in terms of your CV) and smarter (in terms of your research) than the Americans on the academic job market to get a job.[15] There is a latent bias against women and minorities, but there is at least as strong, and likely even stronger bias against foreigners (not even mentioning open restrictions of the kind noted in footnote 15). It is latent, but it makes the CV of Ann Smith simply look better than the CV of Predrag Živojinović. (This of course can be easily tested by doing name

---

13 Anyone who is bothered by this may want to play the following clip of the *Newsroom* series to their children https://www.youtube.com/embed/Y8J7Ug_0N6A?end=202.

14 This may be one of the reasons why so many Americans easily accept Trump's anti-foreigner stance, which actually rests on degrees of "foreignhood", a point addressed below. In this context, it is worth noting that even the personhood and First Amendment rights of non-citizens are legally on rather shaky grounds, see e.g. Michael Kagan, *When Immigrants Speak: The Precarious Status of Non-Citizen Speech Under the First Amendment*, 57 B.C.L. Rev. 1237 (2016), http://lawdigitalcommons.bc.edu/bclr/vol57/iss4/5.

15 Federal funding agencies, like the National Science Foundation, do not make this any easier by heavily restricting the eligibility of non-Americans to their research funds, which are often crucially needed for research projects.

replacement.) And this is not simply Americans vs foreigners cut, it is not a simple binary divide but a matter of degree—it matters "how much" of a foreigner you are. Yes, the Americans may be smarter than the rest, but the Germans, the French (not to mention the English, they are as close as you can get to us, Americans, they even have normal names)... are pretty close to us, not for example like those Eastern Europeans. Predrag Živojinović is still lucky, it can get much worse than Eastern Europeans. Yes my fellow Americans, white males can be, and are, discriminated against, even in academia, even in linguistics, even in syntax, where the influence of Chomsky's political thinking is much stronger than anywhere else due to his prominence in the field.[16] The discrimination is latent, the CV of that American applicant does seem to the committee to be better than the CV of that applicant with a strange name from god knows where (if your country, i.e. your state master, can be at least semibelievably associated with something like *Borat's* Kazakhstan[17]...), it is not open discrimination. (In other words, those search committee members are not openly behaving like the audience in that Texas rodeo in *Borat*, but we are all that rodeo audience, at least to some extent, on the subconscious level[18]). But if you are one of the latter, then you know. Absent proof to the contrary, you are only as smart as your master is deemed to be. That is where you-have-to-be-much-better-than-the-Americans comes into picture, you have to work on that proof to the contrary. And the burden of proof is not the same for everyone. Until recently, linguistics has been not just Indo-European centric, but pretty Euro centric when it comes to the languages which were emphasized in linguistic investigations. Now you start thinking, Germanic, Romance, Slavic. The most prominent linguistics conference in Europe is GLOW. I invite everyone to take any span of 10 years, and then check and count the papers investigating these language groups, and also check the authors of those papers. What they will find is a huge Germanic and Romance vs Slavic discrepancy.[19] Or look at the Slavic faculty members in the North American linguistics program, easily recog-

---

16 This is not to deny the privileged position of white males on different kinds of discrimination scales; the point is that the one under consideration here outranks all the other ones. You are first an American or not.

17 See 2006 movie *Borat: Cultural Learnings of America for Make Benefit Glorious Nation of Kazakhstan.*

18 In spite of not being a "true" American, by spending more than half of my life in the US I have to admit to my current master conditioning working on me at least to some extent too. It should be noted that "true" in "true" American sometimes matters, and sometimes not. In the particular case of guilt by association I noted above, "true" did not matter—I was able to go to the toilet at the airport on my own once I got the American passport (though it may have helped that I had the "right" looks, being white). In the case of smartness/dumbness by association currently discussed, "true" does matter—I am not, and never will be, a "true" American.

19 There is another way this kind of discrimination is displayed. It is perfectly acceptable for Western European linguists to write about Slavic languages without checking the original sources on the phenomena they are writing about, where those original sources are generally Eastern European scholars (who actually work in the West, and publish in the venues in the West, so their work is easily accessible), which sometimes leads to almost laughably incorrect

nizable by those funky Slavic names. I am starting to count, and I am not running out of fingers. If I were to do the same with Western European faculty members, there aren't enough fingers in my whole department to do the counting. Maybe we really are not as smart as you are, maybe our CVs are really not as good as yours (we got our PhDs in the West, so it is not about "inferior" PhDs). Or maybe it is something else. A consequence of the you-are-as-smart/dumb/guilty/etc-as-your-master-is-deemed-to-be syndrome is that accomplishments of your master become your accomplishments. And an inferior state means an inferior human being, as the null hypothesis (i.e. in the absence of proof to the contrary). This smartness/dumb-ness/guilt by association is really the last openly acceptable form of discrimination in the West, and the most prevalent latent form of discrimination. There is also much more of the former than we would like to admit (given that conscious discrimination is more stigmatized than subconscious discrimination for obvious reasons).

One of the main roles of the state is to limit the freedom of movement, as well as the freedom to take a job (the latter is of course part of the former anyway—if you cannot get to X you cannot work in X; still, the latter is even more stringent since being able to get to X does not mean you can work in X). Your freedom of movement is not the same if you are owned by Iran and if you are owned by the US.[20] I don't see many Americans being bothered by this, the way they would be bothered if your freedom of movement were to be limited by other factors, like race, gender, sexual orientation.... Even if you are graciously granted that freedom of movement, why do you have to wait longer in line at passport control at the airport if you are owned by say Nigeria or Ethiopia than if you are owned by an EU country (you also have to deal with those hypocritical smiles of relief from the latter—they don't have to wait like you do). Would the privileged ones, the ones who don't have to wait in line, be equally not bothered by the difference if there was a long line for women (whether they are from Nigeria or EU) and a breeze-through for men (whether they are from Nigeria or EU)? Why is the former kind of discrimination acceptable? Shouldn't they both be unacceptable? The masquerade, the camouflage of the servitude to the state and the interests that the state stands for as the sense of belonging to a larger group somehow also camouflages very open and blatant discrimination.

---

claims by well-known linguists, which could have been easily avoided if the works of Eastern European scholars were deemed as worthy of checking as the works of Western European scholars. That those claims are almost laughably incorrect is only obvious to the Eastern European linguists, who simply accept the situation, they accept that they are not equal. In fact, if they themselves were to do something like this with respect to Romance and Germanic, they would be laughed out of the field.

20 I was practically stateless at one point (when finishing my PhD studies), in the sense that I did not have a valid passport (for a simple reason that the country I came from fell apart). That severely limited my freedom of movement and job options. I could not go to conferences outside of the US, could not apply for jobs outside of the US, even Canada (since I would have to go there for a job talk).

State idolizing, briefly referred to above, is an important part of the masquerade here. It can be more blatant or more perfidious, but it is certainly present and encouraged everywhere, in every country.[21] There are certain forums where it is particularly easy to sell—in particular, sports. Success in sports is in fact considered a high state interest in many countries because of that. Sports are the modern opium for the masses; as such, sports work incredibly well for the purpose of state idolizing. But we should not forget here what the state stands for—it is class/large corporations/authoritarian interests; this is actually what we are idolizing here (without realizing due to the sports camouflage).

I am writing this during the beginning of the coronavirus epidemics in the US, when the freedom of movement of New Yorkers, or those living in Connecticut, like I do, is curtailed (and when even the Right argues, blasphemously from their usual point of view, for strengthening the role of the state in some respects that would come under the short run noted in the beginning of this article). Not very severely, in most cases you can still go somewhere else, you can for example go to Florida but you have to self-quarantine for fourteen days before rejoining the society upon arrival. If this sounds harsh, imagine you are owned by Iran, you have an Iranian passport (or a countless number of other passports). You would jump in joy for this kind of freedom of movement, where you can go anywhere, to any country, just wait for fourteen days upon arrival to rejoin the society. Fourteen days may seem like an eternity for the privileged New Yorkers (and yes, you are all privileged in comparison to .... I will leave it to the reader to fill in the blanks, plenty of options there; a friend of mine who was in Bosnia during the war there, and has a Bosnian passport, only bluntly said this in response to the New Yorkers' coronavirus problems: I've seen worse; another friend of mine from Bosnia, complaining about the discrimination she had to endure in France during the Yugoslav wars, also added, I was still lucky. Imagine I was from… again, fill in the blanks).

In many respects, we are defined by the state we belong to, by who owns us in this respect. This affects even what should be considered basic rights like freedom of movement and freedom to take a job (really everything, your prospects in life, your prospects for health care, education, it can even affect your right to live). You are born into it, through no fault of your own, through no accomplishment of your own. Yet, fault and accomplishment are attached to it, through the smartness/dumbness/guilt…by association.

---

21 The masquerade can be incredibly obvious, especially in authoritarian countries, where one person is in fact the country. This is e.g. the case with the slogans in the former Yugoslavia: *Mi smo Titovi, Tito je naš* ('we are Tito's, Tito is ours'). Another illustration of the absurdity: I was in high school when Tito died. The first morning in school after that, the whole class was uncontrollably sobbing and crying, as if their father died. I found this so absurd that I started uncontrollably laughing (after all, I knew who my father was; he did not die, I saw him in fact that morning when I left for school.).

There is an obvious similarity here with the concept of nobility. This includes the hereditary aspect (you do inherit your citizenship[22]), as well as the existence of legal privileges (like those pertaining to the freedom of movement that is determined by instruments like passports and visas; not to mention that there is a considerable difference in how much help you may get if you get in trouble "abroad"). Much of our life prospects thus end up being determined by a simple accident.

The concept of class as an economic state plays a central role in Chomsky's view of anarchism, issues of class as an economic state inevitably arising all the time within the framework of modern capitalism, which anarchists hope to abolish. The point made here is that the concept of class is broader and to some extent multi-faceted (though class as an economic state is very clearly at its center);[23] what is under discussion here is the concept of class as defined by the country that owns you— it does not at all supplant class as an economic state (though in some respects it does incorporate the aspects of the latter).[24] There is also clear hierarchy, clear inequality in class-by-country. This hierarchy, this inequality, is often neglected, even accepted, by those who do not accept the hierarchy and inequality that comes with the standard (for the lack of a better word) concept of class. Abolishing the state, even weakening the state would also lead to abolishing and weakening the concept of class by country.

As noted above, the concept of class by country incorporates the concept of class as an economic state, which is central to Chomsky's work. Thus, concerning the restrictions on the freedom of movement that are imposed by requiring a passport holder entering another country to have a visa, the poorer a country is the more likely it is that its passport holders will be required to have a visa to enter another country. There are several mobility indexes which measure freedom of movement in terms of visa restrictions imposed on the passport holders of a particular country by other countries. One such index is the Henley Passport index. The three most valuable passports in the 2020 Henley Passport index are those of Japan, Singapore, and Germany. Poor countries, i.e. countries which rank low in terms of GDP per capita, like Somalia, Burundi, Niger, Central African Republic, Congo, South Sudan, Afghanistan, also rank low in the Henley Passport Index.[25]

---

22 There are, however, still countries where women cannot pass their nationality to their off-spring.
23 See also Barry Pateman's introduction to *Chomsky on Anarchism*, AK Press, 2005, p. 10 on class as a cultural state.
24 There is a nod to the state privilege arising from the class-by-country notion in N. Chomsky, *American Power and the New Mandarins*, Pantheon, 1969, p. 28: "The fact is that American intellectuals are increasingly achieving the status of a doubly privileged elite: first, as American citizens, with respect to the rest of the world; and second, because of their role in American society, which is surely quite central, whether or not Bell's prediction proves accurate."
25 For the 2020 Henley Passport Index, see https://www.henleypassportindex.com/assets/2020/Q 1/2020%20HPI%20and%20Global%20Mobility%20Report_200107.pdf. Other factors that matter in this kind of measurements of passport value is whether a country is involved in an

While, as pointed out in the beginning, in the short run abolishing the state may not be a practical goal, the state being needed e.g. to check the power of large corporations, if we are going to check the power of the state itself, which we do need to, we have to keep talking about its absurdity, we need to keep talking about abolishing it as part of that, no matter how impractical this may be in the short run, the goal here being something else, namely to raise the awareness of the absurdity of the concept of state, the concept of ownership by the state as a remnant of slavery, where the master can put us all in the us vs them situation… without either us or them understanding what is really behind that or that it isn't our fight. The true interests of the state (i.e. what is behind the machinery of the state) are even more removed from the citizens now than in e.g. Ancient Greece; many of the overt and covert wars that the US has been engaged in are related to the true interests of its citizens as much as for example the war between the Athens/Second Athenian League and Chios/ Rhodes/Cos/Byzantion in Ancient Greece was related to the interests of the slaves there, who at least knew that it wasn't their fight. More generally, belonging to a state in Ancient Greece involved less servitude to broader interests that have nothing to do with you than it does now. It is important to recall here that the servitude to the state, which most of us willingly subject ourselves to, does not come from "a natural inclination to servitude" but a natural inclination to belong to a larger group, which is taken advantage of in this context. Once this sense of belonging is recognized for what it really is—servitude; more precisely, servitude to what the state represents (class and political interests, large corporation interests, a more localized authoritarian interest)—getting rid of the state becomes part of the struggle for freedom, which is an essential human attribute.

The interests behind the state prey on our natural inclination to belong, taking advantage of it through the concept of "my country" to get us to accept more readily servitude to their interests. What does it really mean when someone says "I'm proud to be an American"? It implies accepting serving the interests behind the machinery of this particular state. It also means taking credit for what you had nothing to do with (e.g. the Declaration of Independence, beating the Nazis in World War Two, getting to the moon… Similarly, "I'm proud to be Greek" means taking credit for the achievements of Ancient Greece, Aristotle, Plato…). The downside of this is that you can also end up taking blame for something you did not do. And none of this was your accomplishment or your fault.

Our state masters determine our freedom of movement, freedom to choose where to work, through fancy instruments called passports and visas, which are used to

---

armed conflict (or more generally politically unstable) and/or perceived to be a likely origin of terrorists.

hide that their real goal is limitations of personal freedom.[26] As such, instruments like passports and visas go against human nature—they restrict personal freedom, hence go against the essential human attribute—struggle for freedom. How would we react if someone were to restrict our freedom of movement, by making traveling from one city to another, say New York to Los Angeles, as difficult and cumbersome as travelling from one country to another? I'm travelling from a city to a city in both cases, why should there be any difference? Why do we so readily accept the difference? The same question can be raised about job prospects. How about making legally getting a job in Los Angeles for a New Yorker as cumbersome as it is as getting a job in London. Why should that be any different? Why are there restrictions on my wanting to travel to Delhi, or work and live in London? Why do we accept that? Why do we allow the interests behind the machinery of the state to put such restrictions on our freedom of movement, job prospects (not to mention the extreme case of those interests forcing us to go and fight in a war), restrictions that we would not accept when it comes to also two arbitrarily picked cities, New York and Los Angeles? Our goal should be to expose and undermine the sense of normalcy in accepting such state imposed restrictions on the freedom of movement (even when they are light). After all, if someone else, not the state, restricts our freedom of movement in this manner, we would not so readily accept it.

Isn't it ironic that there used to be way fewer restrictions on travel and job prospects of the kind noted above?[27] The state-imposed restrictions in this respect are a relatively modern concept, which came with the strengthening of the ownership by the state—the citizens used to be less owned by the state, which actually resulted in more freedom of movement. The concept of a stateless person is also a modern phenomenon—the strengthening of the ownership by the state gave rise to it. Those limitations on the freedom of movement and getting a job noted above are in fact particularly extreme with stateless persons, due to the lack of some of those fancy instruments that are used to legitimize those restrictions. Understanding that

---

26 It's not only that the country you are not a citizen of puts restrictions on you being able to enter the country, minimally requiring you to have a passport, and also often to have a visa, where the country of entrance gets to put additional restrictions on you entering the country (having a visa actually does not guarantee entry, since border crossing authorities are generally allowed to cancel a visa at the border at their discretion), it's also that the country you are a citizen of can put restrictions on getting a passport—being a citizen of a country does not automatically mean you are granted a passport. E.g. in Pakistan, getting a passport requires an interview and signing a religion related oath. In the former Warsaw block countries, passport issuance was not automatic for all citizens, but essentially a privilege and exit visas were required to be able to leave the country. In some countries (e.g. Togo and Montenegro), passport and nationality can be essentially bought with large investments. (In Montenegro this will cost you half-a-million euros; being convicted of a criminal offense will not disqualify you as long as your jail term was not for more than one year).

27 Even as late as 19th and early 20th century in Europe, passports were generally not needed to travel from one country to another.

what the word "foreigner" really means is that the person simply has a different state slave owner should help raise the awareness, hence help deal with the acceptable discrimination of foreigners. Foreigners may be the most discriminated group of people but they are not a protected class under federal laws that define protected classes. National origin discrimination is actually included in the types of discrimination defined in the Title VII of the Civil Rights Act of 1964, hence is covered by the US Equal Employment Opportunity laws, but it is defined in a way that does not include foreigners (i.e. non-Americans) as a class, see in this respect the following quote from the US Equal Employment Opportunity Commission web page[28]: "National origin discrimination involves treating people (applicants or employees) unfavorably because they are from a particular country or part of the world." Furthermore, while the law forbids national-origin based discrimination "when it comes to any aspect of employment, including hiring, firing"[29], it is pretty easy to evade that —this is in fact done quite commonly, but in a way that applies to all foreigners (so in a way that maximizes discrimination), which actually does not go against Equal Employment Opportunity rights since it does not pick on employees that come from particular countries. Essentially, you cannot discriminate against some of them, but you can discriminate against all of them. This is for example easily done by changing the employer's policy regarding sponsorship of visas. A case was just brought to my attention where a very prominent US university terminated employment of a foreigner who the university sponsored for an H-1B visa for a particular job by the university simply deciding that they will no longer sponsor a visa for that job—they will still advertise the same position but foreigners, including the foreigner in question, will no longer be eligible for it; so the position is not eliminated but foreigners are.[30] Were the university to exclude a foreigner from a particular country this way, this would violate Equal Employment Opportunity laws, but excluding all of them is perfectly fine. Many Americans, including self-proclaimed liberals, find this perfectly acceptable. But the situation is utterly ridiculous: the more discrimination there is the more acceptable it is. In other words, when it comes to the foreign-

---

28 US Equal Employment Opportunity Commission: https://www.eeoc.gov/laws/types/nationalori gin.cfm Accessed April 24, 2020.
29 US Equal Employment Opportunity Commission: https://www.eeoc.gov/laws/types/nationalori gin.cfm Accessed April 24, 2020.
30 Peabody Institute of the Johns Hopkins University has simply changed their policies in a way that they no longer support temporary or permanent immigration sponsorship below a certain, newly defined rank. Accordingly, all the foreigner faculty below the rank in question who they brought in with Peabody sponsoring their visas are now fired; in at least one case Peabody is re-advertising the position, so this was not the case of the position being closed. Of course the letter that Peabody is sending says that they "will no longer be able to sponsor" H-1B visas but that happened simply because they decided that they do not want to do that; there is agency hidden behind the carefully chosen word "unable" (they are unable because they don't want to) that is inserted in their letter. The letter also says that the position from which the foreign faculty is being fired will still be advertised and filled.

ers, you cannot discriminate against some of them, but you can discriminate against all of them. Title VII of the Civil Rights Act of 1964, which is supposed to prevent discrimination on the basis of national origin, actually ends up promoting such discrimination since the law ends up encouraging maximizing the discrimination on the grounds of national origin. Say you are a bigot who hates Mexicans and you got a position in charge of human resources in a firm which employs twenty foreigners, eighteen Mexican nationals, and two Russian nationals. It is pretty easy for that bigot to find a legal way (e.g. in the manner described above) to fire those eighteen Mexican nationals as long as the two Russian nationals are also fired.

Consider also affirmative action in the context of immigration. This context is often used to argue against affirmative action in general, or to argue against extending any potential benefits of affirmative action to immigrants, or those born in the US to immigrant parents, even second generation Americans.[31] The crux of the argument concerns the concept of affirmative action where affirmative action is intended to address historical injustices against African Americans (so not as a policy to guarantee diversity by race), hence, the argument goes, affirmative action should not be extended to first or second generation immigrants from say The Gambia or Haiti. But those immigrants are of the same race, their ancestors may also have been slaves (almost a certainty with Haiti), their more immediate economic circumstances have likely been way more dire (considering the difference in the standard of living between e.g. the US and Haiti), the only thing that the argument rests on is really the accident of birth (i.e. where you were born), in fact not even your own accident of birth but your parents' or grandparents'. Why should this kind of accident of birth be treated differently from the accident of birth involved in the concept of nobility, which this country has at least officially eliminated (putting aside the Bushes, the Kennedys of this country as pseudo-nobility)?

The fact is that much of our life prospects are determined by an accident, the accident of where we were born. One of the main roles of the concept of the state is to ensure that. Even when the state recognizes and attempts to ensure the right of every child to have food and get health care almost by definition it attaches the adjective privileged to the children in question by erecting barriers in terms of state borders to "every" in "every child". Even when the state border barrier is no longer there, in the

---

31 For relevant discussion, see for example Nathan Glazer, *Debate on Aliens Flares Beyond the Melting Pot*, The New York Times, April 23, 1995; James Robb, *Affirmative Action for Immigrants: The Entitlement Nobody Wanted*, The Social Contract Press, 1995; Hugh Davis Graham. "Affirmative Action for Immigrants? The Unintended Consequences of Reform." In *Color Lines: Affirmative Action, Immigrants, and Civil Rights Options for America*, ed. by J.D. Skrentny, University of Chicago Press, 2001; Farah Stockman, *'We're Self-Interested': The Growing Identity Debate in Black America.* The New York Times, November 8, 2019; Mary C. Waters and Zoua Vang "The Challenges of Immigration to Race Based Diversity Policies in the United States." In *Diversity and Canada's Future*, ed. by Leslie Seidle, Keith Bantin, and Thoams Courchene, Institute for Research on Public Policy Press, 2007.

US there is the "unqualified immigrant" barrier to federal public benefits. Even when the unqualified immigrant barrier is no longer there, there is the Personal Responsibility and Work Opportunity Reconciliation Act of 1996 barrier.[32] The state does a pretty good job of ensuring the relevance of the accident of your birth.

From the perspective of raising the awareness of discrimination on such grounds, which in many cases flies under the radar (especially if you are fortunate enough to belong to a 'right' state), I applaud countries like Brazil changing their entrance rules for American citizens to match those that the American authorities imposed on their citizens (no matter how much I loathe the possessives in the preceding sentence). Standing in a long line for American citizens at the Rio de Janeiro airport, with citizens from other countries just breezing by, I was hoping that at least some of those angry entitled people waiting in that line will start wondering why this is happening to them. This is the last publicly fully acceptable criterion for discrimination in this country, but apparently only as long as we don't feel it ourselves. There are still blatant racists, chauvinists…(we all know at least one of them—we in fact see him on TV almost daily); discrimination on these grounds is at least officially unacceptable (and, thankfully, often ostracized); discrimination on the grounds of what state master you belong to, on the other hand, is fully acceptable—there is no protected class in this respect, and there can't be as long as the master is involved in determining protected classes. It can go as far as state-sanctioned killing of foreigners, who, as individuals, may not have done anything wrong, in time of war.

In many countries where more than one ethnic group lives there is open discrimination toward some ethnic groups. In Bosnia and Herzegovina, your ethnicity pretty much defines who you are—ethnic-based discrimination is quite open there. In former Yugoslavia it was far less open and widespread but still present; in fact some of that got carried over to the post-Yugoslav states. Before the war, in Slovenia there was a derogatory concept of južnjaci "southerners". The discrimination on the basis of ethnic groups is regularly labeled as unacceptable, but the one based on belonging to particular states often escapes open labeling although it is not different in any way. In fact, it is pretty obvious in the case in question, which is the reason why I am bringing it up. The concept of južnjaci got carried over with Slovenia becoming an independent state—only now it refers to the citizens of different countries. And of course, everyone has their own southerners; all those former Yugoslavs are in fact

---

32 On how the Personal Responsibility and Work Opportunity Reconciliation Act of 1996 and the Illegal Immigration Reform and Immigrant Responsibility Act of 1996 curtail the eligibility of immigrants for public benefits, see for example George J. Borjas, *The Impact of Welfare Reform on Immigrant Welfare Use*, Center for Immigration Studies, 2002 and Tanya Broder. "Immigrant Eligibility for Public Benefits." In *American Immigration Lawyers Association Immigration and Nationality Law Handbook 2005-06*, National Immigrant Lawyers Association, 2005.

southerners for the Germans (and the Germans who live in, and belong to, those southerner states are not quite like the "real" Germans either).

Going back to the responsibility of intellectuals and the activist role that comes with it, when it comes to the state, our goal, the activist goal, should be to undermine the sense of belonging, and eventually to lose the sense of belonging to a state.[33] The slaves in Ancient Rome at least knew they were slaves. The sense of normalcy in accepting state imposed restrictions on the freedom of movement, even when they are light, should also be subverted. In the spirit of that, JFK's cliché "ask not what your country can do for you — ask what you can do for your country"[34] should be replaced with: Ask not what you can do for your country — ask why you have to have a country.

One final passage is in order for the sake of clarification given the beginning of this article. The concept of the state is (morally) abhorrent: regarding the issues discussed in this article, there is no short or long run, it is abhorrent in any run; it is a discriminatory concept, used for open and blatant discrimination, the last fully acceptable form of discrimination in what is called the West, which is simply the privileged class in this form of discrimination. The sense of belonging to the state needs to be undermined now, the discrimination that comes with it, both the officially sanctioned one, like the limitations on the freedom of movement (implemented through passports and visas) and the more perfidious discrimination, illustrated above through guilt/smartness…by association (it is not your fault or an accomplishment that you were born in a particular country; you were not a better person than me because you are an American, I did not become a better person when I got that passport) needs to be confronted and fought right now. Our life prospects should not be so greatly influenced by an accident, the accident of where we were born.

Bibliography

Borjas, George J., 2002: The Impact of Welfare Reform on Immigrant Welfare Use. Center for Immigration Studies.

Broder, Tanya, 2005: Immigrant Eligibility for Public Benefits. In: American Immigration Lawyers Association Immigration and Nationality Law Handbook 2005-06. National Immigrant Lawyers Association.

Chomsky, Noam, 1967: The Responsibility of Intellectuals. In: *The New York Review of Books*. February 23

Chomsky, Noam, 1969: American Power and the New Mandarins. New York.

Chomsky, Noam, 1973: For Reasons of State. New York.

---

33   I lost it but it was easier for me, my state master died.
34   John F. Kennedy's Inaugural Address, January 20, 1961.

Chomsky, Noam, 1996: Free Market Fantasies: Capitalism in the Real World. Talk delivered at Harvard University, April 13.

Chomsky, Noam, 1970: Language and Freedom. In: Proceedings of the University Freedom and Human Sciences Symposium, ed. by Thomas R. Gorman. Loyola University, Chicago. January 8–9.

Chomsky, Noam, 2002: Understanding Power: The Indispensable Chomsky. New York.

Chomsky, Noam, 2005: Chomsky on Anarchism, ed. by Barry Pateman. Oakland

Chomsky, Noam, 2013: On Anarchism. New York.

Herman, Edward/*Chomsky*, Noam, 1988: Manufacturing Consent: The Political Economy of the Mass Media. New York.

Glazer, Nathan, 1995: Debate on Aliens Flares Beyond the Melting Po In:, The New York Times, April 23.

Graham, Hugh Davis, 2001: Affirmative Action for Immigrants? The Unintended Consequences of Reform. In: Skrentny, John D. (ed.), 2001: Color Lines: Affirmative Action, Immigrants, and Civil Rights Options for America. Chicago.

Kagan, Michael, 2016: When Immigrants Speak: The Precarious Status of Non-Citizen Speech Under the First Amendment. In: 57 B.C.L. Rev. 1237.

Kennedy, John F., 1961: Inaugural Address, January 20.

Kostelanetz, Richard, 2006: Review of *Chomsky on Anarchism*. In: Social Anarchism, Issue 39, Baltimore, 39- 43.

Pateman, Barry, 2005: Introduction to *Chomsky on Anarchism*. Oakland.

Robb, James, 1995: Affirmative Action for Immigrants: The Entitlement Nobody Wanted. The Social Contract Press.

Rousseau, Jean J., 1755: Discourse on Inequality.

Stockman, Farah, 2019: *'We're Self-Interested': The Growing Identity Debate in Black America*. In: *The New York Times,* November 8.

Waters, Mary/C./*Vang*, Zoua, 2007: *The Challenges of Immigration to Race Based Diversity Policies in the United States.* In: Seidle Leslie/Keith Bantin Keith/Courchene, Thomas (eds.), 2007: Diversity and Canada's Future. ed. by Institute for Research on Public Policy Press.

Michael Schiffmann

The Soft-Spoken Anarchist:
Chomsky, Populism, and the Question of "From Here to There"

"A Radical Works Beyond the Ivory Tower"[1] is the subtitle of the second of the two books the literary critic and contributor to this book, Robert Barsky, wrote on Noam Chomsky. Chomsky, of course, came to fame, first by giving birth to a revolutionary new type of linguistics, and second, by being one of the most prominent voices of the opposition against the Vietnam war, but it is by now also well-known that in addition to that, Chomsky is an anarchist.

To the political mainstream, or what Chomsky has called "the media and articulate opinion in general,"[2] anarchism is a no-go area of irresponsible thought which, moreover, is bound to lead to actions that are even worse. This may very well be one of the roots of a phenomenon we are bound to find when we look back in history for just a few decades and that is now hard to imagine, namely, that Chomsky used to be a voice in the wilderness for very long periods in his life. He was unable to get a mainstream platform from 1964, when his political activism really began, to 1967, when his now famous essay "The Responsibility of Intellectuals" appeared in the *New York Review of Books*.

After that time, his articles appeared quite frequently in the liberal quality press and his books *American Power and the New Mandarins* (1969),[3] *At War with Asia* (1970),[4] and *For Reasons of State* (1973)[5] reached a relatively wide audience. What is often forgotten is that this was only after the ruling elites in the United States had already begun to turn against the U.S.'s war in Indochina because of the costliness and ineffectiveness of the war.

Once the wars in Indochina ended, leaving behind a terrible trail of destruction that was never acknowledged by the U.S.[6] and left three poor peasant countries in tatters with barely any option for a decent future, the media window for a perceived

---

1 Robert Barsky, *The Chomsky Effect: A Radical Works Beyond the Ivory Tower*, MIT Press 2007.
2 *On Power and Ideology. The Managua Lectures*, South End Press 1987, 130. Unless stated otherwise, the works quoted in the following footnotes are Chomsky's.
3 *American Power and the New Mandarins*, Pantheon Books 1969.
4 *At War with Asia*, Pantheon Books 1970.
5 *For Reasons of State*, Vintage Books 1973.
6 On U.S. guilt in the Indochina wars, arguably the least violent of the U.S. presidents of the last 75 years, Jimmy Carter, made the following astonishing remarks: "The destruction was mutual. We went to Vietnam without any desire to capture territory or impose American will on other people. I don't feel that we ought to apologize or castigate ourselves or to assume the status of

radical such as Chomsky began to narrow as he was shunned by the mainstream media and had to turn increasingly to small independent publishers to get his growing work on politics out. His major 1979 two-volume study *The Political Economy of Human Rights*,[7] co-authored with the late Edward S. Herman and dealing, not just with the aftermath of the U.S.'s wars in Indochina, but also with the brutality of the U.S.'s policy towards the Third World in general, was published by the anarchist collective South End in Boston and got virtually no reviews.[8]

For quite a while, one of the most liberal papers in the country, the *Boston Globe*, had an explicit internal policy of never reviewing any of his books even though he was a quite famous personality and what is called a "local author" who worked and lived right there, in Cambridge and the suburb of Lexington.[9]

For many years, one could summarize the attitude of the mainstream in media and politics towards Chomsky's political work and activities with the words of the British-American journalist, Christopher Hitchens: "Brilliant but unsound; doesn't know when to stop."[10] Chomsky's linguistic credentials were still considered as maybe controversial but unassailable, whereas his critique of U.S. foreign policy was now regarded as, though partly justified during the disastrous Vietnam war, much too far-reaching in its extent and implications.

It was ironically a small booklet by Chomsky simply called *9/11* containing comments and interviews on the terrorist al-Qaida attacks on New York, the aborted Flight 97, and the Pentagon on September 11, 2001, that initiated a changed in this state of affairs.[11] I say "ironically" because I can personally testify to the pseudo-patriotic hysteria that had grasped *official* America at the time. Both I and my part-

---

culpability." News conference on March 24, 1977, cited in many U.S. dailies the following day. Chomsky has quoted parts of this passage multiple times in his work.

7 Noam Chomsky & Edward S. Herman, *The Political Economy of Human Rights*. Volume I: *The Washington Connection and Third World Fascism*. Volume II: *After the Cataclysm. Post-war Indochina and the Reconstruction of Imperial Ideology*. Both South End Press 1979.

8 John Taylor's review in *Third World Quarterly* Vol. 2, No. 3 (July 1980), 561-567, not exactly a mainstream journal, is one of the rare exceptions.

9 In an interview with the progressive radio journalist David Barsamian in February 1990, Chomsky wearily commented: "Take the *Boston Globe,* for example. By the standards of American journalism, it's a very liberal newspaper. Their book review editor a couple of years ago said publicly that she would never allow a South End book to be reviewed. The reason that she gave was that I was a South End author, and as long as I was a South End author, she'd never allow a South End book to be reviewed. My books are not only not reviewed in the *Boston Globe,* but they won't even list them. There's a section on Sunday where they list things by local authors. Like some local author wrote a chapter in a cookbook. They won't even list my books under listings by local authors." *Chronicles of Dissent. Interviews with David Barsamian*, Common Courage Press 1992, 241.

10 Christopher Hitchens, "The Chorus and Cassandra," an article devoted to Chomsky, in Christopher Hitchens, *Prepared for the Worst. Selected Essays and Minority Reports*, Chatto & Windus 1989, 63.

11 In "America's Dumbest Intellectual," *City Journal*, Summer 2002, Stefan Kanfer, an enraged critic, talks about 115,000 sold copies. "It has shown up on the *Boston Globe* and the *Washington Post* best-seller lists, and in Canada, it has rocketed to seventh on the best-seller list. And

ner and my sister, who entered the U.S. with some of the first flights after 9/11, were subjected to the most degrading treatment by the U.S. customs on the mere suspicion that we could be "agitators." Naturally, we then expected to find the U.S. population in an equally fanatic and xenophobic mood, but what we found on the ground, at least during these first few weeks, was starkly different.[12] Almost everywhere we went in New York and Philadelphia, we met with a deep sense of shock rather than rage: "How could this happen to us?" The popular mood seemed better reflected by the sticker that was quite frequently seen in New York, "Our grief is not a cry for war," than by the televised sessions of Congress. This mis-expectation turns out to be important for what I want to sketch out in the following.

1. Beyond the Ivory Tower

Chomsky has been an anarchist since his early youth, a fact that he has often described in personal reminiscences in films and interviews.[13] Given this long-standing background, it is perhaps a little bit surprising that his prodigious output in political articles, interviews, books, and lectures in the 55 years since 1966 contains relatively little on the subject – relatively, that is, because given the enormous amount of time Chomsky spends on these activities, his output here is still quite substantial. But compared to other anarchists, who often write book after book on the roots of class society and aspects of the new anarchist society they wish to replace the current systems based on domination and exploitation with, the distribution of labor in Chomsky's political work is clearly different.

---

as its prominent display at Virgin Records attests, *9/11* is particularly popular with younger readers; the book is a hot item at campus bookstores nationwide." Quoted in Barsky, *The Chomsky Effect*, 67. Also see https://www.city-journal.org/html/america%E2%80%99s-dumbe st-intellectual-12361.html.

12 This story is told in Michael Schiffmann, "A Strange Encounter: Coming to the United States one Week after Nine-Eleven," forthcoming, https://uni-mannheim.academia.edu/MichaelSchiff mann.

13 Chomsky talks about this in the excellent companion volume to the equally named film by Peter Wintonick and Mike Achbar, *Manufacturing Consent, Noam Chomsky and the Media*, Black Rose Books 1994, 49: "By about 1941, I was beginning to go pretty regularly to New York [...] and was hanging around second-hand bookstores on Fourth Avenue, the *Freie Arbeiter Stimme* office [an anarchist publication], etc., picking up literature on all sorts of topics, including the anarchists in the Spanish Civil War." Having already been intrigued by libertarian ideas as a child, he then "learned more about Spanish anarchism, and obtained relevant documentation, from the early 40s." This is a commentary to the corresponding passage in the film at min. 31 ff.

As sketched above, Chomsky really entered the political scene only in 1964 (and, in writing, in 1966),[14] and since that time, he has devoted himself to an endless stream of causes: ending the U.S. wars in Indochina,[15] striving for peace in the Middle East,[16] fighting the U.S.-supported Indonesian invasion in East Timor,[17] struggling against the new Cold War that began with the Reagan administration (with, in fact, already in the latter half of the Carter administration),[18] organizing resistance against the U.S. support for terrorist regimes in Central America and for the terrorist Contra war against Nicaragua,[19] exposing the brutality of Israel's 1982 Lebanon war and the deceptive nature of the U.S.-sponsored "Oslo Peace Process in Israel-Palestine,[20] opposing the NATO war in the Serbian province Kosovo that put the final nail into the coffin for the project of a Yugoslavian state,[21] and one could seamlessly go on with this until today.

Of course, Chomsky, as an anarchist critic of capitalist society, has always been aware that "[d]etermined opposition to the latest lunacies and atrocities" of capitalism in general and U.S imperialism, though it "must continue, for the sake of the victims as well as our own ultimate survival," nevertheless "should be understood as a poor substitute for a challenge to the deeper causes. [...] Protest over Star Wars, massacre in El Salvador, and so on, is a sign of our weakness."[22] In fact, Chomsky's first political book already ends with the conclusion that "[i]t is reasonably clear that unless the commercial and industrial system comes under some sort of popular democratic control, political democracy will be a sham and state power will continue to serve inhuman ends."[23]

We thus find a permanent tension between Chomsky's radical ideas with regard to a necessary fundamental reconstruction of the present oppressive society and urgent current activities to stop immediately occurring atrocities, or, as Chomsky has put it with regard to militarism, "a holding action, rather like putting a band-aid on a can-

---

14 His article "The Responsibility of Intellectuals" first appeared in 1966 in the Harvard University's student journal *Mosaic* and then, in an extended and footnoted form, in February 1967 in the New York Review of Books. See Noam Chomsky "Remarks on the historical context of the essay 'The Responsibility of Intellectuals'," in Nicholas Allott, Chris Knight and Neil Smith, *The Responsibility of Intellectuals. Reflections by Noam Chomsky and others after 50 years*, UCL Press 2019, 5-6.

15 See *American Power and the New Mandarins*, *At War with Asia*, and *For Reasons of State*.

16 *Peace in the Middle East*, Vintage 1974.

17 See chapter 3 of Chomsky & Herman, *The Washington Connection*, and particularly chapter 3.4.4, "East Timor: Genocide on the Sly," *ibid.*, 129-204.

18 *Towards a New Cold War? Essay on the Current Crisis and How We Got There*, Pantheon 1982, *Turning the Tide. U.S. Intervention in Central America and the Struggle for Peace*, South End 1985.

19 *Turning the Tide* and *On Power and Ideology. The Managua Lectures*, South End 1987.

20 *The Fateful Triangle. Israel, the United States, and the Palestinians*, 2nd edition, South End 1999.

21 *The New Military Humanism. Lessons from the Kosovo*, Common Courage 1999.

22 *Turning the Tide*, 250.

23 *American Power and the New Mandarins*, 403.

cer."[24] The greater amount of Chomsky's time has always been devoted to that latter task, and the reasons for him to do so are actually not hard to detect. At a lecture in Hamburg in 1990 which I was able to attend, Chomsky spelled these reasons out most clearly during the Q & A session. A questioner in the audience, who had made a long digression on the importance of science and a scientific approach to everything before he came to his question: "What did he, Chomsky, think of atrocity so and so as a scientist?" But Chomsky did not even bother to go into the question of the merits of science, but stated rather blandly: "I oppose oppression, massacres, atrocities, torture and so on, not because I am a scientist, but because I am a human being!"[25]

Thus, political action (including the writing of books, giving lectures, corresponding with thousands of people, going to demonstrations, going to jail for short periods and risking even substantially longer periods of jail time) comes out of an elementary moral matrix, and as we will see in the next section, it is a morality that Chomsky believes he shares with (virtually) everyone by virtue of being just that, a human being.

Quite beyond all the other features of U.S. state capitalism and imperialism, by 1964 the Vietnam war represented such a monstrosity that Chomsky "began openly resisting" the war, because, in his own words, "it would have been hopelessly immoral not to." And looking back, he even adds that "already much too late; after the US invaded South Vietnam, what we call ethnic cleansing when others are doing it was going on from the early 60s. That was the time to get seriously involved."[26] Chomsky has spoken about this so often that there is no need to further elaborate.

Of course, the elementary moral matrix of which I just spoke also comes into play when one has to decide which kind of oppression emanating from some system, in our case, U.S. state capitalism is the most serious and therefore the most in need to be addressed by a moral agent. As far as that is concerned, there was and is certainly no dearth of horrendous conditions within the borders of the U.S. itself, from the brutal racism Black people were confronted with in the South in the 1960[27] to the perhaps unique phenomenon of mass incarceration of which they are once more the primary victims today,[28] or from the hyper-exploitation of many (once again, mostly

---

24 *Turning the Tide*, 219.
25 Personal recollection.
26 Maya Jaggi, "Conscience of a Nation," *Guardian*, January 20, 2001.
    https://www.theguardian.com/books/2001/jan/20/society.politics.
27 See, among multiple other works, Manning Marable, *Race, Reform, and Rebellion. The Second Reconstruction and Beyond in Black America, 1945 – 2006*, Mississippi University Press 2007.
28 Michelle Alexander, *The New Jim Crow. Mass Incarceration in the Age of Colorblindness*, 2nd edition, The New Press 2012.

Black) U.S. workers from the 1950 to the 1970s[29] to their state of today where either their wages have been frozen at level of the 1970s or they fall prey to the "rustbeltification" of large swathes of former "industrial America" and the ensuing psychological and social consequences such as the opioid crisis.[30]

But even so then – in the 1960s – and now – in 2020 –, there is no doubt that, as Chomsky wrote in his 1985 book *Turning the Tide*, "[t]he real victims of 'America's agony' are millions of suffering and tormented people throughout much of the Third World." And he continues: "Our highly refined ideological institutions protect us from seeing their plight and our role in maintaining it, except sporadically. If we had the honesty and the moral courage, we would not let a day pass without hearing the cries of the victims." This refers, not just to the wars the U.S. has carried and continues to carry out itself, but also to the wars and to the oppression it sponsors and the system it puts into place by this course of action: "We would turn on the radio in the morning and listen to the voices of the people who escaped the massacres in Quiché province [in Guatemala] and the Guazapa mountains [in El Salvador], and the daily press would carry front-page pictures of children dying of malnutrition and disease in the countries where order reigns and crops and beef are exported to the American market, with an explanation of why this is so."[31]

2. The Morality of Human Beings

Given the well-known horrors of the Vietnam war (or actually, the Indochina wars) waged by the U.S., Chomsky's move "beyond the ivory tower" was thus morally well motivated even though in the beginning, it seemed completely hopeless and more like something one "cannot not do" than something that might really have an influence on the course of events.

Chomsky's vivid description of the state of affairs back then is worth quoting at some length:

> The first kind of public, outdoor rally that I spoke to was in October 1965 on the Boston Common. There must have been two hundred or three hundred police – who we were very happy to see I should say, because they were the only thing that kept us from being murdered. The crowd was extremely hostile. It was mostly students who had marched

---

29 For a visual representation, see the Paul Schrader film *Blue Collar* (1978); for Black workers, see Dan Georgakas & Marvin Surkin, *Detroit: I Do Mind Dying. A Study in Urban Revolution*, 3rd, updated edition, Haymarket Books 2012.

30 For frozen and falling wages, see *World Orders, Old and New*, Pluto Press 1994, 140 ff. For a panoramic overview, see Chris Hedges & John Sacco, *Days of Destruction, Days of Revolt*, Nation Books 2012, and Chomsky's *Requiem for the American Dream. The 10 Principles of Concentration of Wealth and Power*, Seven Stories Press 2017.

31 *Turning the Tide*, 170.

over from the university and they were ready to kill you. And [our] demands were so tame.[32]

As Chomsky stepped out of his role as a highly successful university professor with very satisfying professional and personal life – "I was in a very favorable position. I had the kind of work I liked, we had a lively, exciting department, the field was going well, personal life was fine, I was living in a nice place, children growing up. Everything looked perfect" – to return to his much earlier intensely political interests, he realized "that if I returned to these interests, which were the dominant interests of my own youth, life would become very uncomfortable."[33]

But from his early negative experiences in his anti-war activity he never drew a conclusion that is all too tempting for activists who face active hostility, can't find an audience and correspondingly don't see any progress in their cause: Forget about the rest of the population who seem content with their own oppression and unreceptive for the much worse pain of others for which they share responsibility, and raise the ante by using ever more "radical" tactics in your actions against the state, including violent tactics that are bound to increase to hostility of the non-activist part of the population even further.

This kind of reaction is sometimes even labeled – or self-labeled – "anarchist,"[34] but the anarchism Chomsky inherited, essentially unchanged, from his early days is of a very different sort. Moreover, since his beginning acquaintance with anarchism in the 1940, Chomsky had had more than two decades to reflect on it and to deepen its philosophical underpinnings.[35] One crucial difference of this kind of anarchism is the conception of what is loosely called "the people" or the average person – the kind of person that is neither an inhabitant of the academic ivory tower, nor a political activist, nor a part of the educated classes in general.

---

32 *Chronicles of Dissent*, 249.
33 Wintonick & Achbar, *Manufacturing Consent*, 66; in the film, this is at minute 48:20 ff.
34 By this, I do not want to unfairly imply that this is true of all or even of the majority of people regarding themselves as anarchist activists. Quite probably the vast majority of anarchists would adamantly deny that they hold large sectors of the general population in contempt, but actions speak louder than words and people whose views about how things ought to be done and discussed are constantly disregarded by the *actions* of activists will hardly give credence to the *words* of those activists that say otherwise.
35 By the mid-1960s, Chomsky had already had extensive discussions in the early 1950s with his friends Morris Halle and Eric Lenneberg concerning the wrongheadedness of behaviorism with its "plastic" approach to human nature, had published his critique of the leading proponent of this current in psychology, B.F. Skinner ("A Review of B.F. Skinner's Verbal Behavior," in *Language* 35, No. 1 (1959), 26-58) and had become acquainted with the egalitarian and libertarian work of the German linguist, statesman, and philosopher Wilhelm von Humboldt. Along with linguistic work by Humboldt, the German original of the latter's explicitly political work *The Limits of State Action* (Cambridge University Press 1969) is also listed in Chomsky's *Cartesian Linguistics. A Chapter in the History of Rationalist Thought*, Harper & Row 1966, which was written in 1965.

It is a characteristic feature of a whole spectrum of political and economic ideologies (and not just the anarchist currents I just talked about) that they regard the general population as being in need to be guided by others in most important affairs, presumably by people with greater ability or those who know better or those who have the right ideology. This is fairly obvious in parliamentary capitalist democracies which are quite ostensibly governed by an economic elite in the business realm and by a political elite as far as matters of "democracy" are concerned.

In fact, Chomsky has devoted not a few pages of his work to the analysis of the pronouncements of quite liberal proponents of capitalist democracy, pronouncements which make their contemptuous stance towards the majority of the population (and hence, their contempt for the very concept of democracy) glaringly obvious. This is not the place to go into an extended analysis of this topic, but it should be noted that even the title of one of his most important works (co-written with Edward Herman), *Manufacturing Consent*, goes back to an expression coined in the 1920s by "the distinguished [20th century] journalist and political commentator Walter Lippmann," namely, the "manufacture of consent,"[36] which was later almost paraphrased by one of the major figures of public relations at the time, Sigmund Freud's nephew Edward Bernays, who in 1947 talked about the "engineering of consent," which according to him

> quite simply means the application of scientific principles and tried practices to the task of getting people to support ideas and programs. [...] The engineering of consent is the very essence of the democratic process, the freedom to persuade and suggest. [...] A leader frequently cannot wait for the people to arrive at even general understanding [...] democratic leaders must play their part in [...] engineering [...] consent to socially constructive goals and values.[37]

In short, consent needs to be manufactured and engineered from above, from the betters of the population, "to ensure that the population will ratify the decisions of farsighted leaders, who must be free from influence by the unwashed masses."[38]

What is often overlooked is the fact that a range of self-perceived leftist ideologies basically share the same outlook: The "unwashed masses" must be guided by politically educated leaders, even though in this case, the task of these leaders is not the solidification, but rather, the transformation of the status quo.

If one looks at the Leninist concept of the vanguard party which states, in the words of Lenin himself in *What Is to Be Done?* (1902), that without the revolutionary party "[t]he spontaneous working-class movement is by itself able to create (and inevitably does create) only trade-unionism, and working-class trade-unionist polit-

---

36 *On Power and Ideology*, 127.
37 Quoted after *Towards a New Cold War*, 66-67. For 1947 date see fn. 36.
38 *On Power and Ideology*, 127.

ics is precisely working-class bourgeois politics,"[39] meaning that without the outside intervention of party, the working class will fail its mission and will be unable to develop "true" class consciousness, it reads almost like a blueprint of the musings of the theorists of capitalist democracy Walter Lippman and Edward Bernays a couple of decades later.

As mentioned above, other, non-Leninist leftist currents are not always free from this elitist conception of the relation between the "know-it-all" activists and the ignorant, dumbed down masses, and this is exactly where Chomsky's own stance with regard to his fellow citizens, which has not changed or wavered since his very first political writings in the mid-1960s, comes in as a breath of fresh air. My quotes from him on this will therefore disregard chronology.

In *Turning the Tide*, from which I have quoted above repeatedly, Chomsky asks the question why the perpetrators of the many state-sponsored atrocities he has fought over the years, in this case, the masterminds behind the U.S.-sponsored terror wars in Central America in the bloody decade of the 1980s, did not simply call a spade a spade and "and simply tell the American people honestly that we must proceed on our course 'regardless of how many are murdered'[40] because we have higher priorities than the survival of the people of El Salvador?"[41]

Chomsky sees two reasons, one being self-deception to evade seeing unpleasant things when one is looking in the mirror,[42] the other, in my view, Chomsky's core premise for any activity that can achieve positive results – either by mitigating or ending atrocities or by initiating processes that may lead to changes in the direction of less oppression and exploitation and more anarchy and freedom. This reason is that

> elite groups are afraid of the population. They are afraid that people are not gangsters. They know that the people they address would not steal food from a starving child if they knew that no one was looking and they could get away with it, and that they would not torture and murder in pursuit of personal gain merely on the grounds that they are too powerful to suffer retaliation for their crimes. If the people they address were to learn the

---

39 Vladimir Lenin, *What Is to Be Done?* (https://www.marxists.org/archive/lenin/works/download/what-itd.pdf), chapter 3.6 (p. 59, in this internet edition).
40 This phrase goes back to the advice of the political journal *New Republic* to the Reagan administration that it should be *honest* about what it does in Central America and the fact "that military aid must go forth regardless of how many are murdered, lest the Marxist-Leninist guerrillas win." The journal's own stance was: "And indeed, the guerrillas must not win." Editorial, *New Republic*, April 2, 1984, quoted in *Turning the Tide*, 168.
41 *Turning the Tide*, 170.
42 One should not overlook that this, as Chomsky himself has often stressed, is also a reflection of an (already dimmed-down) morality. Few people are able to live with a self-image in which they are just egotistic and selfish. It would be interesting to relate this to the observation as old as Aristotle that humans are "social animals."

truth about the actions they support or passively tolerate, they would not permit them to proceed."[43]

We should note here that what Chomsky writes above involves a kind of Pascalian wager. Just as in Pascal's wager, on which more in a moment, there is not, has not ever been, and cannot be any scientific guarantee for Chomsky's assumption that the rest of the population will be moved to the same kind of activities as his own once the ideological blinders and the lies they are subjected to are removed and effectively countered – quite different from what the man in the audience of Chomsky's Hamburg talk seemed to be suggesting.

No one is more aware of this fact than Chomsky himself, who has repeatedly stressed that a *science* of human nature in both its moral and most other aspects does not yet exist and maybe never will. But that doesn't mean that we can't, and shouldn't, rely on sometimes very well-founded historical research and speculation and subject it to the situation of the Pascalian wager. In Pascal's case, the assumption that God did not exist (which was not lacking in arguments) led to worse outcomes for ourselves than if we believed in His existence, and that is essentially why Pascal suggested to discard non-belief.[44] In a situation in which the morality of our fellow citizens does not in the end correspond to ours, our actions may turn out to be futile, but in the case where we win the wager, there will be ample rewards. As far as I know, Chomsky himself has talked about the Pascalian wager for the first time in 1991, when he wrote: "We are faced with a kind of Pascal's wager: assume the worst, and it will surely arrive; commit oneself to the struggle for freedom and justice, and its cause may be advanced."[45]

In his writings, Chomsky marshals ample evidence for the assumption that his own bet on the fundamental decency of the general population might be the right one. He frequently quotes the results of polls of the U.S. population on a variety of issues, including topics in which sympathy for the plight of others plays a role. Space forbids to quote the numerous examples for the vast gap between the official portrayal of the popular mood by politicians and the media and what the population

---

43 *Turning the Tide*, 170.
44 Pascal's wager is contained in Chapter XLV – "Discourse Concerning the Machine" – of his *Pensées*, in Blaise Pascal, *Pensées and Other Writings*, Oxford University Press 1995. At the beginning (152), he writes: "So we can clearly understand that there is a God without knowing what he is," and he concludes his discourse with the words (156):
But what harm will come to you from taking this course? You will be faithful, honest, humble, grateful, doing good, a sincere and true friend. It is, of course, true; you will not take part in corrupt pleasure, in glory, in the pleasures of high living. But will you not have others?
I tell you that you will win thereby in this life, and that it every step you take along this path, you will see so much certainty of winning and so negligible a risk, that you will realize in the end that you have wagered on something certain and infinite, for which you have paid nothing.
45 *Deterring Democracy*, Verso 1991, 64. Second, enlarged edition 1992.

actually thinks that can be found in Chomsky's work over the years, but two cases concerning areas that have always been close to his heart deserve closer attention.

Ever since the last American left Vietnam from the top of the U.S. embassy on April 30, 1975, there has been a vast and diversified effort to portray the United States as the victim of the war and the peoples of Indochina as the aggressor.[46] Here, President Carter's 1977 observation that the U.S. owes Vietnam no debt because "[t]he destruction was mutual" (see fn. 7) is even at the liberal end of the spectrum; on the other end, there were endless unfounded accusations according to which Vietnam still kept U.S. soldiers in prison, and the threats of renewed U.S. aggression associated with such accusations.[47] Given this political-cultural background, the observation made by Chomsky in a 1993 lecture in Kairo is all the more remarkable. Noting that the effect of the official portrayal of the war "has been complex," he says:

> Public opinion studies show that by 1990, the median estimate of Vietnamese casualties was 100,000, about 5 percent of the official figure; the discovery that Germans estimate Holocaust deaths at 300,000 might elicit some notice and concern, but this passes with no comment. Despite these shocking facts, over 70 percent of the public, unlike the articulate intellectuals, continue to regard the war as "fundamentally wrong and immoral," not a "mistake."[48]

In another lecture years before in Managua (1986), he remarked that

> [s]imilar results hold in many other cases, for example, the 1982 Israeli invasion of Lebanon, approved by a margin of about 3 to 2 by more educated people, opposed by about the same margin by less educated people, who are capable of understanding that aggression and massacre are aggression and massacre, not a legitimate act of self-defense in accord with the highest ideals of Western civilization.[49]

It is important to note that Chomsky's observations also address a logical counterargument against the assumption that the basic impulses of ordinary people are decent: What about all the other polls that show vast chunks, if not the majority of people to be susceptible to all sorts of jingoism, fanaticism, and worse? This observation is certainly also true and can thus not simply be discarded, but the truly remarkable fact about the stance of the U.S. population with regard to the Vietnam war and Is-

---

46 One reflection of this is the endless number of films that have been made about the war and whose content ranges from jingoist celebrations of war to anti-war films, but the vast majority of which have in common that Vietnamese, Cambodians, and Laotians are largely absent in them except in the form of the emblematic "yellow peril." Post-1975 films include *The Deer Hunter* (1978), *Apocalypse Now* (1979), *Purple Hearts* (1984), *Rambo* (1985), *Platoon* (1986), *Gardens of Stone* (1987), *Full Metal Jacket* (1987), and many more since. Needless to say, these films are both artistically and ethically quite diverse, but I know of no prominent film that really tries to show the war from the *Indochinese* perspective.

47 *Necessary Illusions. Thought Control in Democratic Societies*, Pluto Press 1992, 36-37.

48 *World Orders, Old and New*, 96.

49 *On Power and Ideology*, 129.

rael's brutal 1982 Lebanon invasion is that it was taken *despite a massive propaganda to the contrary*.

There is no doubt that propaganda sometimes works, or else it would not be undertaken, but the two examples Chomsky adduces demonstrate that it is possible to resist its onslaught.

3. Why Manufacturing Consent Is Necessary

This latter point directly related to a very important part of Chomsky's political work right from the beginning, namely, the analysis of the portrayal of events by the ruling elites and the media. As Karl Marx famously observed, "The ideas of the ruling class are in every epoch the ruling ideas, i.e. the class which is the ruling material force of society, is at the same time its ruling intellectual force."[50] But for these ideas to take roots in the rest of society, they must be formulated, and this is the natural task of the educated classes – courtiers and clergy in pre-capitalist times, the so-called intelligentsia and the media in our time.

All of Chomsky's political work represents a comparison between facts and their official representation and goes back and forth between them, but there are two major works of his that are systematically devoted to the (mis-)representation of facts by powerful ideological institutions in the service of dominant forces of society, in this case, the modern media: *Manufacturing Consent. The Political Economy of the Mass Media* (co-written with Edward S. Herman, 1988, second edition 2002) and *Necessary Illusions. Thought Control in Democratic Societies* (1989).

In those two books, the authors intend to show how, in "contrast to the standard conception of the media as cantankerous, obstinate, and ubiquitous in their search for truth and their independence of authority," the media actually serve "to inculcate and defend the economic, social, and political agenda of privileged groups that dominate the domestic society and the state. The media serve this purpose in many ways: through selection of topics, distribution of concerns, framing of issues, filtering of information, emphasis and tone, and by keeping debate within the bounds of acceptable premises."[51]

I have previously addressed the likely reasons why the dominant forces of society do not simply openly proceed with the murder and destruction of "Others" in Vietnam, El Salvador, or Nicaragua, citing that it is good for them, or even "us," as the sole rationale but rather resort to all sorts of deception and obfuscation or, in other

---

50 Karl Marx & Frederick Engels, *The German Ideology*, in Karl Marx & Frederick Engels, *Collected Works Vol. 5, 1845-47*, Progress Publishers 1975, 59.

51 Herman & Chomsky, *Manufacturing Consent. The Political Economy of the Mass Media*, Pantheon Books 1988, 2nd edition with a new introduction by the authors 2002, 298.

words, propaganda to hide the very fact that what they are doing inevitably involves just that, murder and destruction. But the ruling system of domination does not only affect victims in the Third World (or in the ample sections of U.S. society that closely resemble Third World conditions). Exploitation and oppression of the majority of the population are also at the very center of the domestic systems over which these elites rule.

The mere fact that these forms of oppression and exploitation are less severe than those inflicted elsewhere does not, however, make them any less real. What the propaganda system must thus drive out of people's hearts and minds is not just sympathy for others, but also, and perhaps even more crucially, sympathy for *themselves*. Conditions of unfreedom in which one's life is not based on autonomous self-determination but on having to more or less blindly follow the orders of others must be psychologically inculcated as natural and inevitable state of affairs which to oppose would not only be futile but might even lead to a worse situation than the one which one started from.

This is the point to go into some of Chomsky's reflections on human nature that go beyond the observation that "elite groups are afraid of the population" because "[t]hey are afraid that people are not gangsters."[52] These reflections underpin Chomsky's version of Pascal's wager, the wager that a more just and free future is possible, in an even deeper sense. They are connected to his linguistic work, even though he is at pains to stress that they do not directly follow from it. It is well-known at least to linguists that a core insight of Chomsky's linguistics is the virtually unlimited creativity human language allows for,[53] a creativity that is, according to an early insight by the German linguist Wilhelm von Humboldt, based on the "infinite employment of finite means."[54] Or as Chomsky explains it:

> Language is a process of free creation; its laws and principles are fixed, but the manner in which the principles of generation are used is free and infinitely varied. Even the interpretation and use of words involves a process of free creation. The normal use of language and the acquisition of language depend on what Humboldt calls the fixed form of language, a system of generative processes that is rooted in the nature of the human mind and constrains but does not determine the free creations of normal intelligence or, at a higher and more original level, of the great writer or thinker.[55]

What is crucial here is the free creations of *normal intelligence*; the "process of free creation" we are talking about here is in no way limited to great writers or thinkers or other extraordinary human beings. In his 1966 book *Cartesian Linguistics*, Chom-

---

52 See above and footnote 43.
53 This is elaborated by the linguist David Adger in a very accessible recent book, *Language Unlimited. The Science behind Our Most Creative Power*, Oxford University Press 2019.
54 Wilhelm von Humboldt, *On Language*, Cambridge University Press 1988, 91.
55 "Language and Freedom," in *The Chomsky Reader* (ed. James Peck), Pantheon Books 1987, 152.

sky even traces this conception back to Descartes who he says "maintains that language is available for the free expression of thought or for appropriate response in any new context and is *undetermined* by any fixed association of utterances to external stimuli or physiological states."[56] For Descartes, this non-determined character of human language use was the clearest proof that humans (as distinct from animals, who he considered to be automatons)[57] indeed possess freedom.

Just as the assumption that "people are not gangsters," the observation that human language use is free cannot be literally proven, even though the massive evidence for "the diversity of human behavior, its appropriateness to new situations, and man's capacity to innovate – the creative aspect of language use providing the principal indication of this –" was suggestive enough for "Descartes to attribute possession of mind to other humans, since he regards this capacity as beyond the limitations of any imaginable mechanism." And Chomsky adds that Descartes seemed to be suggesting that

> a fully adequate psychology requires the postulation of a "creative principle" alongside of the "mechanical principle" that suffices to account for all other aspects of the inanimate and animate world and for a significant range of human actions and "passions" as well.[58]

Ideas like this were further developed much later by Wilhelm von Humboldt, even though the latter himself apparently did not draw any connections to his linguistic observations. In his 1792 work *The Limits of State Action*, von Humboldt develops a speculative theory of human nature in which the concept of freedom is once more of central importance: "I have felt myself animated throughout with a sense of the deepest respect for the inherent dignity of human nature, and for freedom, which alone befits that dignity." But in his vision, von Humboldt goes far beyond abstract musings:

> [M]an never regards what he possesses as so much his own, as what he does; and the laborer who tends a garden is perhaps in a truer sense its owner, than the listless voluptuary who enjoys its fruits. [...] [I]t seems as if all peasants and craftsmen might be elevated into artists; that is, men who love their labor for its own sake, improve it by their own plastic genius and inventive skill, and thereby cultivate their intellect, ennoble their character, and exalt and refine their pleasures. And so humanity would be ennobled by the very things which now, though beautiful in themselves, so often serve to degrade it. [...] But, still, freedom is undoubtedly the indispensable condition.[59]

---

56 *Cartesian Linguistics*, 60. Italics mine.
57 *Ibid.*, 59.
58 *Ibid.*, 61.
59 Quoted in "Language and Freedom," 149-50, Wilhelm von Humboldt, *The Limits of State Action*, Cambridge University Press 1969, 24.

It is hard to imagine a vision in a starker contrast to the capitalist society with its deeply alienating effects which was still only on the horizon when von Humboldt wrote these lines. Elsewhere, Chomsky has summarized this, following Bakunin, as "an instinct for freedom." And he further comments: "Whether the instinct for freedom is real or not, we do not know. If it is, history teaches that it can be dulled, but has yet to be killed."[60]

If von Humboldt's sketch of the essence, the nature, and the actual needs of human beings is anywhere near accurate, as Chomsky certainly believes, it is indeed small wonder that in a situation where the need for freedom and self-determination are denied to the overwhelming majority of the population, a vast ideological machinery must be put in place to obscure and deny this fact, or else convince people that "there is no alternative."

Once more, Chomsky can often show that it is hard to manufacture consent and to dull the instinct for freedom. To give just one of many striking examples, after five years under Reagan, polls regularly indicated that "the public would support a tax increase devoted to New Deal and Great Society programs, contrary to widespread beliefs. Support for equal or greater social expenditures was about 80% in 1980, and increased by 1984." Despite massive propaganda, massive majorities supported social and environmental programs over military spending and opposed a ban on abortion. Perhaps even more impressively, a decade earlier, pollsters had found "that the overwhelming majority believe that workers and the community should control business enterprises,"[61] echoing interests and concerns that were articulated by von Humboldt almost two hundred years before. This was so despite the fact that virtually no one in the political system or the media advocated these positions.

4. From Oppression to Liberation

There was thus a reason why my own, my partner's and my sister's fears about the spontaneous reaction of the U.S. population turned out to be unfounded or, at the very least, exaggerated,[62] even though, given the amount of immediate official warmongering and propaganda, the mood we experienced on the ground couldn't prevail for very long. Even so, it was still remarkable that Chomsky had his very first bestseller with 9/11 and that highly critical books such as Ziauddin Sardar and Merryl Wyn Davies' *Why Do People Hate America?*[63] and Ahmed Rashid's not quite so

---

60 *Deterring Democracy*, 397, 401.
61 *Turning the Tide*, 241.
62 It must be admitted, though, that our observations were limited to the culturally liberal big cities New York and Philadelphia.
63 Ziauddin Sardar & Merryl Wyn Davis, *Why Do People Hate America?* Icon Books 2002.

critical, but nevertheless serious and essential book *Taliban*[64]also became instant bestsellers.

The U.S. attack on Afghanistan followed 9/11 almost immediately, but it took the Bush administration 18 more months and a massive campaign of lies about weapons of mass destruction to soften public opinion up to the point where it could begin its disastrous invasion of Iraq on March 20, 2003.[65] As Chomsky had dryly remarked in a 1977 lecture in Holland: "One problem is that in a democracy, the voice of the people is heard. Therefore, it is necessary to find ways to ensure that the people's voice speaks the right words."[66]

In recent political discourse, the term "populism" has gotten a bad name in left-liberal circles because of its association with right-wing demagogues such as Marine Le Pen in France, Geert Wilders in the Netherlands, Nigel Farage in the UK, and of course Donald Trump in the United States. Populist movements, the British *Guardian* noted in a hardly unrepresentative article in 2016 (on the pending re-election of the "populist" leftist Jeremy Corbyn as the leader of the UK's Labour Party), have "a disdain for elites and experts of all kinds," assume that politics must simply "put into action the will of the people," and most dangerously, propose "straightforward, simple solutions to what are in fact complex problems."[67] In other words, populist movements make irresponsible promises to the naïve masses who might then be tempted to follow them because of their detachment of what is actually possible.

It should not surprise us by now that in the few instances Chomsky mentions the terms "populism or "populist" at all in his works,[68] they have a positive rather than a negative connotation. As he generally does, here, too he sticks to the dictionary sense of the term as opposed to the one used in the jargon of political discourse: "a

---

64 Ahmed Rashid, *Taliban. The Story of the Afghan Warlords*, Pan Books 2001.
65 On this point, see, among many others, Sheldon Rampton & John Stauber, *Weapons of Mass Deception. The Uses of Propaganda in Bush's War on Iraq*, Robinson 2003.
66 "Intellectuals and the State," in *Towards a New Cold War*, 65.
67 Julian Baggini, "Jeremy Corbyn is a great populist. But that's no good for our democracy," *Guardian*, July 25, 2016, https://www.theguardian.com/commentisfree/2016/jul/25/jeremy-cor byn-populist-democracy-mps.
68 In *American Power and the New Mandarins*, he talks about "the strong populist element in *early* Chinese Marxism" (137, emphasis mine), in *The Washington Connection and Third World Fascism*, Chomsky and Herman mention the hostility of the Brazilian post-1964 military dictatorship to "to any sort of populism" (101) and later on the "Free World scene of military elites repressing populist or mild reformist tendencies and using systematic and institutionalized terror to allow a redistribution of income upward and outward", as in Vietnam, being one of the reasons for the ferociousness of the U.S. on that country (103). Other positive remarks on "populism" concern the East-Timorese movement FRETILIN, whose activities to achieve independence from the U.S.-supported colonial state Indonesia Chomsky has invested enormous personal efforts to support because a literal genocide of the East-Timorese population was at stake. For "populism," in turn quoting East-Timor specialist Jill Jolliffe, see *ibid.*, 140, and for the East-Timorese resistance being faced with genocide, the whole subchapter of the book, 3.4.4, "East Timor: Genocide on the Sly," 129-204, and John Pilger, *Distant Voices*, Vintage 1994, Section 6: "East-Timor" (233-323).

political approach that strives to appeal to ordinary people who feel that their concerns are disregarded by established elite groups."[69] Given everything that was said above, this is of course exactly the kind of approach that can lead to the liberation of the majority of the population from the exploitation and oppression it is subjected to in a capitalist society – and in fact, it doesn't take much of a genius to see that it is the only such approach.

It is however, an approach that raises a very important question, that shouldn't be dismissed as mere propaganda by elitist liberals, and that question is: Who exactly is going to do the appealing in the "political approach that strives to appeal to ordinary people"? The subtext in articles such as the one from the *Guardian* quoted above is mostly that this is either done by leftist or rightist "leaders" who manipulate the masses into more or less blindly following certain goals: xenophobia in the case of Le Pen et al. in the case of the right, and "socialism" in the case of Corbyn, Bernie Sanders and others on the left.

The crucial thing that this perspective leaves out is the Chomskyan one. The one time he mentions populism more than just in passing is the case of the populist People's Party in 19th century which had been, according to Chomsky, "depicted in scholarship as a primitive, proto-fascist and anti-Semitic movement", but on which he then goes on to quote the historian Gabriel Kolko to the effect that it should more accurately be described as "the most truly libertarian social force relative to [...] the regions in which it temporarily emerged as a factor."[70]

To learn more about this, one can turn to Chomsky's close friend and fellow activist, the historian Howard Zinn's account of this movement in his acclaimed *A Peoples History of the United States* which makes crystal clear that the most pertinent character of the much denigrated People's Party's populist movement was that it was "for the people, of the people, and by the people." It was not a movement of intensely dissatisfied people stirred up by demagogues who told them what to think or do, but locally organized by people of a wide spectrum of opinions that ranged from parochial and sometimes bigoted impulses to defend oneself against "the big nobs" to outright socialism imbued with interracial solidarity.[71]

What clearly comes across from both Kolko's and Zinn's descriptions of the populist movement is that it represented an attempt – or rather, a multiplicity of attempts – at *self*-liberation. This is the reason why Kolko calls it a "truly *libertarian* social force" – here, masses of people with little formal education and little in the way of well-known leaders who stuck out from the rest organized themselves to pursue

---

69 Oxford English Dictionary, quoted at https://www.lexico.com/definition/populism.
70 *Turning the Tide*, 224, quoting Gabriel Kolko, *Main Currents in Modern American History*, Pantheon Books 1984, 26; the whole U.S. Populist movement is described on pages 25-29.
71 See Howard Zinn, *A People's History of the United States*, Longman 1980, 280-89, where Zinn quotes multiple participants in the movement, a hallmark of all of Zinn's brilliant historical work.

goals which, if pushed to their logical limits, amounted to a political and economic self-management of society.

There have of course, been many movements in history that show parallels to or even went far beyond the short-lived and heterogeneous populist movement of the People's Party in the United States which essentially ended in 1896 when its remnants effectively merged with the Democratic Party.[72] These movements range from the Levellers, particularly the Diggers or "True Levellers" in England in the 17th century who fought, not just for political democracy and equality but for the abolition of private property and a society completely free from domination[73] to the anarchist movement in Spain particularly of the period of the Spanish civil war from 1936 to 1939 whose often very successful attempts to put their ideals into practice were in the end brutally suppressed both from within and without the republic they had fought for.[74] As the experience of the Spanish anarchists has had a great influence on Chomsky, here is a flavor of it from George Orwell's *Homage to Catalonia*:

> It was the first time that I had ever been in a town where the working class was in the saddle. Practically every building of any size had been seized by the workers and was draped with red flags or with the red and black flag of the Anarchists. […] Every shop and café had an inscription saying that it had been collectivized; even the bootblacks had been collectivized and their boxes painted red and black. Waiters and shop-walkers looked you in the face and treated you as an equal. Servile and even ceremonial forms of speech had temporarily disappeared. […] In outward appearance it was a town in which the wealthy classes had practically ceased to exist. […] Above all, there was a belief in the revolution and the future, a feeling of having suddenly emerged into an era of equality and freedom. Human beings were trying to behave as human beings and not as cogs in the capitalist machine.[75]

This lengthy quote should at the same time serve to show what Chomsky regards as the essence of anarchism, namely, the liberation of people from oppression in ways that is compatible with the nature of humans as inescapably social beings. Illegitimate forms of authority should be dismantled, but this is not an individualist enterprise, as "anarchists have typically believed in a highly organized society, just one that's organized democratically from below."[76]

---

72 *Ibid.*, 288.
73 For more on this, see Jim Fox, "1642-1652: The Diggers and the Levellers" on the anarchist website libcom.org, https://libcom.org/history/1642-1652-diggers-levellers, and in greater detail Hans-Christoph Schröder: *Die Revolutionen Englands im 17. Jahrhundert*, Suhrkamp 1986.
74 This is described in what Chomsky considers by far the best book by George Orwell, namely in the latter's travelogue *Homage to Catalonia*, Penguin 2000.
75 *Ibid.*, 2-3. An overlapping passage is also quoted at much greater length in "Objectivity and Liberal Scholarship," in *American Power and the New Mandarins*, fn. 90, 145-46.
76 *Understanding Power*, The New Press 2002, chapter 6: "Community Activists," 199. This book is a unique collection of Chomsky's discussions with audiences and activists over a period of ten years from 1989 to 1999 edited by Peter R. Mitchell and John Schoeffel.

At the core of it is the principle of autonomous individual and collective self-determination, and this is also where the key for the transition from a repressive society based on domination to a (more) liberated one lies. Chomsky has often spoken against the concept of "leaders," intellectual or otherwise, who regard it as their mission to guide the unenlightened masses to a brighter future; one of the first times I saw him speak in Germany, he even felt compelled to remark "I was not the leader of the U.S. peace movement [against the Vietnam war]," just to avoid potential misunderstandings.[77]

It is in people's organizing "democratically from below" that the hope for winning the Pascalian bet on a better future lies. But this will inevitably involve people from all walks of life and all sorts of current ideological predilections; there cannot, and should not be a uniform movement of the population where everyone agrees on everything. This is also one of the reasons why Chomsky has always rejected to speculate about the concrete form a future anarchist society might take: "I don't feel in a position – and even if I felt I was, I wouldn't say it – to know what the long-term results are going to look like in any kind of detail: those are things that will have to be discovered, in my view,"[78] even though he has welcomed the speculations of others – recognizing them as just that, speculations.[79]

As deeply ingrained structures of oppression will of course not simply go away at the first push, Chomsky thinks that the first and foremost lesson has to be that people expecting success in their various struggles must be prepared to be in it for the long haul. In one of his many interviews with Chomsky, radio journalist David Barsamian asks him: "But you warn that victories don't come quickly. So we're not in a sprint here. It's a marathon," and Chomsky responds in a similar vein to what he has stressed over many years:

> It's a marathon, and one in which you often go backward. There's regression, too. The last thirty years have been in some respects a period of regression, although in popular activism it's been an expansion. History is never simple.[80]

Elsewhere, he has stated the same thing even briefer: "Nothing is going to work pretty soon, at least if it's worth doing, nor has that ever been the case."[81]

---

77 Personal recollection; this was at the Hamburg event referred to in fn. 25.
78 *Ibid.*, 201.
79 E.g., Michael Albert & Robin Hahnel, *Looking Forward: Participatory Economics for the Twenty First Century*, South End Press 1991.The back flap text of the book says: "Albert and Hahnel agree with Noam Chomsky that 'The task for a modern industrial society is to achieve what is now technically realizable, namely, a society which is really based on free voluntary participation of people who produce and create, live their lives freely within institutions they control and with limited hierarchical structures, possible none at all'."
80 *Power Systems. Conversations on Global Democratic Uprisings and the New Challenges to U.S. Empire. Interviews with David Barsamian*, Metropolitan Books 2013, 176.
81 Again, in conversation with Barsamian. *Class Warfare. Interviews with David Barsamian*, South End Press 1996.

This is true for the struggle for particular goals such as raising the minimum wage, pushing LGBT rights and advancing environmental protection or against particular atrocities such as the U.S.'s Indochina wars in the 1960s and 1970s and its support for the murderous wars against the populations of Central America in the 1980s, but even more so for the much more encompassing and general struggle for a free and just society as envisaged by anarchist principles.

I think it's important to note that in the latter case in particular, a logical case has to be made: No anarchist or libertarian society could even *exist* without the continuous and active participation of its population in its management, and it makes still less sense to assume that it will somehow fall from heaven without such permanent activity.

Perhaps less than in any other case, free societies are managed "all by themselves," i.e., by the majority assuming that the management of society is the task of someone else, i.e., some extra-class of people, the task of people Chomsky's friend Mike Albert has called the coordinator class: government bureaucrats, white collar workers, forepersons, etc.[82] With regard to this aspect, the goal of an anarchist society is the eradication of the division of labor as far as possible.

At the same time, for the emergence of a free society, the struggles against the various kinds of exploitation, domination, and oppression must somehow meet and recognize themselves in each other, and this is often where the difficulties really begin because in a society that is radically built on competition, this competition is inevitably bound to show up in the struggle *against oppression* as well.

As the struggle against oppression is hard and demanding, there can often be a fierce fight over scarce resources both in the wider – attention, attendance at events, active participants in the movements – and the narrower – financial sense. There are multiple forms of oppression and domination that only partly overlap, and solidarity between them does not come for free and certainly not automatically.

In this regard, the British activist Milan Rai, who has worked with Chomsky and has done some extraordinary peace work himself,[83] has to contribute an observation that has stuck with me ever since I first read it. It concerns the organization RESIST

---

82   In one of his latest books, Albert describes this class in the following way: "But in between the lowly laborers and lordly capitalists, this contending view says there is a third class, the coordinator class, which includes those who do mainly empowering work, unlike workers at the bottom who do overwhelmingly disempowering, rote, and tedious work." He estimates the percentage of this class at roughly 20 percent. Michael Albert, *Practical Utopia. Strategies for a Desirable Society*, PM Press 2017, 22.

83   See, inter alia, Milan Rai, *War Plan Iraq: 10 Reasons Against War with Iraq* (which includes a chapter by Chomsky), Verso 2002, a book full of essential arguments supporting the British movement against the participation of the UK in the U.S.-directed Iraq war, a movement that almost succeeded in both preventing the UK's participation in the war and in bringing the Blair government down. See Milan Rai, "Introduction: Tony Blair Wobbled – We Almost Derailed the War," in Milan Rai, *Regime Unchanged. Why the War in Iraq Changed Nothing*, Pluto Press 2004, xix-xxvi.

that Chomsky co-founded with other friends such as the Dutch-American writer Hans Koning and which was heavily involved in direct resistance against the Vietnam war such as the October 20, 1967, March on the Pentagon:

> At a RESIST meeting in New York, a hostile group of draft resisters came to demand control of RESIST's finances – apparently opposed to the "diversion" of money to draft counselling and advisory groups. After some acrimonious debate, Chomsky suggested that a representative of the group come to the RESIST office in Boston the next day and examine their files, and decide which groups should not have been given money. When the files had been inspected, the resisters saw that money was being passed on to Black groups in Mississippi who wanted to develop anti-draft work and so on, and they withdrew their objections.[84]

What counts as "important for the struggle" in a given situation cannot be determined by dogma, but must be subject to negotiation. Chomsky's colleague Lois Kampf, to whom this report is originally due, "notes that everyone else at the meeting was just angry – Chomsky was the only one with a constructive proposal."[85]

The contradictions between the various kinds of struggle can be big and small, and for a unified movement for a better world for all to develop, it is extremely important that people become aware of each other's respective plight, regardless of how different from their own it might be, a conception that Chomsky, along with others, has come to call "intersectionality." As we will see right away, for Chomsky, at least in a capitalist society as ours, the question of the ownership of the means of production and therefore, the mode of production, has always been central because it affects all members of society, but for him, that could never mean that other forms of vile repression such as patriarchy or racism can be degraded to the status of "secondary contradictions,"[86] as certain dogmatic tendencies of the post-1960s "New Left" were tempted to treat them:

> As [U.S. founding father] John Jay put it, the country should be governed by those who own it. [...] That's at the core of things. [...] On the other hand, it's certainly worth overcoming the other forms of oppression. For people's lives, racism and sexism may be much worse than class oppression. When a kid was lynched in the South, that was worse than being paid low wages.[87]

Nevertheless, he adds: "So when we talk about the roots of the system of oppression, that can't be spelled out simply in terms of suffering. Suffering is an independent dimension, and you want to overcome suffering."[88]

---

84 Milan Rai, *Chomsky's Politics*, Verso 1995, 195 Fn. 94.
85 *Ibid.*, based on an interview with Kampf at the MIT, April 22, 1993.
86 I don't know much about the U.S. in this regard, but this was certainly the case in Germany.
87 *The Prosperous Few and the Restless Many*, Odonian Press 1993, 71.
88 *Ibid.*, 71-72.

There is thus no question for Chomsky that oppression, exploitation, and domination must be fought on all fronts at the same time, a conception that is articulated today under the rubric of "intersectionality." Chomsky has always been the first to stress the importance of each of those struggles in their own right, but as he says in his most recent book, properly understood intersectionality is the first step to overcome the isolation between these struggles:

> For activists, there are strong temptations – understandable, valid – to devote intense efforts to critical issues in the immediate focus of their work. But linkages with other social struggles are real, not just at home but globally. All can gain by considered and careful initiatives to pursue "intersectionality" and solidarity.[89]

Nowhere is this truer than in the two areas that Chomsky currently considers as the most urgent ones, namely, the struggle against the increasing danger of a nuclear war and the struggle against climate change, both questions that involve the survival of the species itself. As in other areas, here, too, progress can be achieved even without overcoming capitalist society as a whole: "Even within the current structure of power, there's plenty of latitude for pressure and changes and reforms." As always, this progress is reached by the activity of increasingly larger sectors of the population as "any institution is going to have to respond to public pressure – because their interest is to keep the population more or less passive and quiescent, and if the population is *not* passive and quiescent, then they have to respond to that."[90]

But as mentioned above, even if the population wins this or that important victory, the central question of capitalist class rule – the fact that even seemingly democratic politics is, in the words of the U.S. philosopher John Dewey which Chomsky has often quoted, no more than "the shadow cast on society by big business" – will not go away, and therefore

> [r]eforms are of limited utility; democracy requires that the source of the shadow be removed, not only because of its domination of the political arena, but because the very institutions of private power undermine democracy and freedom.[91]

Political, cultural, and social movements overlook this fact at their peril. If intersectionality fails, they might even find themselves at each other's throat, having completely lost sight of the ominous source of the shadow that Chomsky mentions in his Dewey quote. Here, a personal reminiscence seems to me to be quite instructive with regard to Chomsky's approach to this matter. The first time I was able to get an impression of Chomsky from a little bit more up close was in Zurich in 1992, where he gave a talk as part of a series organized by the leftist *Wochenzeitung* (*WoZ*) under the rubric "Brave New World Order."

---

89   *Internationalism or Extinction*, Routledge 2020, 84-85.
90   Teach-In: Evening," in *Understanding Power*, 76.
91   *World Orders, Old and New*, 87.

One day after he had spoken before and discussed with a large crowd in the community center Rote Fabrik, he participated in a demonstration organized by the local anarchist scene on the occasion of the so-called Los Angeles Riots that followed the acquittal of four policemen who had almost beaten the Black motorist Rodney King to death the year before[92] by an almost purely white jury. During the riots, more than fifty people were killed and hundreds of buildings were burned. The organizers of the demonstration hailed the events as harbingers of a coming revolution in the United States, a fact that clearly came across in the banners, leaflets, and speeches at the demo. I am wondering to this day what they made of the speech that Chomsky gave after he had taken the time to march along with the demonstrators for the whole time – or at least the excerpts below:

> The current riots in the U.S. are, I am afraid, not a struggle for freedom. They are just a reaction to the fact that a large part of the population has become superfluous. We describe the rioters as Blacks, [...] but we must not forget the ideological aspect. In the U.S., it is not allowed to use the word class – that is taboo.
>
> The resentment and the fears that are reflected in the jury trial are a typical phenomenon among oppressed people who are frightened to death by each other. Thus, they are diverted from their real oppressors and hate each other instead. That's normal, and for the rulers [...], that is not a bad result.[93]

He also pointed to the fact that poverty among *all* ethnic groups, including whites, was spreading with accelerating speed, and since the 1990s he has not tired of pointing to the fact that the wages of all U.S. workers have been stagnant or declining since the early 1970s. In his 1996 book *Class Warfare*, he even bitterly complained – something that he very rarely does – that the U.S. left was not doing its task in this regard.

Talking about people such as Timothy McVeigh, a veteran of the U.S.'s 1991 Iraq war who felt let down and betrayed by the federal government to such an extent that he blew up a federal building in Oklahoma, killing 168 people and maiming hundreds of others, Chomsky said:

> But these paramilitary organizations that are called militias – people like the Timothy McVeighs, who are they? They're mostly white, working-class men with something like high school educations. They're pretty much the kind of people who were building the

---

92 This gruesome event happened to have been taped by a bystander with a video camera; without the tape, the case would probably not even have gone to trial. The video is at https://www.yout ube.com/watch?v=sb1WywIpUtY.

93 I am quoting and retranslating here from the discussion following Chomsky's speech at the Rote Fabrik, where he said essentially the same things as at the demonstration a day later: "Unordnung in der Ordnungsmacht. Die Situation der USA," in Christina Koch (ed.), *Schöne neue Weltordnung. Die Zürcher Veranstaltungen*, Rotpunktverlag, 216-17. Other contributors to the Zurich series of events and thus to the book included Samir Amin, Tony Benn, Eduardo Galeano, Louisa Hanoune, Boris Kagarlitsky, Fatima Mernissi, Vandana Shiva, and Jean Ziegler.

[radical industrial union founded in the 1930s] CIO sixty years ago. Why aren't they doing something similar now? It's an organizer's dream, but they're not being organized.[94]

And talking about a worker at a solidarity event he and his interviewer David Barsamian had attended three weeks before, he elaborated:

> He [was] describing his picture of what he wanted his life to be and thought it ought to be. [...] [I]f that life is taken away from [people like him] and the possibilities of their having a meaningful existence with serious work and family life and the rest of what he was saying [...] they're going to go in one of two directions. Either they too will be doing something like joining paramilitary groups, or some other destructive activity [...] or they will be the people who will rebuild the civil society that's being dismantled and restore some semblance of a democratic system.[95]

The roots of the current "Trump phenomenon" where those who have been spit out by the capitalist system and are cast as "deplorables" by liberal elites fall into despair and resort to destructive responses, such as the one reflected in the opioid crisis, or by becoming the fan base of a person who is not only a certifiable sociopath, but recognizably their class enemy, reach indeed far back.

The reason why so relatively few activists, both in the U.S. and elsewhere, have been willing to deal with the capitalist system itself and its consequences may very well be that it is the hardest to dislodge: it is the power system where the concentration of power has reached its utmost level. Nevertheless, for people who want a truly free society, the question cannot be avoided. It is of enormous importance if the husband of a woman in some offshore factory where she works twelve hours a day seven days a week begins to treat her as a human being and if she is no longer discriminated against because of her "race," but her fingers will still be chopped off by the machine if she lets her thoughts wander too much while she devotes half of her lifetime to increasing the company's profit.

5. Revolutionary Reformism

From all the above, it seems to me, and I think Chomsky would agree, that revolutionary change towards a society free of oppression moves in concentric circles: You begin with singular issues, move on to solidarity with others who are concerned with similar issues, and you end up by saying that the guiding principle – the dismantling of illegitimate authority should apply all across the board: We don't just want the bread or the cake, we want the bakery.

---

94 *Class Warfare*, 111.
95 *Ibid.*, 111-12.

A very radical change, and it is from this fact that the question how we get from here to there gains its pertinence. For revolutionaries – and one is a revolutionary if one subscribes to such a sort of change – it is tempting to assume that radical solutions demand "radical means," that is, in certain opinions, one or another form of violence. There are of course many examples for violent revolutions in history, not least the Spanish revolution particularly in the years 1936-37, but it is far from clear that what was achieved by violence was the best or most important part in them.[96]

Moreover, already in his first book Chomsky pointed to a sobering fact that should give advocates of violence pause: "One who pays some attention to history will not be surprised if those who cry most loudly that we must smash and destroy are later found among the administrators of some new system of repression."[97] Examples for this are too numerous to cite; a particularly sad case is represented by many liberation movements in the third world which, once in government, turned out to be as repressive as their colonial predecessors, even though the repression took a different form.

Like most people, however, Chomsky is not a pacifist, so for him the question of violence is a *practical* one. The question that arises here is twofold: The first has already been addressed in the previous paragraph, namely, does not the use of violence and the militarization of resistance inherently foster authoritarian tendencies that run counter to the goals of a libertarian revolution? This was certainly true in the Spanish civil war, where the non-Anarchist parts of the republic conspired against the Anarchist revolution and constantly cited "military necessities" in the struggle against the Franco troops to do so.[98]

The second question is whether violent means to fight government, corporate, or other forms of oppression are even feasible in a highly developed country such as the U.S, and here, Chomsky's answer is clearly no (this "no" doesn't include various forms of resistance that *the state* characterizes as violent, such as blockades, protection against police violence, etc.). In a dialogue with a listener of David Barsamian's radio talk show who wanted to know what he thought about the opportunities the 2nd amendment gives U.S. citizens to defend themselves against the state, Chomsky first pointed out that in the U.S., citizens have ways to influence the government, ways they don't have (so far) with regard to big business, and then commented:

> As for guns being the way to respond to this, that's outlandish. […] If people have pistols, the government has tanks. If people get tanks, the government has atomic weapons. There's no way to deal with these issues by violent force, even if you think that that's

---

96 The Terror in the French Revolution would be an interesting subject to study in this regard.

97 "Introduction," *American Power and the New Mandarins*, 18.

98 "Objectivity and Liberal Scholarship," in *American Power and the New Mandarins*, 115. Ironically, Chomsky argues that the authoritarian policy of the central republican government, which it invariably justified with the military situation, actually undermined the military resistance against Franco.

morally legitimate. Guns in the hands of American citizens are not going to make the country more benign. They're going to make it more brutal, ruthless and destructive.[99]

But there is still another important reason why violence as a tactic rarely works. Once violence becomes a tactic, an established mode of activism, the violence used will tend to obscure the very issue that the activism tried to call attention to. This has been Chomsky's stance since the very beginning of his own activism, where he often engaged in non-violent civil disobedience, but he has made the point quite forcefully again recently with regard to the massive Black Lives Matter protests following the abuse and murder of yet another Black man, George Floyd, by the police.

According to him, the effect of the Los Angeles riots in 1992 was, "as usual, [...] to shift public attention to rioters: We have to have more law and order, more force; that's the typical response to protests once they become violent."[100] Instead of clarifying the issues to a larger public, these tactics are obscuring them, which is why they should be rejected. On the other hand, Chomsky has, to the best of my knowledge, never even once joined the ranks of the hypocrites of official politics and the media who are using the violence to do the obscuring.

In his 1970 essay "Language and Freedom," echoing Kant who defended the French Revolution *despite* the Terror, Chomsky denounces both terror and violence, but also makes the crucial observation: "Yet no person of understanding or humanity will too quickly condemn the violence that often occurs when long-subdued masses rise against their oppressors, or take their first steps toward liberty and social reconstruction."[101]

We could thus summarize Chomsky's approach to the question of how we come from here to there, from a highly exploitative and often very repressive capitalist society to a society in which the majority of the population is finally allowed to fulfill its needs to live a free, creative life, as one where this struggle is guided by the principle of an ever-increasing level of (largely) non-violent mass activity of the population itself.

This leaves us with a final topic that has been contentious among radicals for more than hundred years, the question of reform or revolution, or in other terms, of working inside the system or outside and against it. For Chomsky, that has never been a serious question. As he said in a discussion already quoted above, "I don't really see why that [simply working for certain demands] should make any difference: what you try to do is advance the principles. Now, that may be what some peo-

---

99   *Secrets, Lies and Democracy*, Odonian Press 1994, 37-38. Given all that has happened in between, now, twenty-five years later, these remarks have an eerie ring to them.
100   "Trump Wants to Destroy Organised Human Life: Noam Chomsky," internet interview with Vijay Prashad, June 3, 2020, https://www.youtube.com/watch?v=RiTl0moYYeQ.
101   "Language and Freedom," in *The Chomsky Reader*. 145.

ple call 'reformism' – but that's kind of like a put-down: reforms can be quite revo-lutionary if they lead in a certain direction."[102]

This conception is remarkably similar to the ideas developed by one fellow con-tributor to the 1992 Zurich series of events, the Russian dissident Boris Kagarlitsky, who spent time in jail for his activities under the Soviet regime and who, in his 1990 book *The Dialectic of Change* on progressive transformations in countries both of the East and the West, also saw a "revolutionary-reformist process" at work in whose "multi-stage character, we must inevitably acknowledge the necessity of tem-porary retreats."[103]

In the process, the "left" – those who are advancing the cause of freedom and equality – must use any means at their disposal to advance the options and possibili-ties of the population even in a society which is not yet free. The important thing is to always pave the road without losing sight of where one wants to lead it to. Chom-sky has forcefully argued that at the present stage, that even involves voting for a corporate Democrat with a terrible record such as Joe Biden.

Curiously, the question of whether one should vote for a Democrat instead of a Republican, not vote at all, etc., has been splitting the U.S. left for at least the last twenty years, and voting for the Democrat – or whoever is perceived to be the better candidate – has been contemptuously called "LEV," or lesser evil voting, which is supposed to be reformist, a betrayal of principle, or worse.

Chomsky's answer to this leads us straight back to his ecumenical approach which doesn't, in principle, distinguish between small ("reformist") steps and huge ("revolutionary") advances, provided that they are pushes in the right direction:

> There is an official doctrine that politics reduces to voting in an election, and then going home to leave matters to others. [...]
> The traditional left doctrine is very different. It holds that politics consists of constant ac-tivism to resist oppression, not only from government, but from even harsher private power, and to develop people's movements to promote justice and popular control of in-stitutions. Every few years an event comes around called an "election." One takes a few minutes to see if there is a significant difference between the candidates, and if there is, to take another few minutes to vote against the worst one and then get back to work.[104]

---

102 "Community Activists," *Understanding Power*, 201.
103 Boris Kagarlitsky, *The Dialectic of Change*, Verso 1990, 332. Unfazed by the series of defeats the international left had suffered at the end of the 1980s, Kagarlitsky concluded the main part of his book with words that remind one of the Pascalian wager:
    The outcome of the contemporary world crisis depends on the ability of progressive forces to present humanity with a genuine alternative. The advantage of the present epoch is that, along with its difficulties and misfortunes, it also provides a chance of real change. This is the posi-tive side of the crisis. The Chinese indicate this concept by the unity of two hieroglyphs: "danger" and "opportunity." The question is which one comes out on top (333).
104 "We Must Not Let Masters of Capital Define the Post-COVID World," interview with C.J. Polychroniou, *Truthout*, July 1, 2020, https://truthout.org/articles/chomsky-we-must-not-let-m asters-of-capital-define-the-post-covid-world/. Or as Chomsky's friend over many years,

6. Coda

My best opportunity to meet Chomsky as a person and to observe his interactions with others has been in 2004 when he was awarded the Carl von Ossietzky Prize of the city of Oldenburg, Germany and I was invited to give a speech. It is still not clear to me how he got the prize as the official persons who had awarded it – apart from the late journalist Eckart Spoo who had suggested Chomsky – seemed to have very little interest in him while he was there.

This was certainly not true of the many hundreds of others who came to the events where he spoke – the official ceremony, a very well attended podium discussion with visitors from all over Oldenburg and beyond, and a morning event with students from local high schools. It was here that one could see Chomsky's idea about a society of equals free from domination in action. It was a pleasure to watch Chomsky coming alive again after the relatively tedious podium discussion because he could speak directly to a bunch of law students who had asked to see him, and it was equally refreshing to see how high school students fearlessly held their ground if they disagreed with Chomsky's responses to their contributions.

But to me, his whole approach to the question I have tried to address in this essay seems to be encapsulated in the lunch, and the discussions at the lunch, I and a number of friends were able to have with him before the podium discussion. We were about a ten people; Noam, myself, my partner, my sister, an Iranian poetess who had always dreamt to meet Chomsky, a young student who was obviously – but in different ways – in love with both the poetess and Chomsky, one of the pioneering German publishers of Chomsky's books, Wolfgang Haug. Given the diversity of the participants, the discussions had a truly far range and went from the prison conditions in Iran to vegetarianism (as some of us, including Chomsky, were eating fish or meat) to even more serious theoretical issues, such as the practical feasibility of anarchism which we were all sure would be called into question by most of the people who would share the podium with Chomsky in the evening.[105]

The nonchalant response Chomsky had for these concerns has stuck with me ever since: "You only need to look at the current situation. Is that sane? How could anar-

---

Howard Zinn formulated it: "There's hardly anything more important that people can learn than the fact that the really critical thing isn't who is sitting in the White House, but who is sitting in – in the streets, in the cafeterias, in the halls of government, in the factories. Who is protesting, who is occupying offices and demonstrating – those are the things that determine what happens." Howard Zinn, "The Signs of Resistance," interview by Anthony Arnove, *Socialist Worker*, February 16, 2001, quoted in Lance Selfa, *The Democrats. A Critical History*, Haymarket Books 2008, 238 fn. 3.

105 Most of the above represents personal recollections. The German-language documentation of the event as well as the organization of the event itself owes a lot to the city official Gerda Grebe. See Stadt Oldenburg, *Dokumentation Carl-von-Ossietzky-Preis 2004*, Stadt Oldenburg 2005.

chy, the removal of domination of one set of people over another, make it worse? Anarchism isn't chaos, violence, and destruction. Anarchy is sanity."

The absence of the exploitation, repression, torture, alienation, domination of some by certain others is sanity. Who could object to that statement?

And the best part of it is perhaps that we are already there,[106] and have always been: Everything that happens, will happen, or come about in the future depends on us and our own activity. The Golden Age, if it exists or can come about, is in ourselves and in our own hands.[107]

It is upon us to act on this insight.

Bibliography

Achbar, Mark & *Wintonick*, Peter, 1992: Manufacturing Consent: Noam Chomsky and the Media (film).

Achbar, Mark (ed.), 1994: Manufacturing Consent: Noam Chomsky and the Media. The companion book to the award-winning film by Peter Wintonick and Mark Achbar. Montréal: Black Rose Books.

Adger, David, 2019: Language Unlimited. The Science behind Our Most Creative Power. Oxford: Oxford University Press.

Albert, Michael, 2017: Practical Utopia. Strategies for a Desirable Society. Oakland, CA: PM Press.

Albert, Michael & *Hahnel*, Robin, 1991: Looking Forward: Participatory Economics for the Twenty First Century. Boston: South End.

---

106 Chomsky has always stressed the necessity for activists to lay the groundwork before they push for far-reaching goals. But at the same time, he has often pointed to the fact that for large parts of the populations of the industrial democracies, radical ideas frequently lie just beneath the surface. Among the most interesting cases are efforts by U.S. workers at taking over and self-managing factories abandoned by their owners in "rust-belt" places such as Ohio, documented inter alia in Gal Alperovitz, *America Beyond Capitalism. Reclaiming Our Wealth, Our Liberty, and Our Democracy*, Wiley 2005, which is briefly discussed in *Occupy*. Zucotti Park Press 2012, 94-95. In February 1990 (*Chronicles of Dissent*, 247-48), Chomsky commented on such issues:
The 18th-century revolutions have not been consummated. Even the texts of classical liberalism were talking about things like wage slavery, people being condemned to work under command instead of working out of their own inner need and not controlling the work process. That's at the core of classical liberalism. That's all been completely forgotten. But that ought to be revived. That's very real. That means an attack on the fundamental structure of State capitalism. I think that's in order. That's not something far off in the future. In fact, we don't even have to have fancy ideas about it. A lot of the ideas were articulated in the 18th century, even in what are the classical liberal texts and then later in at least the libertarian parts of the socialist movement and the anarchist movement. I think that is a very live topic which ought to be faced.

107 I stole this idea from Alexander Cockburn, *The Golden Age Is in Us. Journeys and Encounters*, Verso 1995.

Alexander, Michelle, 2012: The New Jim Crow. Mass Incarceration in the Age of Colorblindness, 2nd edition. New York: The New Press.

Allott, Nicholas, *Knight*, Chris & *Smith*, Neil, 2019: The Responsibility of Intellectuals. Reflections by Noam Chomsky and others after 50 years. London: UCL Press.

Alperovitz, Gal, 2005: America Beyond Capitalism. Reclaiming Our Wealth, Our Liberty, and Our Democracy. Hoboken, NJ: Wiley.

Baggini, Julian, 2016: "Jeremy Corbyn is a great populist. But that's no good for our democracy." In: Guardian, July 25, 2016, https://www.theguardian.com/commentisfree/2016/jul/25/jeremy-corbyn-populist-democracy-mps.

Barsky, Robert, 2007: The Chomsky Effect: A Radical Works Beyond the Ivory Tower. Cambridge, MA: MIT Press.

Chomsky, Noam, 1959: "A Review of B.F. Skinner's Verbal Behavior." In: Language 35, No. 1 (1959), 26-58.

Chomsky, Noam, 1966: Cartesian Linguistics. A Chapter in the History of Rationalist Thought. New York: Harper & Row.

Chomsky, Noam, 1969: American Power and the New Mandarins, New York: Pantheon.

Chomsky, Noam, 1969a: "Introduction." In: *Chomsky*, Noam, 1969: American Power and the New Mandarins. New York: Pantheon, 3-22.

Chomsky, Noam, 1969b: "Objectivity and Liberal Scholarship." In: *Chomsky*, Noam, 1969: American Power and the New Mandarins. New York: Pantheon, 23-158.

Chomsky, Noam, 1969c: "The Responsibility of Intellectuals." In: Chomsky, Noam, 1969: American Power and the New Mandarins. New York: Pantheon, 323-366.

Chomsky, Noam, 1970: At War with Asia, New York: Pantheon.

Chomsky, Noam, 1973: For Reasons of State. New York: Vintage.

Chomsky, Noam, 1974: Peace in the Middle East. New York: Vintage.

Chomsky, Noam, 1982: Towards a New Cold War? Essay on the Current Crisis and How We Got There. New York: Pantheon.

Chomsky, Noam, 1982a: "Intellectuals and the State." In *Chomsky*, Noam, 1982: Towards a New Cold War. New York: Pantheon, 60-85.

Chomsky, Noam, 1985: Turning the Tide. U.S. Intervention in Central America and the Struggle for Peace. Boston: South End.

Chomsky, Noam, 1987: The Chomsky Reader, *Peck*, James (ed.). New York: Pantheon.

Chomsky, Noam, 1987a: "Equality. Language Development, Human Intelligence, and Social Organization." In: *Chomsky*, Noam, 1987: The Chomsky Reader. *Peck*, James (ed.). New York: Pantheon, 183-202.

Chomsky, Noam, 1987: "Language and Freedom." In: *Chomsky*, Noam, 1987: The Chomsky Reader. *Peck*, James (ed.). New York: Pantheon, 139-155.

Chomsky, Noam, 1987: On Power and Ideology. The Managua Lectures. Boston: South End.

Chomsky, Noam, 1992: Chronicles of Dissent. Interviews with David Barsamian. Monroe, ME: Common Courage Press.

Chomsky, Noam, 1992a: Deterring Democracy, second, enlarged edition, London: Verso.

Chomsky, Noam, 1992b: Necessary Illusions. Thought Control in Democratic Societies. London: Pluto Press.

Chomsky, Noam, 1992c: "Unordnung in der Ordnungsmacht. Die Situation der USA." In: *Koch*, Christina (ed.), 1992, Schöne neue Weltordnung. Die Zürcher Veranstaltungen. Zurich: Rotpunktverlag, 193-226.

Chomsky, Noam, 1993: The Prosperous Free and the Restless Many. Berkeley, CA: Odonian Press.

Chomsky, Noam, 1994: Secrets, Lies and Democracy, Berkeley, CA: Odonian Press.

Chomsky, Noam, 1994: World Orders, Old and New. London: Pluto.

Chomsky, Noam, 1996: Class Warfare. Interviews with David Barsamian. Boston: South End.

Chomsky, Noam, 1999: The Fateful Triangle. Israel, the United States, and the Palestinians, 2nd edition. Boston: South End.

Chomsky, Noam, 1999: The New Military Humanism. Lessons from the Kosovo. Monroe, ME: Common Courage.

Chomsky, Noam, 2001: 9/11. New York: Seven Stories.

Chomsky, Noam, 2002: Understanding Power. *Mitchell*, Peter R. & *Schoeffel* (eds.). New York: The New Press.

Chomsky, Noam, 2002a: "Community Activists." In *Chomsky*, Noam, 2002: Understanding Power. *Mitchell*, Peter R. & *Schoeffel* (eds.). New York: The New Press, 177-223.

Chomsky, Noam, 2002b: "Teach-In: Evening." In *Chomsky*, Noam, 2002: Understanding Power. *Mitchell*, Peter R. & *Schoeffel* (eds.). New York: The New Press, 70-105.

Chomsky, Noam, 2012: Occupy. New York: Zucotti Park Press.

Chomsky, Noam, 2013: Power Systems. Conversations on Global Democratic Uprisings and the New Challenges to U.S. Empire. Interviews with David Barsamian. New York: Metropolitan Books.

Chomsky, Noam, 2017: Requiem for the American Dream. The 10 Principles of Concentration of Wealth and Power. New York: Seven Stories.

Chomsky, Noam, 2019: "Remarks on the historical context of the essay 'The Responsibility of Intellectuals'." In: *Allott*, Nicholas, *Knight*, Chris & *Smith*, Neil, 2019: The Responsibility of Intellectuals. Reflections by Noam Chomsky and others after 50 years. London: UCL Press, 5-6.

Chomsky, Noam, 2020: Internationalism or Extinction, London: Routledge.

Chomsky, Noam, 2020: "Trump Wants to Destroy Organised Human Life: Noam Chomsky," internet interview with Vijay Prashad, June 3, 2020. See: https://www.youtube.com/watch?v=RiTl0moYYeQ.

Chomsky, Noam, 2020: "We Must Not Let Masters of Capital Define the Post-COVID World," interview with C.J. Polychroniou. In: Truthout, July 1, 2020, https://truthout.org/articles/chomsky-we-must-not-let-masters-of-capital-define-the-post-covid-world/.

Chomsky, Noam & Herman, Edward S., 1979: The Political Economy of Human Rights. Volume I: The Washington Connection and Third World Fascism. Boston: South End.

Chomsky, Noam & Herman, Edward S., 1979: The Political Economy of Human Rights. Volume II: After the Cataclysm. Postwar Indochina and the Reconstruction of Imperial Ideology. Boston: South End.

Cimino, Michael, 1978: The Deer Hunter (film).

Cockburn, Alexander, 1995: The Golden Age Is in Us. Journeys and Encounters, London: Verso.

Coppola, Francis Ford, 1979: Apocalypse Now (film).

Coppola, Francis Ford, 1987: Gardens of Stone (film).

Editors of the New Republic, 1984: "Editorial." In: New Republic, April 2, 1984.

Fox, Jim: "1642-1652: The Diggers and the Levellers." See: https://libcom.org/history/1642-1 652-diggers-levellers.

Furie, Sidney J., 1984: Purple Hearts (film).

Georgakas, Dan & *Surkin*, Marvin, 2012: Detroit: I Do Mind Dying. A Study in Urban Revolution, 3rd, updated edition. Chicago, IL: Haymarket Books.

Hedges, Chris & *Sacco*, John, 2012: Days of Destruction, Days of Revolt. New York: Nation Books.

Herman, Edward & *Chomsky*, Noam, 2002: Manufacturing Consent. The Political Economy of the Mass Media, 2nd edition with a new introduction by the authors. New York: Pantheon.

Hitchens, Christopher, 1989: Prepared for the Worst. Selected Essays and Minority Reports. London: Chatto & Windus.

Hitchens, Christopher, 1989a: "The Chorus and Cassandra." In: Hitchens, Christopher, 1989: Prepared for the Worst. Selected Essays and Minority Reports. London: Chatto & Windus, 58-77.

Holliday, George, 1991: "Rodney King Beating Video." See: https://www.youtube.com/watch ?v=sb1WywIpUtY.

Humboldt, Wilhelm von, 1969: The Limits of State Action. Cambridge: Cambridge University Press.

Humboldt, Wilhelm von, 1988: On Language. Cambridge: Cambridge University Press.

Jaggi, Maya, 2001: "Conscience of a Nation." In: Guardian, January 20, 2001, https://www.th eguardian.com/books/2001/jan/20/society.politics.

Kagarlitsky, Boris, 1990: The Dialectic of Change. London: Verso.

Kanfer, Stefan, 2002: "America's Dumbest Intellectual." In: City Journal, Summer 2002, https://www.city-journal.org/html/america%E2%80%99s-dumbest-intellectual-12361.htm l.

Koch, Christina (ed.), 1992: Schöne neue Weltordnung. Die Zürcher Veranstaltungen. Zurich: Rotpunktverlag.

Kolko, Gabriel, 1984: Main Currents in Modern American History. New York: Pantheon.

Kotcheff, Ted, 1985: Rambo (film).

Kubrick, Stanley, 1987: Full Metal Jacket (film).

Lenin, Vladimir, 1903: What Is to Be Done? See: https://www.marxists.org/archive/lenin/wor ks/download/what-itd.pdf.

Marable, Manning, 2007: Race, Reform, and Rebellion. The Second Reconstruction and Beyond in Black America, 1945 – 2006. Jackson, MS: Mississippi University Press.

Marx, Karl & *Engels*, Frederick, 1845: The German Ideology. In: *Marx*, Karl & *Engels*, Frederick, 1976, Collected Works Vol. 5, 1845-47. Moscow: Progress Publishers.

Marx, Karl & *Engels*, Frederick, 1976, Collected Works Vol. 5, 1845-47. Moscow: Progress Publishers, 19-584.

Orwell, George, 2000: Homage to Catalonia. London: Penguin 2000.

Oxford English Dictionary: "Populism." See: https://www.lexico.com/definition/populism.

Pascal, Blaise, 1995, Pensées and Other Writings. Oxford: Oxford University Press.

Pascal, Blaise, 1995a: Pensées. In: *Pascal*, Blaise, 1995: Pensées and Other Writings. Oxford: Oxford University Press, 1-181.

Pilger, John, 1994: Distant Voices. New York: Vintage 1994.

Rai, Milan, 1995: Chomsky's Politics. London: Verso.

Rai, Milan, 2002: War Plan Iraq: 10 Reasons Against War with Iraq. London: Verso.

Rai, Milan, 2004: Regime Unchanged. Why the War in Iraq Changed Nothing. London: Pluto.

Rai, Milan, 2004a: "Introduction: Tony Blair Wobbled – We Almost Derailed the War." In: *Rai*, Milan, 2004: Regime Unchanged. Why the War in Iraq Changed Nothing. London: Pluto, xix-xxvi.

Rampton, Sheldon & *Stauber*, John, 2003: Weapons of Mass Deception. The Uses of Propaganda in Bush's War on Iraq. London: Robinson.

Rashid, Ahmed, 2001: Taliban. The Story of the Afghan Warlords. London: Pan Books.

Sardar, Ziauddin & *Davies*, Merryl Wyn, 2002: Why Do People Hate America? London: Icon Books.

Schiffmann, Michael, forthcoming: "A Strange Encounter: Coming to the United States One Week after Nine-Eleven." See: https://uni-mannheim.academia.edu/MichaelSchiffmann.

Schrader, Paul, 1979: Blue Collar (film).

Schröder, Hans Christoph, 1986: Die Revolutionen Englands im 17. Jahrhundert. Frankfurt/M.: Suhrkamp.

Selfa, Lance, 2008: The Democrats. A Critical History. Chicago, IL: Haymarket Books.

Stadt Oldenburg, 2005, Dokumentation Carl-von-Ossietzky-Preis 2004. Oldenburg: Stadt Oldenburg.

Stone, Oliver, 1986: Platoon (film).

Taylor, John, 1980: "Reviewed Work: The Political Economy of Human Rights." In: Third World Quarterly Vol. 2, No. 3 (July 1980), 561-567.

Zinn, Howard, 1980; A People's History of the United States. London: Longman.

Zinn, Howard, 2001: "The Signs of Resistance," interview by Anthony Arnove. In: Socialist Worker, February 16, 2001.

Other works not cited but recommended:

Chomsky, Noam, 2003: Radical Priorities. 2nd, enlarged edition. Montréal: Black Rose Books.

Chomsky, Noam, 2004: Language and Politics. Otero, Carlos P. (ed.), 2nd, expanded edition. Choco, CA: AK Press.

Chomsky, Noam, 2015: What Kind of Creatures Are We? New York: Columbia University Press.

Collins, John, 2008: Chomsky. A Guide for the Perplexed. London: Continuum.

Grewendorf, Günther, 2006: Noam Chomsky. Munich: Beck.

Haley, Michael C. & *Lunsford*, Ronald F., 1994: Noam Chomsky. New York: Twayne Publishers.

Schiffmann, Michael, 2008: absolute Noam Chomsky. 2nd edition. Freiburg: orange press.

Smith, Neil & *Allott*, Nicholas, 2016: Chomsky. Ideas and Ideals. 3rd, expanded edition. Cambridge: Cambridge University Press.

Human Rights and the Notion of Freedom

Juan Uriagereka[1]

Culture as a Human Right—within the National State Framework

The 1885 Berlin (or Congo) Conference initiated the *Scramble for Africa*.[2] Organized by Bismarck, aside from the new German Empire (after the Franco-Prussian war) and a unified Italy, it included the British and French empires. Less central (Austro-Hungarian, Ottoman) as well as emergent empires (Russia, the US) were also present, plus the waning (Spain, Portugal) and smaller ones with a financial spine (the inventors of the Stock Market Belgium & Holland, Denmark, and Sweden-Norway). The summit's rationale was to avoid war among civilized nations. French prime minister Jules Ferry declared how "the higher races have . . . a duty to civilize the inferior races,"[3] the reason no African group belonged at the gathering. The spirit of that symposium was inspired by the US Manifest Destiny doctrine:[4] stemming from the liberal revolutions and the eventual abolition of slavery, "civilizing" meant addressing the failures of the *Ancien Régime* by applying new freedoms. This was especially so for the freedom to exploit world resources, which the Industrial Revolution demanded. While war among the *superior races* was not averted, 90% of Africa did become occupied until the great wars of the 20th century.

In the present piece, I want to concentrate on the fact that all mighty nations, as we know them today, were either present at that conference or scrambling to be there. Hostilities with those absent, Japan most vividly, led to direct confrontation with Russia and ultimately various 20th century alliances. Many of today's other powerful nations, as represented in the G20 (which includes all of the above or their alliances, like the European Union) emerged from the aftermath of the world wars, also traceable to that conference. Less obviously, other groups in the Western hemisphere had sought nationhood arguably as much as Germany or Italy had, without success. In Eurasia, the situation was most interesting within the Middle East, the United Kingdom, and the Iberian Peninsula, which I will focus on. I do this because

---

1 This piece is meant more as personal commentary than academic reflection. I appreciate helpful comments from Ignacio Alcover, Günther Grewendorf, Juan Luis Guillén, Viola Miglio, and Subashree Rangaswami, none of whom should be held responsible for any errors or misrepresentations on my part, nor as subscribing any of my ideas.
2 See Chamberlain 2010 for historical context.
3 "Il faut dire ouvertement que les races supérieures ont un droit vis-à-vis des races inférieures. Je répète que les races supérieures ont un droit, parce qu'il y a un devoir pour elles. Elles ont le devoir de civiliser les races inférieures." Said in the French Chamber of Deputies, July 28, 1885. As quoted in Sévillia 2003:396.
4 On American expansionism after the revolution, see Mark 2014.

of relative familiarity with the latter and also because Noam Chomsky—whose philosophy of the state and democracy the current volume focuses on—has often talked about these particular instances.

1. Rights and Freedom

I will start with Chomsky's 2002 address to a Kurdish audience,[5] which continues to be pressing today. Of course, Turkey—who was present in the Berlin conference as the Ottoman empire—remained a state after the conflicts of the 20th century, while the Kurds still lack one (despite the fact that they have been seeking it since the 1830's). This particular lecture is significant, also, because of the immediate legal reaction it received from Turkish authorities (see fn. 5).

Chomsky started his talk by reminiscing on being asked about his views on the right to one's mother tongue. "As a linguist," he said (p. 47), "I have no opinion about the matter." This is qualified as follows: "As a human being there is nothing to discuss. It is too obvious. The right to use one's mother tongue freely in every way that one wants—in literature, in public meetings, in any other form—that is a primary essential human right." Here I wish to reflect on the origins of such a right. Particularly since Chomsky also said in that talk, in response to a request to define freedom (p. 53): "I would not even try. It's a fundamental basic concept that we understand but we can't define. . . Freedom is what we make of it. If we stand against repression, authority and illegitimate structures, we are expanding the domain of freedom."

The issue is important because the human right to one's culture clearly presupposes one's freedom to exercise it. It then becomes vital, if not to formally define, at least to contextualize the origin and development of the relevant notions, to display them against the background of democracy. In a people-based government, broadly characterized culture is of the essence, so as to have informed citizens prepared to meaningfully affect their collective lives. Past authoritarian societies—either by accident or by deliberate design—may have lacked the practical means to have reliable information distributed over the population, to affect their participation in decision-making. In contrast, a progressive society is supposed to build on human creativity (e.g. to read or transmit and question evidence by any relevant means) and dignity (e.g. to distribute work, wealth, or societal needs) to build a viable future. In any

---

5 Chomsky visited Diyarbakirin in February 2002, while in his visit to Turkey so as to observe the trial of his publisher Fatih Tas (who had published Chomsky's work documenting over 30,000 killings, since 1984 alone). The content of his speech, with audience reactions, is reproduced in Coates 2002. Reuters reported on February 18, 2002, how a "Turkish security court began examining evidence against U.S. academic Noam Chomsky for allegedly fomenting separatism during a visit to Diyarbakir."

event, it is because these dynamics can be rather subtle that we need to reflect on them, since in conflicts like the one between the Kurds and the Turks, one group's freedoms may be seen as infringing on the other's.

2. A Brief History of Liberalism

Nation-states start with the 18th Century liberal revolutions, which echo earlier insurrections. Since the European Renaissance, these ranged from anti-Castilian Valencian (1519-23, 1702-15), Catalan (1640-52, 1687-89), and other revolts (*Comuneros* in Castile (1520-22), or liberation revolts in the Netherlands (1566-648), Portugal (1640), Naples (1647), Sicily (1672-8)); to a variety of uprisings in early European colonies—through anti-Habsburg (Bohemia (1618-25), Moravia (1640-44), Magnate Conspiracy (1664-70), Hungary (1703-11)); anti-English (Irish (1594-603, 1641, 1798) and Scottish (1685, 1745-46)); or anti-Russian (Bashkir (1676) and Cossack (1707-09)) rebellions. Each of these is a confrontation between cultures, the winners being the empires gathering in the Berlin Conference. Obviously, the matter is not just cultural: during the same period, economic struggles were present in the various French confrontations with commoners (1648-53), the peasant wars in Hungary (1514), Slovenia (1515), Friesland (1515-23), Germany (1524-25), Sweden (1542, 1596-97, 1743), and Russia (1606-7, 1773-75), or the slave rebellion in Malta (1749). All of it before the famous bourgeois revolutions in England (1642, 1688), the American colonies (1776), and the momentous French (1789) revolution, with global consequences affecting all the empires after the domino effect of the Napoleonic Wars.

The *Ancien Régime* was directly challenged in all those instances, as expected from the intellectual contributions of Rousseau, Voltaire, Diderot, Hume, Kant, Montesquieu, or Adam Smith. The emerging societal conditions, after the expansion to the colonies (that driving the Transatlantic Slave Trade)[6] and the incipient industrial revolution led to the Public Sphere.[7] This is at the birth of the media, stemming from the printing press: newspapers, journals, masonic lodges, reading clubs in coffee houses, all sanctioned an intellectual class to build on the contradictions of the European empires and their turf wars—coupled with rampant taxation to finance their aftermaths. The new capitalist order could not be based on the older paradigm,

---

6　Aside from providing relevant references, Esposito 2015 argues that resistance to malaria by Africans, as opposed to native populations in the American continent, was a leading factor behind this well-planned aberration. Of course, socio-economic conditions in West Africa, as well as a prevalent internal slave trade, were also key factors.
7　The notion comes from Habermas 1962, which created the discipline of media studies. Papastephanou 2012 explores Habermas's (somewhat debatable) uses of some of Chomsky's linguistic notions in his approach.

and in fact the countries where a bourgeoisie emerged and consolidated through international trade, industry, and the creation of flexible financial institutions, clearly played a more important role than those in which the bourgeoise were disdained or even confronted. Hence, the leading role in Berlin of England, France, or the Flanders ex-colonies, as well as Germany and Italy (and, ultimately, Japan) feeling short-changed of their would-be privileges in that context.

Liberalism sprung from that post-Renaissance chaos, replacing hereditary privilege with the enlightened ideas of democracy and the system of law, together with bourgeois markets against aristocratic monopolies or trade barriers. That necessitated a notion of state where such principles can be endorsed, with individual protections. The 1789 "Bill of rights" (to life, liberty & property) was thus enacted, with ingredients of what eventually morphed into Roosevelt's 1941 "four freedoms" (of speech, to worship, from want and fear). The "nation-building" process—for nations supported by empires—is the way to secure, in short, a new world order. The state had little to do with human needs, though; it pertained to the needs *of the citizen*, as had been the case in the Athenian (city state) democracy before. That allowed state laws to separate between free citizens and those at their service (non-citizens), women among the latter. Of course, given the philosophical underpinnings of the system based on various freedoms, the slave-trade became too hard to justify. It was more practical, in any case, to focus the production of raw materials in a continent where the subjects could be safely controlled at a distance.

The Napoleonic wars happened as a reaction from counter-revolutionary aristocratic movements, but also a power struggle with the British Empire—with a liberal class of their own and complex local geopolitics (e.g., vis-à-vis Ireland) and colonies the world-over to control.[8] The liberation domino effect in the Americas was patent throughout the 19th century, fueled by the scientific/philosophical critique of the establishment, to bring about constitutionalism.[9] Due to the anti-religious and uniformizing approach that the French pushed wherever their armies landed, many also began to explore unified nationalistic identities, for the first time (the case for the Kurds, but also for Germans or Italians) or with a new emphasis on sentiments that had never been equally tested (e.g. in Spain or Scandinavia). Virtually every "nationalist" conflict lingering in the 21st century can be traced back to these dynamics, as is evident in Eurasia or the Americas. In Africa, the mess was compounded by the fact that the nations that eventually emerged correspond to the Berlin Conference divisions, lacking any connection to traditional cultures. The Cold War only added to

---

8 See Jupp 2003 for perspective and references.
9 See Lindsay 1917 for skepticism on the relationship between classical liberalism and actual constitutionalism.

the tragedy, thus immersing the Congo (for instance) in further atrocities after independence, having experienced a true colonial holocaust.[10]

By the mid 19th century, liberal contradictions themselves were amply spotted and analyzed, leading to the emergence of radical ideologies.[11] Conflicts among those— as well as imperialistic clashes—steered nations towards the great confrontations of the 20th century, in which liberal democracies (generally) emerged winners in the West, while communist *régimes* did in the Eastern periphery of Europe and Asia. Former colonies, the Arab world, and emergent African nations generally had the kind of alignment "choice" during the Cold War that Russian roulette provides. While radical ideologies opposed colonialism, it is questionable just how much they did to liberate the oppressed.[12] Each major confrontation, in any event, resulted in peripheral liberations: the first World War, in the Bolshevik revolution; the second, in the Chinese one, as well as Indo-Pakistani emancipation; the South East Asian wars, in local revolutions all the way out to Latin America and Africa. The process is still unfolding and uncertain, with the Arab Spring relating to the Gulf Wars,[13] presently with more shadows than lights. All the while, confrontation between the war winners (after the possibility of self-destruction reached planetary scope) underlies the Cold War and even the *Internet Wars* in present iterations.[14]

This brings us to today, when the fundamentals of our Information World (if we may so describe the one including powers from the old 1st and 2nd worlds combined) have obviously kept their liberal roots. The challenges are still concentrated on what, as a suitable antonym, may be characterized as "the Other World": including what used to be called the 3rd World and the *precariat*.[15] Behind a façade of "democracy" (for former 1st World countries) or a "welfare state" (for former 2nd World countries)

---

10 The term "holocaust" is used by Hochschild 1998, when documenting casualties in the order of ten million. Post-colonial wars, starting with Lumumba's Western-led removal and assassination, soon after his being elected Prime Minister, led to the dictatorial Mobutu regime and, three decades later and after the Rwandan genocide, to the Congo Wars of the 1990's. These are often also described as yet another holocaust with a death toll in the order of five to six million (see e.g. Cooper 2013 a, b).

11 The First International, for a point of measure, was founded in 1864 (following the widespread European revolutions of 1848), with its initial Geneva congress held in 1866.

12 Although the legacy was loaded. Jedwab et al. 2017 argue how the purposes of colonial railroads, for instance, were military domination, mining, and crash crops to connect agriculturally rich areas—rather than local needs. This is the infrastructure inherited throughout a continent, From Egypt to South Africa. It is not easy to "start over" when previously existing foundations would need to be torn apart, often in a hostile geopolitical environment.

13 See the chapters in Krieg 2019 for perspective.

14 See Hanson 2015 for an attempt to analyze the relevant military, political, economic, and sociological effects.

15 Classic Marxist theory spoke of the *lumpen proletariat* as an underclass devoid of class consciousness. The term *precariat* was popularized in Standing 2011, as referring essentially to the class depicted in the recent movie *Parasites*. Large segments of the precariat are behind the current populist push in Western societies (Foti 2017).

—and either way blandishing "human rights" as the banner—Information World states have veered for (at least) influence in relation to the Other World.

3. Culture in the Context of other Freedoms

Regarding Chomsky's point that freedom is *what we create*, which is ultimately a cultural notion of freedom, the original *Bill of Rights* certainly did not speak of culture itself being a right. Then again, the 2007 United Nations *Declaration on the Rights of Indigenous Peoples* (UNDRIP) does.[16] Efforts along these lines date back to proposals made to the League of Nations, the precursor of the UN created after WWI. In 1923, the Chief of the Iroquois League and the founder of the largest Maori religion in New Zealand explicitly asked from the League an acknowledgement of basic sovereignty, self-government, and the ability to pursue their beliefs; they were ignored at the time.[17] Such efforts only continued in the UN after the 1970's, especially so after the 1997 reorganization of the Department of Economic and Social Affairs (DESA) into its current form.

Even though the Declaration starts its preamble by affirming that "all doctrines, policies and practices based on or advocating superiority of peoples or individuals on the basis of national origin or racial, religious, ethnic or cultural differences are racist, scientifically false, legally invalid, morally condemnable and socially unjust...", it is not a binding document. While that preamble admits how "indigenous peoples have suffered from historic injustices as a result of . . . their colonization and dispossession of their lands, territories and resources, thus preventing them from exercising . . . their right to development in accordance with their own needs and interests," and that such rights were "affirmed in treaties, agreements and other constructive arrangements with States...," there is no way to enforce what is historical fact, or even common sense, as the preamble also recognizes how "respect for indigenous knowledge, cultures and traditional practices contributes to sustainable and equitable development and proper management of the environment." Still, the document is more than anyone had been able to achieve to date, in several generations of grassroots organizations pushing for the agenda.

Just for perspective, the Declaration (see fn. 16 for a link), speaks of: (i) self-determination of indigenous individuals and peoples (Articles 1 - 8; 33 -34), (ii) culture protection through practices, languages, education, media, religion (9 - 15, 16, 25, 31); (iii) ownership of type of governance and to economic development (17 -

---

16 The declaration, with a historical overview and several FAQs, can be found in the UN site, for the Department of Economic and Social Affairs (DESA) pertaining to Indigenous Peoples, in the following link: https://www.un.org/development/desa/indigenouspeoples/declaration-on-th e-rights-of-indigenous-peoples.html.

17 See Sabatello & Schulze 2014:163.

21, 35 -37); (iv) general health rights (23 -24); and (v) protection of subgroups (e.g. the elderly, women, children – 22); but most controversially also (vi) land rights: from ownership (even reparation – 10) to environmental issues (26 -30, 32). It is this last point that makes the Declaration virtually impossible to implement at present.

Notable democracies initially opposing UNDRIP include Australia, Canada, New Zealand, and the US. This was largely on the basis of aboriginal laws conflicting with general ones within relevant states, divergences and clashes with present land-owners, general resources, intellectual property rights—even a definition of what counts as "indigenous". For example, Canadians described the document as "un-workable in a Western democracy under a constitutional government, [inasmuch as] you are balancing individual rights vs. collective rights".[18] Curiously Ukraine, which initially abstained (like the Russian Federation) from endorsing the Declaration, eventually changed course in response to the Russian annexation of Crimea (after taking the Crimean Tatars as indigenous). After pressure from native American President Evo Morales and *mestizo* President Hugo Chávez (both invited to play that role in 2007), leaders who had questioned the Declaration settled on the document being "aspirational".

It is worth citing from the UN Press Release on the occasion of the Declaration's signing (September 13, 2007).[19] The UK ambassador is reported to have said how the document is…:

> … not intended to impact in any way on the political unity or territorial integrity of exist-ing States. . . [A]rticles . . . on redress and repatriation . . . apply . . . only in respect of such property or of such ceremonial objects and human remains that [are] in the owner-ship or possession of the State. . . [T]he Declaration [is] non-legally binding and . . . [has no] retroactive application on historical episodes. National minority groups and other ethnic groups within the territory of the United Kingdom and its overseas territories [do] not fall within the scope of the indigenous peoples to which the Declaration [applies].

This hardly needs to be editorialized—coming from one of the countries favoring the document. It goes without saying that the only legal bite would have to be estab-lished in terms of countries signing UNDRIP, the first of which was Bolivia, and de-veloping national laws based on it.

Experts emphasize opportunities and challenges. For example, Karen Engle echoes Chomsky's ideas about freedom being a construct, when arguing in her 2011 that UNDRIP…

> . . . pushes the liberal human rights paradigm by explicitly referring to the right to self-determination, embracing collective rights, and expressing an understanding of the inter-relationship between rights to heritage, land, and development. . . On the other hand, it represents the continued power and persistence of an international human rights

---

18 In what follows, reactions and overall analysis are from Engel 2011.
19 The press release is here: https://www.un.org/press/en/2007/ga10612.doc.htm.

paradigm that eschews strong forms of indigenous self-determination and privileges individual civil and political rights. . . UNDRIP signifies both the possible expansion and continued limitation of human rights and the perpetuation of certain biases, including the suggestion that cultural rights . . . are outside the domain of human rights.

The political nightmare of any *global* declaration is hard to fathom. For instance, on behalf of the African Union, and apparently pressured by Western democracies opposed to the text, in 2006 Namibia pushed for a non-action resolution.[20] This was given that "the vast majority of the peoples of Africa are indigenous to the African Continent" and the claim that "self-determination only applies to nations trying to free themselves from the yoke of colonialism." One wonders whether self-rule doesn't arise for African minorities,[21] but the conflict in point resulted in further compromises in 2007, in relation to whether self-government should correlate with statehood.

Engle 2011 also emphasizes significant changes in the UNDRIP drafts. The 1993 sketch of the declaration included an additional provision on the right to self-determination that listed the areas over which indigenous peoples would have control: "culture, religion, education, information, media, health, housing, employment, social welfare, economic activities, land and resources management, environment and entry by non-members". Then a change was made for the Human Rights Council's consideration of the declaration; what remains in the adopted version arguably watered down that understanding of self-determination by instead stating that it guarantees the "right to autonomy or self-government in matters relating to their internal and local affairs, as well as ways and means for financing their autonomous functions." Moreover, Compromise Article 46 prevented the declaration from being construed as: ". . . authorizing or encouraging any action which would dismember or impair totally or in part, the territorial integrity or political unity of sovereign and independent States". As Engle puts it:

> External forms of self-determination are off the table for indigenous peoples, and human rights will largely provide the model for economic and political justice. The 1993 version . . . [instead] included collective rights of indigenous peoples to "maintain and develop their distinct identities" collectively and individually (Article 8), "to determine their own citizenship in accordance with their customs and traditions" (Article 32), and "to determine the responsibilities of individuals to their communities" (Article 34).

Evidently, that touches upon the issue of property, which is key to the liberal perspective at large. Can indigenous rights to culture and property undermine individual rights? What position should states take in instances of stolen goods (e.g. art master-

---

20 See Engel 2011:229, also for the following quotes.
21 Like the San peoples of the Kalahari Desert, spreading over Botswana, Namibia, Angola, Zambia, Zimbabwe, Lesotho, and South Africa (some 100,000 individuals, who managed to survive the area since the Paleolithic).

pieces, by the Nazi or Napoleonic troops)? Should precedents in that regard, presently often discussed at international arenas (e.g. the marbles stolen from the Parthenon) have any bearing on decisions about invaded land? Moreover, do relevant crimes, if clearly typified, prescribe after a time, particularly across generations? For that matter, should inheritors of stolen property be requested to relinquish it? These questions have obvious moral, but no simple socio-economic, answers, and are live at least within the 1st World: from Georgetown University owning up to having sold hundreds of slaves in 1838,[22] to liberal candidates to the US Democratic Nomination openly discussing reparations for African Americans, an idea that used to be limited to the political agenda of the Black Lives Matter movement. Identical issues arise in terms of land-rights, such as those presently being raised by the Mapuche communities in Argentina.[23] Examples abound the world-over.

The idea of culture as a human right, in sum, emerged strongly at the end of the 20th century, partly as a consequence of a better understanding of culture as a human trait (after the development of anthropology, linguistics, and the social sciences in general) and also as a result of expanding human rights more generally: from women's voting and other rights to various civil liberties, including those related to disabilities. Indigenous rights advocates have also broadened the liberal model of human rights to incorporate a collective right to culture, given the alarming rate at which endangered languages are dying, which ought to be considered separately.

4. Nationalism and Culture

Writing for *National Geographic*, Strochlic 2018 leads her piece by boldly stating how "every two weeks a language dies." That makes 2600 by the end of this century, a third of the extant ones; those are decline rates in the order reported for biodiversity since the Industrial Revolution.[24] If it weren't tragic, it would be curious how the same period we have been examining should have had comparable consequences for the earth's environment and its cultures alike. It cannot be an accident that the languages of the empires present in Berlin in 1885 should all have well insured futures,

---

22 Thus, solidifying their endowment fund. This is a malaise affecting most US universities, particularly if we extend the matter to land stolen from Native Americans, often part of the so-called land grants (Ambo 2017).

23 This was in relation to land stolen as recently as 1879, during the Conquest of the Desert in Patagonia by the Argentinean army, which Pérez 2011 directly describes as genocide; on current land issues, see e.g. Carroll 2011.

24 For the Intergovernmental Science-Policy Platform on Biodiversity and Ecosystem Services Global Assessment, see https://www.un.org/sustainabledevelopment/blog/2019/05/nature-decli ne-unprecedented-report/.

in terms of speaker numbers.[25] These thirteen, for the most part closely related, languages (0.18% of the world's) account for 20% of today's speakers. Moreover, except Turkish, they are all Indo-European. The other languages with massive numbers of speakers, and thus also secured futures, are all spoken in former empires or major colonies of the fourteen countries where the dominant languages were spoken, with populations large and powerful enough to stage successful independent processes.[26] As it happens, the rest of the world (some 20% of its population) speak the remaining >90% of languages, from several language families.

Since only serious efforts to revitalize endangered languages can revert such trends, the question is whether corresponding struggles can succeed in stateless nations. Still, mention of nationalism is frowned upon in academic circles. While this may be a reaction to *nationalsozialismus* or the *sovietization* of socialism, there could be further elitist elements to the disdain. Thus, the Europeans traditionally denigrated the perceived nationalistic naïveté of Americans, Asians, or Africans more recently—particularly when emergent nations had been former colonies. Meanwhile, a nationalist sentiment is easy to observe in present populisms across the globe, from Brazil to India. Within that trend, for nations with remote possibilities of becoming a state (like the Kurds and many others that are not even fighting for the privilege) the liberation idea is at best aspirational, and largely met with contempt by the established states, if not worse. In that context, it seems overly simplistic to equate nationalism for the dominant powers (the US, China, the European nations, England, Japan…), or even mere world players (India, Pakistan, Iran, Australia, Canada, Brazil, Egypt, Indonesia…), with the aspirational nationalisms of the stateless cultures, whether in a liberation process or otherwise.

Even from a less-elitist perspective, losing the world's cultures beyond one's own may seem unimportant to those not suffering from starvation or who think of themselves as already educated. One might worry about the nature and direction of that "education" but, like freedom, this too seems to be what one creates. A significant majority could argue that, as a result of the liberal revolutions, they are no longer strictly in the precariat, even if proportions, in world-wide terms, may not have changed. No one can predict, in any case, whether the equations supporting the (neo-)liberal world dynamics that the dominant cultures have created are sustain-

---

25 Adding native and 2nd language speaking, the list of languages spoken in the Berlin Conference nations with current numbers of speakers is: English: 1,150M; Spanish 560M; French 280M; Russian 260M; Portuguese 245M; German 110M; Turkish 88M, Italian 85M; Dutch 29M; Swedish 14M; Hungarian 13M; Swedish 6M; Norwegian 5.5M.

26 Languages with >25M present speakers fall into that description, accounting for 60% of the world's population: Mandarin: 1120M (other languages of China ~700M); Hindi 610M (other languages of India ~1000); Arabic 580M; Indonesian 200M (other languages of Indonesia 200M); Japanese 126M; Korean 95M, Vietnamese 76, Urdu 70, Farsi 52, Swahili 50, Hausa 44, Polish 40, Yoruba 38, Burmese 33, Sunda 32, Ukrainian 27, Igbo 27, Uzbek 25M.

able.[27] No one even knows if they *require* a precariat, whether within a state or elsewhere.[28]

The only thing clear is that market economies flourished in the period we are discussing. While the role thereof for capital and labor can hardly be denied, it is perhaps less obvious how the Scramble for Africa was really a race for competitive resources, where the cost was essentially only in infrastructure, as opposed to the raw materials themselves or the price of extracting them. It is never trivial to get a financial equation to yield positive, let alone efficient, results in a competing market, but it is obviously much harder if the initial resource conditions make the manufacturing process more expensive than one's rivals'. Eurasian powerhouses in Berlin were seeking an advantage in these markets, and part of the reason the conference ultimately failed—if not in raping Africa, in securing peace even amongst Eurasians—is because it may have been mathematically very hard to keep those markets in equilibrium. In any event, the system is way too complex for anyone to really establish anything, beyond informed speculation.

It is perhaps unreasonable to expect answers to such complex questions from the precariat, since it often lacks stable and sustainable access to the basic human rights of minimal health, let alone education. Which paradoxically leaves those in charge with the task of imagining solutions that may infringe on their privileges. To make matters even more nuanced, well intentioned expectations towards the precariat and their rights, not just to human dignity, but also to their (often ancestral) culture, more often than not clash against their own disdain for that very culture, particularly if seen as associated to the causes behind their poverty, disease, illiteracy, and so on. Direct contact with groups in need of desperate support often brings surprises for the well-meaning "helpers", since it is hard for distressed individuals to think in terms of protecting a way of life that may be portrayed to them as defunct. It is not uncommon, also, for mixed families to be created in which some members seek traditional ways of life, while others root for a different path instead: integration into the inevitable mainstream.

The UN Press release about UNDRIP (see fn. 19) speaks in terms of the rights of "the world's 370 million native peoples", vastly underestimating reality if "hybrid" situations are taken into consideration. For contrast, while in South America alone present first-peoples are in the 60M range, if the "mestizo" are considered too, the numbers jump to 225M, and adding people from partial African descent (e.g. Simón

---

27 The precise model in Motesharrei, Rivas, & Kalnai 2014 makes relevant predictions: long-term societal collapse is inevitable (in the model) when facing excessive class inequality (labor exploitation) or resource depletion.

28 Even though liberal economists like Paul Krugman (e.g. 2008) raise the issue of whether economic equations demand a middle class that stays as a precariat, to find radical critiques one still needs to resort to Chomsky & Herman 1988 or go into popular books like Varoufakis 2017, where some of the basic questions are posed.

Bolivar himself), to some 340M—totaling 64% of the population, as compared to 33% of a European descent.[29] Such numbers in Latin America are roughly equivalent to those for the "native peoples" that the UN officially recognizes for the world. If we run similar calculations for the rest of humanity, it is easy to find similar proportions, even more dramatically in some areas. One needs to remember, also, that generally those of European descent tend to remain among the ruling classes, while the rest linger within the precariat. This leads to all sorts of internal struggles about the perceived conflict between the traditional way of life vis-à-vis putative paths towards economic survival.[30]

It is nothing short of miraculous how a few cultures, especially when surrounded by elements of what I am calling the Information World, have found ways to push this agenda to center stage. This is apparent in Canada (mainly through Quebec) within the Americas and New Zealand with the Maori population. It is also seen in the Middle East within the Israeli/Palestinian conflict, and very generally in various places within Europe—some having originated as nations within the last couple of decades, within what was once part of the 2nd World. It is anyone's guess, also, whether situations like *Brexit* may lead to further pushes for, in particular, Scottish nationalism (to remain within the European Union) and Irish nationalism (to unify Ireland), or where the Catalan and Basque conflicts are ultimately leading, among a few other visible ones within Europe. While the sociological reality of these forms of nationalism is patent, it is intriguing to consider them beyond their own borders. Does an individual in, say, the Scottish Highlands suffer discrimination the way someone in a Navajo reservation still obviously does? And does it ultimately matter if the conditions differ—or can experiences relevantly reach across cultures?[31]

Strictly, no nation in the modern state sense existed until the 19th century, even those that had been empires. The so-called *Spains*, for instance, designated in plural several kingdoms (Castile, Aragon, Navarre…) that at best had powerful strategic alliances among them to run their domains. Cases similar to the ones already mentioned of Germany and Italy can be discussed within the contexts of the Austro-Hungarian, Russian, or Ottoman empires. At the same time, other communities with less momentous consequence for the official history of Eurasia gained consciousness of their socio-cultural and economic reality at that time, like the "historical nationalities" within present-day Spain (Catalan, Basque, Galician). It was largely a matter of chance and geopolitics whether that self-awareness resulted in a full-blown state. Castilian imperialism was patent even towards neighboring countries, like Portugal. After having entered a dynastic alliance between 1580 and 1640 (the Iberian Union),

---

29 See Meade 2010:6.
30 See Wearne 1996 for some contemporary ways of characterizing what it is to be first-people at present.
31 See Mabry et al 2013 for various contrasting studies in the case of Europe.

an invasion and ensuing war took place until the 1668 Treaty of Lisbon resulted in a renewed Portuguese independence.[32] A comparable process in Catalonia ended in 1652, sealed with promises for autonomy and respect for traditional customs.[33] So, counterfactually, it could have been just as likely for the Eastern portion of Iberia to become an independent country at that time as it was for the Western one—we may have then been talking, nowadays, about a Portuguese issue, instead of a Catalan one.

That said, and regardless of which foundational myth is brought to bear on the discussion of each relevant instance, very few innocent bystanders exist among those just mentioned. Portugal's imperialistic reach is well known, as it is their role in initiating the Atlantic Slave Trade—not in vain were they invited in the Congo Conference. Catalonia certainly followed suit, even as a more or less autonomous entity with the plural *Spains*. The powerful bourgeoisie that fueled the revival of Catalan culture in the 19th century, without going any further, made their riches benefitting directly from the colonial trade, including slaves in the most successful instances. One cannot, in any case, simplistically equate a culture, even if oppressed by another, with the racial or ethnic plights that are relatively easy to spot elsewhere, at least from a certain "anthropological distance". In the case of Iberia, the racial and ethnic admixture is so miscellaneous since the Neolithic (if not earlier) that it is impossible to delineate ethnic groups, much as revivalists of old foundation myths would want otherwise.

The same can be said about the totality of the Mediterranean basin, with islands of ancient populations where one least expects them (e.g. the Berber). In that context, passionate separations like the one between the Israeli and the Palestinian are less ethnic than ultimately *ad-hoc*, with religion amplifying the effect—not even that being enough in some instances, like the conflict between Sunni vs. Shiite Muslims. The point is that, once one moves beyond tribal groups that amalgamate in terms of a continuum of coalescing indicators, it becomes impossible to delineate any characteristic function to designate political legitimacy for a group.[34] This was a conflicting element, for example, among the Basques, after they started abandoning, already in the Middle Ages, ancient religious (pagan) forms, and territorial chieftains aligned with different noblemen. By the time of the post-Napoleonic civil wars in Spain, Basques were divided in terms of whether they supported the liberals (in the cities) or the conservatives (in the villages); among the latter, whether they did so via preserving old traditions, including the language, or banking on the realities of Spain, in which the kingdom of Navarre had mostly integrated.[35]

---

32 The Iberian union has been a topic of discussion for centuries, approaching a voluntary reality in various instances throughout history; see Pérez Isasi 2014 for a perspective and references.
33 See Stradling 2002.
34 See Leerssen 2006 on the difference between cultural and political nationalism.
35 See Suárez Zuluaga 2007 on the general theme of Basque in-fighting.

Those were, in short, *Basques against Basques*, and it would be at least parochial to call one of the subgroups "more Basque" than the others. That is precisely what happened, however, all through the 20th century. One must not forget that, of the territory that, for example, the Basque Nationalist Party takes as historically aspirational (the partially Basque-speaking French areas, what is currently the Basque Autonomous Community in Spain, *and* the Chartered Community of Navarre), almost half supported the Francoist uprising against the Spanish second republic.[36] Were those Basque? Surely, they were at least of Basque descent, even if they would not have seen themselves as aligning with Basque nationalism. These sorts of divides have lasted to our days elsewhere too, and will continue to surface in comparable instances.

The most obvious situations of discrimination within the context of the Information World pertain to communities without a territorial claim by the time of the liberal revolutions. A case in point within Europe are the Romani peoples. Despite having distinct languages and cultures of great influence, and been part of the Western experience since Antiquity, their place within the European Union is effectively that of new African immigrants. Aside from annihilation during the Nazi Holocaust, these communities faced and keep encountering virtually automatic expulsion, either from cities or, as the case may be, entire states. Their precariousness is interesting in Spain, where the post-dictatorship (1978) Constitution guarantees the rights of languages that correspond to a "historical territory". The Spanish *gitanos* have no such territory, despite having lived within the area for well over half a millennium and the fact that, in all of Iberia, at least a million could be counted (in established communities within Andalusia, Portugal, Catalonia, and Basqueland).[37] With relevant caveats, similar issues can be raised elsewhere.

5. Any Lessons Learned?

Returning to his talk to the Kurds and issues raised in that context, Chomsky referred positively to the situation in Spain that we have commented on here, as an example of what can be done with language and culture recovery. It is undeniable that—especially in Catalonia and Basqueland—serious efforts since the last dictatorship (which banned the use of Catalan and Basque, the languages "of the traitor provinces") have resulted in vibrant bilingual societies, exhibiting social indicators

---

36 In fact, it was through Navarre that Franco's co-conspirator, General Mola, was able to subdue the newly created Basque Government in 1937—by building on the *requeté* Navarrean force.
37 See Brunescu 2014 and Sigona & Trehan 2009 (with a chapter on Spain) for recent perspectives on the Roma.

that place them ahead of comparable communities within Spain.[38] Can such experiences be exported to instances with fewer resources, outside the 1st World?

It would be good to have a positive answer, for no one wants to fight for independence if it amounts to nothing tangible, for the emergent national or autonomous entity. The issue boils down, then, to whether it may be possible to establish a fruitful relation between the notions of *culture* and *state*, so that the ensuing structure is not just stable, but sustainable, internally and towards its neighbors. Chomsky himself seems ambivalent about the prospect, particularly at present.[39] In 2002, speaking to the Kurds, he spoke of a "healthy development" in Europe:

> . . . the erosion of the nation-state system with increasing regionalization. In areas from Catalonia to Scotland, there is a revival of traditional languages, cultures, customs and a degree of political autonomy leading towards what may become—and I think should become—an arrangement of regional areas that are essentially autonomous within a federal framework. In fact something like the old Ottoman empire. There was a lot wrong with the Ottoman empire, but some things about it were basically correct: mainly, the fact that it left a high degree of regional autonomy and independence within a framework, which unfortunately was autocratic and corrupt and brutal, but we can eliminate that part, and the positive aspects of the Ottoman empire probably ought to be reconstructed . . . [p.52]

In that context, Chomsky also spoke of a "Europe of the Regions":

> . . . a federation of regional areas with their own language, culture, political autonomy within a bigger federation. And that's extremely healthy. . . Your personal identity is very closely tied to your native language. If this is a language which is not permitted to be freely used for communication, for talk, for expression, for literature, for song, for any purpose, that's an infringement on your fundamental human rights. And it diminishes you as a person. [p. 53]

All of that was in the early days of the European Union, a decade after the creation of the euro and when no one could foresee a second Gulf War, a world financial crisis, immigration tragedies of recent decades—partly behind Brexit—or the specifics of a pandemic. Of course, life and entropy happen. And it is up for grabs whether, as in previous crises, this will result in the birth of new countries (e.g. a Scotland or a unified Ireland) or it will even be possible for the European Union to survive, let alone allow for regional autonomy to foster personal identities. At present, while COVID19 has put any other matters to the side, a negotiation table is supposed to sit

---

38 Artola et al. 2018:15 report how "the richest regions are Madrid and the Basque Country, with real GDP per capita above 30,000 € in year 2017. Next are the CCAA in the North-East: Navarre, La Rioja, Aragon and Catalonia, where GDP per person exceeds 25,000 €. The third cluster includes regions with an income between 20,000 and 25,000 € per capita, including regions in the North-West and the Valencian Community and Murcia. Finally, the CCAA in the South (Andalusia, Extremadura and Castilla-La Mancha) are below the 20,000 € threshold."

39 In several recent talks and podcasts, while criticizing holding Catalan leaders as political prisoners, Chomsky has also spoken critically of the Catalan process of independence, which he likened to Brexit.

members of the new coalition (left-wing) government in Spain with members of the Catalan *Generalitat*—that being essentially the political association that Franco staged his putsch against in 1936.[40] While opinion polls swing with contextual circumstances (including the very political process and its various stages: elections, demonstrations, trials, etc.), there is no overwhelming majority in either Catalonia or Basqueland for absolute independence, as opposed to some compromise solution (federal or otherwise). The separatist tendency, however, seems stronger among the youth, especially in Catalonia. What is also clear, in any event, is that the combination of independent-federalist-autonomous forces (supporting what one may describe as cultural nationalism) is overwhelming in both areas, vis-à-vis e.g. Galicia.[41]

---

40 That is, the Popular Front in 1936 (in Catalonia, Leftist Front) included the Spanish Socialist Workers' Party, the Communist Party of Spain, together with other leftist parties and unions, plus the Catalan and Galicia nationalists; the Basque nationalists went to the elections on their own, and already during the Spanish Civil War, during which they opposed Franco's putsch, were able to secure an autonomy statute for a few months, until the first official Basque Government was militarily defeated. The present coalition government of Spain is formed around the Spanish Socialist Workers' Party, the post-financial crisis leftist party United We Can (which integrates other leftist organizations, including the descendants of the Communist Party of Spain), together with support or acquiescence (abstention) from virtually all (local) nationalist parties. To be precise, there are also nationalist (Popular Party) and Ultra-nationalist (Vox) Spanish parties, which together with the neo-liberals (Citizens) constitute the opposition.

41 Results of the 2019 general elections (to the Spanish Parliament) in the three "historical territories" are interesting in this regard (in brackets, groups with insufficient percentages for parliamentary representation):

2019 General Elections	Radicals	Socialists	Liberals	Conservatives	Spanish Nationalists	Local Nationalists (Left)	(Right)
Catalonia	21%	20.5%	5.6%	7.4%	6.3%	22.6%	13.7%
Basqueland	15.4%	19.2%	(1.1%)	(9%)	(2.4%)	19%	32%
Galicia	12.7%	31.3%	(4.3%)	32%	(7.8%)	8.1%	

Note how the traditional left (socialists, radicals) range between 36% (for Basqueland) and 44% (for Galicia), while the traditional right (liberals, conservatives) do from 10.1% (and no representation for Basqueland) to 36.3% (for Galicia). This wide variation is contingent on the ideology of local nationalists. In Catalonia, those constitute 36.3% of the electorate (in a ~2:1 ratio for the leftist groups); in Basqueland, 51% of the electorate (in a ~2:3 proportion for the rightist groups); and in Galicia, 8.1% of the electorate, all leftist. If one considers mere left/right ideology, without examining nationalism, the proportions are as follows: Catalonia ~3:2, Basqueland ~11:9, Galicia ~13:11. In other words, ideologically these communities lean to the left (more so towards the East), and the local nationalist sentiment is weaker towards the West. There is no rightist nationalist sentiment in Galicia and the Spanish ultra-nationalists only obtained a token representation in Catalonia, with a 6.3 of the electorate, while for Spain as a whole their percentages were around 15%. It is noteworthy, also, that half the socialists in these communities and virtually all of the radicals support at least federalist position. That said, it is fair to assume support for such an approach (either directly or as better than mere autonomy) along the following lines: Catalonia: ~70% vs. ~20% (~10% neutral); Basqueland: ~77.5% vs. ~12.5% (~10% neutral); Galicia: ~27% vs. ~57% (~16% neutral).

Back in 2002, Chomsky also mentioned terrorism, often associated to these sorts of processes—although it has been mostly absent from the Catalan process. After his customary critique of the term (technically deployed for the weak and desperate, while powerful states use it rampantly and without remorse), Chomsky wondered about the strategic effectiveness of conventional violence, as the state tends to avail itself of more (and more efficient) weapons. Then, in response to a question about "the secret" behind his militance, he said:

> For hundreds of years in the US, as elsewhere, people have been struggling hard to en-large the domain of freedom and justice and there have been successes. And the result is that people like me are lucky. We can enjoy the privilege of enjoying the freedom that has been won. These are not gifts, they are not in the Constitution, they are not in the Bill of Rights. . . Take any nice words you like, you have to give them their meaning, and the meaning is given by struggle and commitment. And it has been done over the centuries to a very significant extent. The result is that people in the US have freedom to a larger ex-tent. The secret is to have a history behind you of people who dedicated themselves to creating a relatively free society. That's the secret. [p. 54]

Now, once again part of the paradox behind that "secret" seems to be that, without at least some power, it is hard to request, let alone gain, any of these freedoms. In the Spanish instances we have been discussing, it hardly seems accidental that the Cata-lan region was once an empire as its own kingdom, and even the Basque region has consistently been an economic powerhouse—even if it virtually lacked nationalist oligarchs (unlike Catalonia). It seems to be no accident, either, that these two regions fought on the side of decentralization during the las Spanish Civil war and also against Spanish centralism during the civil wars of the 19th century.[42] It is curious to note, also, how nationalism stemming from the state is often taken not to exist at all, as if relevant tendencies reflected just normalcy. In the case of the Spanish conflicts, the percentage of Spanish nationalists could be guesstimated at around 40%.[43] So the challenge in these conflicts is whether, beyond addressing their own particular agenda, the cause for cultural rights in general can be pursued from particular gains conquered by minorities from the established states. For example, in Iberia, it re-mains to be seen whether Basque and Catalan conflicts, with undeniable results for

---

42 For context on those wars, see Sabanadze 2010. The confrontations are often presented in purely dynastic terms, in the context of the tensions between liberals and conservatives after the Napoleonic wars. While that is a key dimension to the conflicts (which lasted for a total of 14 years: 1833-1840, 1846-1849, and 1872-1876), progressive historians also point out a fur-ther one, based on the historical privileges associated to the regions still in (relative) turmoil, which the post-revolutionary European order saw as regressive.

43 The present Spanish parliament presents a proportion of about 15% of representatives with an ultra-nationalist Spanish ideology; among the 21% of conservatives probably around 80%, among the 7% of liberals, around 50%, and among the 28% of the socialists, around 20%, are at least moderately nationalistic in Spanish terms. For a more scientific assessment of these (fairly hard to ascertain) proportions, see the analysis by Spanish social scientist Kiko Llaneras at https://elpais.com/politica/2017/10/11/ratio/1507747264_973195.html.

the respective populations, have any bearing on, in particular, the Romani problems we have also pointed out.

These tensions may also be behind why Chomsky does not want to commit to linking his professional work as a linguist on human creativity (via grammaticality and its account in ultimately biological terms) with his passion for human dignity (via the pursuit of freedom). The link is, if I read him correctly, not a matter of natural law. *It has to be won.* A related matter is how to achieve that goal for oneself, while at the same time not infringing on the freedoms of others. In the end, this may have no simple solution within the context of the state that democratic societies have built. If it does exist, Chomsky does not seem to know it, and neither do I. Although I do think that it is part of the responsibility of intellectuals to put our thinking to the task. For it would seem as if beings engaging in grammaticality judgments (talking entities) should have enough critical creativity to understand that privilege is not just unsustainable, but ultimately also existentially lame. It is perhaps once we accept the sheer fun of our diversity that we can begin to embrace what makes us different as much as we share what unifies us.

That view is not universal, even when pushing us to absurd situations. French authorities—inheritors of the Napoleonic tradition that sought to impose *liberté, égalité, fraternité* by force—have a problem with *burkas*, even when face coverings are imposed to deal with COVID19. It requires no commentary that a woman in France can be fined for wearing a black traditional veil more rapidly than for not wearing a white mask, amidst a pandemic. The challenge for the next generation will be to observe and act upon such contradictions, which stem from the still to be properly defined *democracy equation.* What will it take to demonstrate how democracy for a few (e.g. men owners) is not democracy at all? States stretch philosophical credibility in terms of definitions of citizen to address such difficulties, adding provisos as the case may be to make the definition less inclusive (birth, ancestry, time of residence, etc.). We already know that "democracies work" when given unlimited resources and no conflict for the beneficiaries—but are those anything but aristocracies? The real question is how to realize inclusive democracies, and what that may entail for an organization not just of states, but also across nations. When I say this is a *question*, I mean that I do not know the answer.

The current world is one of great possibilities for some, for instance having democratized access to markets (given certain perks, including funds to invest and education to understand how). As such, that is neither good nor bad: it depends on the nature of what is traded and how it is produced. The current Global Market is allowing products to arrive at our own door, one of the ways the middle classes in the 1st World have mostly stayed healthy during the pandemic—with members of the precariat delivering from food to packages with essentials. Many of us are even sharing bits of stock in the entrepreneurial companies, directly or through funds for our basic social capital (education, health, retirement funds) that otherwise would be lost to inflation. At what price, though, in terms of where the companies we own stock at operate? So it is, anyway, that many in the Information World are managing to leave the lesser casts to join the Welfare State, no less than as partial owners. This is, in fact, having been convinced that we need not just the basics our parents fought for, but also the various whims that fuel market economies. Similarly, for our kids: having accessed the middle class via some meritocracy, we now pay for tutors (coaches, college visits, etc.) to make sure they need not earn their way up; just as aristocrats did with their privileges and offspring. The next goal could be Faustian immortality.[44]

It is logically possible that other cultural and economic commodities—stemming from communities already formed through social media and the like—may find ways into a more participatory democracy in which cultural and economic clashes can at least be discussed in a genuinely civilized way: not as a means to steal wealth and resources from one another, but as a way to construct a diverse future together. Whether that logical possibility materializes into something tangible will probably depend on the next generation. Hopefully, they will be given a chance to find a way of redefining democracy in this new era of unthinkable potential. The Greta Thunberg generation does have some remarkable individuals, even if there have always been Iqbal Masihs or Malala Yousafzais; these are, in any case, our children, and theirs is our future. Hopefully, aside from individual acts of great courage, they will encounter their place within the constructs we are passing on to them, which came from our own ancestors.

Nothing more than that are cultures, really: ways of seeing and being, preserved in our collective memories. In the end, we all seem to have a right to our own, hopefully without annihilating those of others. The alternative is, in any case, entirely unclear. After all, it is through these memories, and alternate realities that we conjure based on them and their limitations, that we initiated our human odyssey to start with. If that sounds like a linguist speaking (of memories, generating representations, and all that...), it is because, well, that is what I guess I am.

Bibliography

Ambo, Theresa, 2017: California Tribal Nations and the University: Examining Institutional Relationships, Responsibility and Reciprocity. UCLA doctoral dissertation.

Artola, Concha/*Fiorito*, Alejandro/*Gil*, María/*Pérez*, Javier/*Urtasun*, Alberto/*Vila*, Diego, 2018: Monitoring the Spanish Economy from a Regional Perspective: Main Elements of Analysis. Banco de España Documents Ocasionales 1809.

---

44 According to Harari 2015, not an exaggeration.

Bunescu, Ioana, 2014: Roma in Europe: The Politics of Collective Identity Formation. Burlington.

Carroll, Rory, 2011: Argentinian founding father recast as genocidal murderer. In: The Guardian, Jan 13, 2011.

Chamberlain, Muriel, 2010: The Scramble for Africa. New York.

Coates, Ken, 2002: The New American Century? London.

Cooper, Tom, 2013: Great Lakes holocaust: the first Congo War, 1996-1997. Havertown.

Cooper, Tom, 2013: Great Lakes conflagration: the second Congo War, 1996-1997. Havertown.

Engle, Karen, 2011: On Fragile Architecture: The UN Declaration on the Rights of Indigenous Peoples in the Context of Human Rights. In: European Journal of International Law, 22-1.

Esposito, Elena, 2015: Side Effects of Immunities: the African Slave. European University Institute Working Paper, October 29, 2015.

Foti, Alex, 2017: General Theory of the Precariat: Great Recession, Revolution, Reaction. Amsterdam.

Habermas, Jürgen, 1962 (1989 translation): The Structural Transformation of the Public Sphere: An Inquiry into a category of Bourgeois Society. Cambridge.

Hanson, Fergus 2015: Internet Wars: The Struggle for Power in the 21st Century. Haberfield.

Harari, Yuval, 2015: Homo Deus: A Brief History of Tomorrow. New York.

Herman, Edward/*Chomsky* Noam, 1988: Manufacturing Consent: The Political Economy of the Mass Media. New York.

Hochschild, Adam, 1998: King Leopold's Ghost - A Story of Greed, Terror and Heroism in Colonial Africa. New York.

Jedwad, Remi/*Kerby*, Edward/*Moradi*, Alexander, 2017: How colonial railroads defined Africa's economic geography. In: Michalopoulos S./E. Papaioannou E. (eds.), 2017: The Long Economic and Political Shadow of History, Volume 2. London.

Jupp, Peter, 2003: The British State and the Napoleonic Wars, 1799-1815. In: Rowe, Michael (ed.), 2003: Collaboration and Resistance in Napoleonic Europe. Berlin, p.213-237.

Krieg, Andreas, (ed.), 2019: Divided Gulf: Anatomy of a Crisis. London.

Krugman, Paul, 2008: The Return of Depression Economics and the Crisis of 2008. New York.

Leerssen, Joep, 2006: Nationalism and the cultivation of culture. In: Nations and Nationalism, v. 12, n.4, 559-578.

Lindsay, Matthew, 2017: The Presumptions of Classical Liberal Constitutionalism. In: Iowa Law Review Online 219.

Mabry, Tristan/*McGarry* John/*Moore*, Margaret/*O'Leary*, Brendan (eds.), 2013: Divided Nations and European Integration. Philadelphia.

Mark, Joy, 2014: American Expansionism, 1783-1860: A Manifest Destiny? Hoboken.

Meade, Teresa, 2010: A History of Modern Latin-America. Oxford.

Papastephanou, Marianna, 2012: Exploring Habermas's Critical Engagement with Chomsky. In: Human Studies v. 35, n.1, 51-76.

Motesharrei Safa/*Rivas*, Jorge/*Kalnay*, Eugenia 2014: Human and nature dynamics (HANDY): Modeling inequality and use of resources in the collapse or sustainability of societies. In: Ecological Economics v. 101, 90-102.

Pérez, Pilar, 2011: Historia y silencio: La Conquista del Desierto como genocidio no-narrado. Corpus, v. 1, n.2, 1-9

Pérez Isasi, Santiago. Literature, Iberism(s), Nationalism(s): Notes for a History of Literary Iberism (1868-1936). *452° F* 11, 64-79.

Sabanadze, Natalie, 2010: Globalization and Nationalism: The Cases of Georgia and The Basque Country. Budapest.

Sabatello, Maya/Schulze, Marianne, 2014: Human Rights and Disability Advocacy. Philadelphia.

Sévillia, Jean, 2003: Historiquement Correct. Paris.

Sigona, Nando/*Trehan*, Nidhi (eds). 2009: Romani Politics in Contemporary Europe: Poverty, Ethnic Mobilization, and the Neoliberal Order. New York.

Standing, Guy, 2011: The Precariat: The New Dangerous Class. London.

Stradling, Richard, 2002: Philip IV and the Government of Spain, 1621-1665. Cambridge.

Strochlic, Nina, 2018: The Race to Save the World's Disappearing Languages. *National Geographic*, 16 Apr. 2018

Suárez Zuluaga, Ignacio, 2007: Vascos contra vascos: Una explicación ecuánime de dos siglos de Lucha. Barcelona.

Varoufakis, Yanis, 2017: Talking to my Daughter about the Economy: A brief History of Capitalism—how it Works and how it Fails. New York.

Watson, Cameron, 1996: Folklore and Basque nationalism: language, myth, reality. In: Nations and Nationalism, v.2, n.1, 17-34.

Wearne, Phillip, 1996: Return of the Indian: Conquest and Revival in the Americas. Philadelphia.

Jean Bricmont

Freedom of Speech, Chomsky and France

Introduction

A basic tenet of democratic theory is that democracy can only function if it exercised by an "informed citizenry". Given the way our media work we are very far from being in that situation. However, one of the preconditions (necessary but not sufficient) for the citizenry to be informed is freedom of speech. Is at least that precondition fulfilled in the modern liberal democracies of Western Europe? We will concentrate here on the case of France.

Freedom of speech seems to be taken very seriously in France; see for example the large demonstrations following the murder by Islamist fanatics of *Charlie Hebdo* staff members in January 2015. Newspapers regularly publish protests against censorship or attempts at censorship by groups of self-styled radical students, Muslims or people of African descent.

Yet, there is less than meets the eye, as we shall try to show here. And a campaign waged against Noam Chomsky that started in 1980 and which is not completely over illustrates the ambiguity if not the hypocrisy of the "defense of free speech" in France.

Of course, everybody in France is for free speech; but most people accept that there must be "exceptions" or "limits". The issue is what those limits are and what justifies them. All defenders of free speech agree that personal insults, slander and incitement to illegal actions (for example violence) are not covered by free speech.

But the issue becomes interesting when one considers opinions about society, politics, religions, history, sciences, pseudo-sciences, social or ethnic groups, etc. Article 19 of the Universal Declaration of Human Rights states: "Everyone has the right to freedom of opinion and expression; this right includes freedom to hold opinions without interference and to seek, receive and impart information and ideas through any media and regardless of frontiers.

This article does not say that those opinions should not be racist, sexist, homophobic or antisemitic and even less that they should not be considered as such by certain groups of people who might feel "offended" by someone else's opinions.

In fact, in 1976, the European Court of Human Rights gave a verdict concerning "The Little Red Schoolbook", a "radical" book addressed to schoolchildren and criticizing the family and the schools, that directly addressed the issue of offensiveness, by writing in its verdict:

> "Freedom of expression constitutes one of the essential foundations of such a society, one of the basic conditions for its progress and for the development of every man. Subject to paragraph 2 of Article 10 (art. 10-2), it is applicable not only to "information" or "ideas" that are favorably received or regarded as inoffensive or as a matter of indifference, but also to those that offend, shock or disturb the State or any sector of the population. Such are the demands of that pluralism, tolerance and broadmindedness without which there is no democratic society"[1].

In France, this conception is nowadays often considered radical and even "American" by reference to the First Amendment of the U.S. Constitution. Sometimes people reply that those views were also those of Voltaire, but they were very clearly stated by Robespierre who, in 1791, explained why freedom of speech is necessary in order to discover truth:

> "The freedom to write can be exercised over two objects, things and people. The first of these objects includes all that concerns the greatest interests of man and society, such as morals, legislation, politics, religion. ... Now, it is nature itself which wants the thoughts of every man to be the result of his character and his spirit, and it is nature itself which has created this prodigious diversity of minds and characters. The freedom to publish one's opinion can therefore be nothing other than the freedom to publish all contrary opinions. You must either give it this breadth or find a way to make the truth come out first of every human head in its purest and most naked form. It can only emerge from the struggle of all ideas, true or false, absurd or reasonable. [...] If those who make laws or those who apply them were beings of a higher intelligence than human intelligence, they could exercise this power over thoughts; but if they are only men, if it is absurd that the reason of one man should be, so to speak, sovereign over the reason of all other men, any penal law against the manifestation of opinions is nothing but absurdity.[2]"

Laws against Incitement to Hatred

In France there are two laws that limit free speech; the first one was introduced in 1972 and is called the Pleven law, by the name of the minister of Justice at that time. It punishes those who have, by speech, writing, images or other similar means, "provoked discrimination, hatred or violence against a person or group of persons because of their origin or their belonging to a particular ethnic group, nation, race or

---

1 Handyside v. The United Kingdom, https://hudoc.echr.coe.int/eng#{%22itemid%22: [%22001-57499%22]}.
2 Discours sur la liberté de la presse, par Maximilien Robespierre, 11 may 1791. Available on : The Project Gutenberg EBook of Discours par Maximilien Robespierre.

religion". Discrimination and violence can be considered illegal actions but what does "hatred" mean?

Unfortunately, there is no shortage of people who have preferences for one human group (usually their own) over other groups. If we want to "combat" these feelings and the "prejudices" that underlie them, shouldn't we first allow them to be expressed?

More fundamentally, at what point do such feelings become hatred? Where the offense is ill-defined, the reign of arbitrariness begins. The main quality of the law, which is practically its definition, is that the law must be the same for everyone. If we abandon this principle of equality, we fall back into the arbitrariness of power, against which the law is supposed to protect us. One of the most fundamental arguments in favor of freedom of expression is that while illegal actions can be defined with some precision, human thought is far too flexible to characterize thoughts as illegal while preserving this principle of equality.

Let us quote again Robespierre:

> "Indeed, it is an indisputable principle that the law cannot impose any punishment where there cannot be an offense that can be precisely characterized and recognized with certainty; otherwise the destiny of citizens is subject to arbitrary judgments, and freedom is no longer. Laws can affect criminal actions, because they consist of sensitive facts, which can be clearly defined and ascertained according to sure and constant rules: but opinions! their good or bad character can only be determined by more or less complicated relations with principles of reason, of justice, often even with a host of special circumstances. I am accused of a theft, a murder; I have the idea of an act whose definition is simple and fixed, I question witnesses. But I am told of an incendiary, dangerous, seditious writing; what is an incendiary, dangerous, seditious writing? Can these qualifications be applied to the person presented to me? I see here a host of questions that will be abandoned to all the uncertainty of opinions; I find no more facts, no witnesses, no law, no judge; I see only vague denunciation, arguments, arbitrary decisions.[3]"

The problem posed by the Pleven law is seriously aggravated by the fact that this law recognizes the right of any association that proposes, "by its statutes, to combat racism" and has been "declared for at least five years", to become a civil party in any lawsuit related to this law.

Let me briefly consider three examples of abuses that this aspect of the Pleven law renders possible and even unavoidable.

---

3 Ibidem.

Daniel Mermet is a long-time radio journalist who had his own program called "Là-bas si j'y suis" (Over there if I'm there) on *France Inter*. He was fired in 2014 and now runs a program with the same name on his own channel.

At the start of his radio shows, he used to pass on messages left by listeners on his answering machine. One day, in June 2001, during a series of broadcasts devoted to the Israeli-Palestinian conflict, among the forwarded messages was this one: "What is this deadly power that delights in the killing of children and mutilation, that justifies the unacceptable day after day with criminal excess and that has the infamous arrogance to call us racists when we timidly dare to protest against this unworthy conduct? What is it about these hypocrites who wield the shield of anti-semitism with such virtuosity when all we want to do is remind them that, for the past fifty years, they have been reproducing the horrible injustice they have suffered in homeopathic doses? I am fiercely anti-Zionist. I am not anti-Semitic in any way. "

Following this, Daniel Mermet was sued for defamation and incitement to racial hatred by *Avocats sans frontières* (Lawyers without Borders), the *Union des Étudiants Juifs de France* (UEJF -- Union of Jewish Students of France) and the LICRA (International League against Racism and Antisemitism)[4]. He was definitively acquitted at the end of 2006, after almost five years of legal proceedings, worries, negative media exposure, etc. The simple fact of winning long drawn-out lawsuits does not eliminate the damage caused.

How can the statements cited here be interpreted as inciting to racial hatred? They are clearly aimed at a "deadly" political power, i.e. the Israeli state. The fact that Israel has chosen to define itself as a "Jewish" state does not make criticism of its government's policies anti-Semitic, any more than criticism of, say, the Chinese government would be *ipso facto* anti-Chinese in a racist sense.

The listener also speaks of "hypocrites who wield the shield of antisemitism," including associations that use that shield to silence criticism of the government in question. Can there be a better illustration of this use than the prosecution of Daniel Mermet?

According to the transcript of the hearings in *Le Monde*, the famous French philosopher Alain Finkielkraut, a witness for the prosecution, puts forward an argument that illustrates one of the fundamental intellectual confusions of this form of "anti-racism": "95% of Jews in France are Zionists, in the sense that they have a solidarity of destiny with Israel. To banish this State from humanity, as a fascist or a

---

4 Le journaliste Daniel Mermet assigné pour "incitation à la haine raciale" Des associations juives accusent le producteur de France-Inter d'avoir diffusé des propos d'auditeurs à caractère antisémite, *Le Monde*, June 1, 2002.

Nazi one, is to exclude, under the mask of anti-racism, all those who, as Jews, support it. "

Let's leave aside the fact that we don't know which opinion poll Alain Finkielkraut refers to. Likewise, criticizing a military occupation by a state is not the same thing as "banishing" that state from humanity.

Alain Finkielkraut's remarks nevertheless raise a fundamental problem: supporting a State's internal or external policy is a political choice. The fact that a given human group, defined in ethnic, national or religious terms, supports a certain policy does not in itself make opposition to that policy racist. If all Germans after 1870 approved the annexation of Alsace-Lorraine, or if all Catholics, at some point in history, were opposed to the separation of Church and State, then refusing this annexation or wanting this separation is still a political position and is not anti-German or anti-Catholic in the sense of an "exclusion" of a given human group. And the same would be true for Jews and Israeli policy, even if all French Jews approved all Israeli policies (which is certainly not the case).

The Siné Affair

Maurice Sinet whose *nom de plume* is Siné was one of the most famous and radical French cartoonist. He was violently opposed to the Algerian war and one of the symbols of the 1968 rebellion. Siné had a column in the famous weekly *Charlie Hebdo*. He wrote, on July 2, 2008, about Jean Sarkozy, son of the then French President Nicolas Sarkozy: "He has just declared that he wants to convert to Judaism before marrying his fiancée, who is Jewish and the heiress of Darty's founders. He will go a long way in life, this little one![5]"

We can read in *Libération* of June 23, 2008: "Patrick Gaubert, president of the LICRA and friend of Nicolas Sarkozy, [...] notes that today, Nicolas Sarkozy's son, Jean, has just got engaged to a Jewish woman, heiress of the founders of Darty, and is considering converting to Judaism in order to marry her.[6]"Where is the difference between the two texts? Only in Siné's irony: "He will go a long way in life, this little one! "

To put things in perspective, Siné also once drew a nun masturbating herself with a crucifix in her vagina and calling the drawing "the religion". He also wrote about veiled muslim women: "I've never been very tolerant, but it doesn't get any better and, at the risk of being seen as politically incorrect, I admit that more and more Muslims irritate me and that, the more I come across the veiled women who prolif-

---

5 Darty is a famous chain of appliances stores.
6 Christophe Ayad et Antoine Guiral, «Sarkozy comme chez lui en Israël» *Libération*, June 23 2008.

erate in my neighborhood, the more I feel like kicking them violently in the ass![7]".
All this is of course viewed as legitimate "criticisms of religion".

Conversion for opportunistic reasons is a recognized phenomenon, especially concerning marriage. When the husband or the wife is rich, it always provokes sarcasm, with or without Siné. But it was enough for this sarcasm to be about a marriage where the rich wife is Jewish, for this icon of the French cartoon to be fired from *Charlie Hebdo* and prosecuted in court for incitement to racial hatred.

Siné was reproached for the fact that the rumor of Jean Sarkozy's conversion to Judaism was false. But he was not the one who had invented the rumor and Siné always maintained that if the conversion had been to Islam or Catholicism, concerning a marriage to a wealthy person adhering to either of these religions, he would have made fun of it just as much.

Unsurprisingly, the French philosopher Bernard-Henri Lévy, a witness for the prosecution at the trial, wrote of the case: "Behind those words, a French ear could not fail to hear the echo of the most rancid antisemitism." Notwithstanding this testimony, the courts fortunately acquitted Siné and ordered Charlie Hebdo to pay Siné a generous severance package.

On the other hand, *Charlie Hebdo*'s director, Philippe Val, who has since become director of *France Inter*, could write the following without being at all rebuked :

> "If we look at a map of the world, going eastwards: beyond the borders of Europe, that is to say Greece, the democratic world stops. There is just one small advanced confetti in the Middle East: it is the State of Israel. After that, nothing more, all the way to Japan. ...] Between Tel Aviv and Tokyo, arbitrary powers reign, whose only way to maintain themselves is to maintain, among populations that are 80% illiterate, a fierce hatred of the West as democracies.[8]"

I suppose this is just a geopolitical opinion[9].

The Morin-Naïr-Sallenave Case

The French sociologist Edgar Morin, together with the intellectual Sami Naïr and the writer Danielle Sallenave, signed an op-ed in *Le Monde* on June 4, 2002, entitled: "Israel-Palestine: the Cancer". They were prosecuted for "incitement to racial hatred" for two passages in the article:

> "It is hard to imagine that a nation of fugitives, from the longest persecuted people in the history of mankind, having suffered the worst humiliations and contempt, is capable of

---

7 *Charlie Hebdo*, June 11, 2008.
8 *Charlie Hebdo*, July 26, 2006.
9 And a false one, since no country situated "between Tel Aviv and Tokyo" has an illiteracy rate of 80%.

transforming itself in two generations not only into a people who are 'domineering and sure of themselves', but, with the exception of an admirable minority, into a contemptuous people who take satisfaction in humiliating others."

"And here we have the incredible paradox. The Jews of Israel, descendants of the victims of an apartheid called ghetto, ghettoize the Palestinians. The Jews who were humiliated, despised, persecuted now humiliate, despise, persecute the Palestinians. The Jews who were victims of a ruthless order impose their ruthless order on the Palestinians. The Jews who were victims of inhumanity display terrible inhumanity. The Jews, scapegoat for all evils, scapegoat Arafat and the Palestinian Authority, blamed for attacks that they are denied the power to prevent.[10]"

It was at his press conference in June 1967, following Israel's lightning victory in the Six Day War, that Charles De Gaulle famously first spoke of "an elite people, sure of themselves and dominating". According to his son, he "would have liked to be able to say the same thing about the French.[11]"

The incriminated passages were cited out of context, since, in their second opening sentence, the authors of the article wrote: "This logic of contempt and humiliation is not peculiar to the Israelis, it is peculiar to all occupations, where the conqueror sees himself superior to a people of sub-humans." Thus, it is Israeli Jews who are targeted and not Jews in general, and moreover, Israelis are criticized only because they behave in the same way as other occupiers. The authors also compared the situation in Palestine to France's "colonial repression" during the Algerian War. One has to wonder whether anyone has been sued for "incitement to racial hatred" for condemning "the Americans" when writing comparably virulent condemnation of U.S. policy in Vietnam or Iraq, or of "the French" in condemning France's policy in Algeria, when it is obvious that it is not the whole of those populations that are being criticized but only those who design and execute such policies.

Oddly enough, in all three cases above, the persons being sued were situated on the left or the far left, where people are the most insistent on the necessity to fight "racial hatred" even by restricting free speech. But the most spectacular victim of this desire for censorship coming from the left is indeed Noam Chomsky.

The Faurisson Affair

To understand the origin of Chomsky's problems in France, we have to go back to 1978-1979, when Robert Faurisson, professor of literature at the University of Lyon, published various articles setting out his thesis on the non-existence of gas chambers

---

10 Edgar Morin, Sami Naïr, Danielle Sallenave, Israël-Palestine: Le cancer, *Le Monde,* June 4 2002.
11 Philippe De Gaulle, *De Gaulle, mon père. Entretiens avec Michel Tauriac*, Paris, Plon, 2004, volume 2, p. 323.

in the Nazi concentration camps. On December 29, 1978, *Le Monde* had published a letter from Faurisson on "the problem of the gas chambers". The letter began by recalling that early reports of homicidal gas chambers in Nazi concentration camps at Oranienburg, Buchenwald, Bergen-Belsen, Ravensbrück and Mauthausen had all turned out to be unfounded, which showed that rumors could be mistaken. Faurisson had visited Auschwitz-Birkenau and reported that he found no evidence of gas chambers used to kill people. Whereas every other aspect of the installations was well documented, Faurisson said he found "no order of construction, no study, no orders, no blueprint, no bills and no photos" of gas chambers used for extermination purposes. He concluded, "The nonexistence of 'gas chambers' is good news for poor humanity. A good news that it would be wrong to keep hidden any longer."

This publication provoked not only protests, but all kinds of harassment and even physical attacks on Robert Faurisson, as well as court proceedings. In reaction to this, a petition was circulated demanding that "the university and the government do everything possible to ensure his safety and the free exercise of his legal rights". Among the 500 signatories was the name of Noam Chomsky.

Noam Chomsky, who called Nazi policy toward the Jews "the most fantastic outburst of collective insanity in human history,"[12] has consistently stated that his support was strictly limited to the defense of Robert Faurisson's freedom of expression, and in no way implied a defense of the content of that expression. This did not prevent Noam Chomsky from becoming the target of attacks equating him with Robert Faurisson, as if the distinction between the defense of freedom of expression and the defense of the particular ideas expressed was incomprehensible in certain French intellectual circles.

At the time I was hardly aware of this controversy. I was living in the United States, where I taught and did research in theoretical physics. But I had read Chomsky and I was very interested in his philosophical and political writings. Paradoxically, I rediscovered in him the French tradition of the Enlightenment, which at the time had faded from memory in its country of origin.

When I returned to Europe a few years later, I discovered that the name of the man whom the New York Times (who never liked him) called "arguably the most important intellectual alive today"[13] was impossible to mention in France because of the Faurisson affair. This case illustrates the problem of secondary censorship, or the slippery slope, i.e. that from the moment one prohibits certain statements, one tends to prohibit others that are "close" to the censored statements and to amalgamate the defense of freedom to express statements with the statements themselves. Chomsky's exclusion from the French intellectual scene for almost twenty years is what

---

12 Noam Chomsky, His right to say it, *The Nation*, February 28, 1981.
13 Paul Robinson, The Chomsky Problem, *New York Times*, February 25, 1979.

led me to become interested in the controversy that had produced this incongruous situation.

Following the articles he had published in 1978-1979, Robert Faurisson was prosecuted by the LICRA, the MRAP (*Mouvement contre le racisme et pour l'amitié entre les peuples* -- Movement against Racism and for Friendship among Peoples) and various associations of deportees and resistance fighters who felt they had suffered moral prejudice as a result of these publications. In 1981, Robert Faurisson was sentenced to pay a symbolic franc and the costs of publication of the judgment. The grounds for the judgment were quite remarkable: the court recognized that it had "neither competence nor quality to judge history" and that the historian has "full and complete freedom" to present his views; but it nevertheless criticized Robert Faurisson for having lacked "the prudence, objective circumspection and intellectual neutrality that are required of the researcher he wants to be" and, even more remarkably, for having "with an uncommon thoughtlessness but with a clear conscience, allowed others to use his speech with the intention of apologizing for war crimes or inciting racial hatred."

It is quite remarkable to condemn not what was said, but the use made by others of what was said, without specifying who those others were, or indicating the means by which "others" could have been prevented from using what one wrote for purposes not necessarily those of the author.

Noam Chomsky reacted at the time in rather strong terms:

"In a display of moral cowardice, the court then claimed that it was not restricting the historian's right to express himself freely, but only punishing Faurisson for using it. By this shameful judgment, the state is given the right to determine an official truth (despite the protests of the judges) and to punish those guilty of 'irresponsibility'. If this does not trigger massive protests, it will be a black day for France.[14]"

Needless to say, there were absolutely no protests. The conviction was upheld on appeal in 1983, but with different justifications. On the one hand, the court reaffirmed the incompetence of the courts in matters of history and the principle of freedom of research, but concerning Robert Faurisson himself, it wrote that : "Nor is it permissible to assert, in view of the nature of the studies in which he engaged, whether he dismissed the testimony out of thoughtlessness or negligence, or whether he deliberately chose to ignore it. Moreover, no one can, as it stands, convict him of lying when he lists the multiple documents he claims to have studied and the organizations he allegedly investigated for more than fourteen years. That the value of the conclusions defended by Mr. Faurisson is therefore a matter for the sole appreciation of experts, historians and the public. »

---

14 Noam Chomsky, *Réponses inédites à mes détracteurs parisiens*, Paris, Spartacus, 1984.

Nevertheless, the court reproached Robert Faurisson for stepping outside the realm of historical research by using the word "lie" in regard to the genocide and for "seeking to mitigate the criminal nature of the deportation". The court considered that these positions were "hurtful" to the survivors and convicted Faurisson on these grounds.

It is obvious that this kind of judgment can only be selective: what is to be done if people feel "hurt" when faced with statements about the "positive role" of colonization, or statements favorable to U.S. or Israeli policy, to wars in the Middle East, or to wars in Indochina? It is not easy to escape Robespierre's principle: "The freedom to publish one's opinion cannot be anything else than the freedom to publish all contrary opinions."

Chomsky's Involvement in the Faurisson Affair and his Slandering

In an article published by *Esprit*[15] in September 1980, Pierre Vidal-Naquet declared that the petition signed by Noam Chomsky was scandalous because "it does not at any time ask whether Faurisson is telling the truth or not". Clearly, if one had to assess the truth of a controversial statement before defending a person's right to express it, this defense would become practically impossible, if only for reasons of time: at the very least, the statement would have to be studied and possibly translated.

Pierre Vidal-Naquet unwittingly admitted as much when he remarked in regard to Arthur Butz, an American revisionist whose work preceded that of Robert Faurisson: "Refuting Butz? It is possible, of course, it is even easy, provided one knows the case, but it is long, it is tedious." In any case the defense of freedom of expression should not be concerned with whether the victim of censorship "tells the truth or not".

The "scandal" caused by the petition forced Noam Chomsky into an epistolary exchange not only with Pierre Vidal-Naquet, but with a number of French intellectuals and newspapers. A trace of these exchanges can be found in *Réponses inédites à mes détracteurs parisiens*, published by an anarchist publishing house, *Spartacus*. This book includes unpublished or truncated letters from Noam Chomsky sent to newspapers such as *Le Monde*, *Le Matin de Paris*, *Les Nouvelles Littéraires*, as well as an interview given to *Libération* but which was not published because the translation made by that newspaper had distorted its content.

The fact that an intellectual with Noam Chomsky's international reputation could not obtain the right to respond to the attacks against him in the French press and

---

15 A monthly publication, founded in 1932 by the personalist thinker Emmanuel Mounier, and having originally a left-wing Christian orientation.

could only find a very marginal publisher for his "responses" did not seem to bother Pierre Vidal-Naquet, who mentions the book "published, alas, by the Spartacus publishing house." It would evidently have been better, in the eyes of Pierre Vidal-Naquet, if Noam Chomsky's answers had not been published by anyone.

Among those epistolary exchanges, Noam Chomsky wrote a text setting out his arguments about freedom of expression and gave the text to a friend in Paris, telling him to do with it what he wanted. The friend was Serge Thion, a specialist on Cambodia and a long-time anti-colonial activist. He had got to know Robert Faurisson at that time and saw fit to publish this text as an "notice" ("*avis*" in french) at the beginning of the defense brief published in book form by Robert Faurisson in 1980, in response to the legal proceedings against him.

Following outraged protests from certain French intellectuals, Noam Chomsky asked the publishers to withdraw his text from Robert Faurisson's book. But too late. He was later to state that this withdrawal request was the only mistake he had made in the whole affair[16]. This publication gave to Pierre Vidal-Naquet, and many others, the opportunity to renew their attacks on Noam Chomsky. For almost a quarter of a century, Chomsky's name would be associated in a sort of whispering campaign with that of Robert Faurisson, and Chomsky's writings, particularly his works on U.S. policy in Central America and the Middle East, would become de facto impossible to publish in France until the middle of the 1990s.

But what is really "scandalous", to use his favorite word, in Pierre Vidal-Naquet's position, is that he denies that the attacks on Robert Faurisson constitute an attack on freedom of expression. Pierre Vidal-Naquet considers that "the conditions under which Faurisson was led to leave Lyons [...] are certainly regrettable, as I have said, but his freedom of expression, subject to the laws in force, was in no way threatened". He also considers that the proceedings initiated by the LICRA and other associations against Robert Faurisson "do not prevent him from writing or being published." Following that logic, the Soviet state did not prevent a certain number of dissidents from being published (in the West), it punished them only when this happened. Even if the sanctions here are less severe than there, prosecuting, damaging the career of, or in any way intimidating an individual because of his opinions is a form of repression of freedom of expression.

The height of distortion was reached when Pierre Vidal-Naquet rhetorically asked whether Chomsky was demanding that "the display and sale (of Faurisson's works) be imposed at the doors of the synagogues" – a totally absurd notion.

Despite his claim to consider freedom of expression to be "the highest and least questionable of principles," Alain Finkielkraut wrote in *Libération*, on January 16, 1981, that the prosecution of Robert Faurisson was part of "the normal exercise of

---

16 See the documentary *Manufacturing Consent: Noam Chomsky and the Media*; Directors: Mark Achbar, Peter Wintonick,1993.

freedom of expression" in "all democratic countries, including the United States". He did not seem to realize that such a prosecution would have precisely no chance of success in the United States, nor in many other countries.

In the same article, Alain Finkielkraut wrote: "For our Chomskians, the Nazi genocide is no longer part of reality; it has stopped taking place. It has now entered another realm: that of tastes and colors. One can believe in it or not, depending on the climate, the whim, the digestion, the temperament, as one believes in Santa Claus or in the victory of the left. " Yet this is the exact opposite of the views of Chomsky, who has never hidden his total opposition to the idea that there are no factual truths or that "everything is equally valid".

Chomsky himself quotes amusing comments on his involvement in that affair:

> "Cavallari [Paris correspondent for the *Corriere della Sera*] went on to explain that my rage against 'French culture' derives from its refusal to accept the theory that linguistics proves that 'the Gulag descends directly from Rousseau' and other imbecile ideas he chooses to attribute to me for reasons best known to himself. In *Nouvel Observateur*, Jean-Paul Enthoven offers a different explanation: I support Faurisson because my 'instrumentalist theory of language, the "generative grammar"…does not allow the means to think of the unimaginable, that is the Holocaust.' He and Cavallari, among others, explain further that my defense of Faurisson is a case of the extreme left joining the extreme right, a phenomenon to which they devote many sage words. In *Le Matin*, Catherine Clement explains my odd behavior on the ground that I am a 'perfect Bostonian,' 'a cold and distant man, without real social contacts, incapable of understanding Jewish-American humor, which relies heavily on Yiddish.' Pierre Daix explains in *Le Quotidien de Paris* that I took up left-wing causes to 'clear myself' of the reactionary implications of my 'innatism.' And so on, at about the same level[17]."

The campaign against Chomsky seems never to end: in November 2016, Chomsky was supposed to receive a prize for his work in linguistics, awarded by the International Society of Philology in a room of the French National Assembly, a prize previously awarded to such personalities as Roman Jakobson and Umberto Eco.

At the last minute, the National Assembly announced that the prize could not be awarded on its premises. Finally the prize was awarded on the premises of the Centre Wallonie-Bruxelles, a centre for the promotion of artists and creators from the French-speaking part of Belgium.

The most detailed justification for the cancellation of Chomsky's invitation to the National Assembly was provided by the well-known French journalist Frédéric Haziza. Haziza's comments are worthy of mention, as they illustrate the religious attitude that some people adopt towards the Holocaust and their contempt for the facts.

Haziza begins by asserting that "Chomsky has been a faithful supporter of Holocaust deniers, including Robert Faurisson, for 36 years," which repeats the usual

---

17   Noam Chomsky, His right to say it, *The Nation*, February 28, 1981.

confusion between supporting someone's freedom of expression and supporting what they say.

Haziza goes on to write that:

> "Chomsky reoffends in 2010 when he signs with Soral, Dieudonné, Bruno Gollnisch... or Robert Ménard, a petition initiated by Paul-Éric Blanrue and Jean Bricmont, two anti-Semites and Holocaust deniers. A petition calling for the repeal of the Gayssot Act and the release of a certain Vincent Reynouard, then imprisoned after multiple convictions for apology of war crimes and for contesting crimes against humanity.[18]"

Vincent Reynouard is indeed a far-right militant and Holocaust denier but he was put in jail for almost a year purely for his opinions, and if one objects to the repression of opinions, it is normal to object to such imprisonment.

More absurd still, Haziza considers "that honoring Chomsky in the Assembly would have been a challenge to the Gayssot law voted on July 13, 1990 in this very place by the deputies". In what way would the mere presence of a foreigner hostile to a French law be tantamount to "calling it into question"?

And Haziza ends as though a sacrilege had been avoided: "Not honoring Chomsky in the National Assembly simply preserved the dignity of this place, symbol of the values of the Republic."

Finally, it should be noted that, at the time of the Faurisson affair, none of the great French intellectuals associated with the "anti-totalitarian" and more or less libertarian movement of the 1960s and 1970s, such as Michel Foucault, Jacques Derrida, Pierre Bourdieu, Claude Lefort, Cornelius Castoriadis, Gilles Deleuze, Felix Guattari, Edgar Morin, André Gorz, François Furet, André Glucksmann, Paul Thibaud, Philippe Sollers Jean-Marie Domenach, Bernard-Henri Lévy, made the slightest protest against the prosecution of Robert Faurisson.

What is even more remarkable is the fact that none of them said even a word against the smear campaign against Noam Chomsky, when it was not difficult to find out what really happened - with the petition as with the "opinion" published at the beginning of Faurisson's defense brief. It leaves one perplexed as to the depth and coherence of their anti-totalitarian convictions. The fundamental principles of the Republic were undoubtedly better defended, during the Faurisson affair, by an American libertarian than by the entire French intelligentsia of the time, which chose to ignore the principles it claims to uphold.

---

18 To be precise, I did not initiate the petition and Chomsky did not sign it, but made a separate statement protesting Reynouard's imprisonment for opinion.

The 1983 judgment against Robert Faurisson did not satisfy his opponents. Pierre Vidal-Naquet complained that this judgment "recognized the seriousness of Faurisson's work, which is a crowning achievement, and, in short, condemned him only for having acted maliciously by summarizing his theses in slogans", which is true. The logic of the 1983 judgment was that, since the historian's freedom was complete, as long as the Holocaust deniers expressed their opinions more cautiously than Robert Faurisson had done, they did not have to be prosecuted.

This is probably why, in 1990, legislation introduced by Communist deputy Jean-Claude Gayssot was adopted which provides for punishing denial of crimes condemned by the post-war Nuremberg trials – in effect, meaning the Holocaust – with up to one year's imprisonment and a fine of 45 000 euros, not counting the payment of damages and court publication costs. Later jurisprudence states that the law applies "even if [such denial] is presented in veiled or dubitative form or by way of insinuation.[19]"

It is nevertheless worth noting that most people keep their opinions to themselves or their friends, when those opinions are unpopular, marginal, or politically incorrect. So who is going to dare admit publicly that he has doubts about the existence of the gas chambers, when he knows that he faces a year's imprisonment and a fine of 45 000 euros? This implies that one can never be certain of the sincerity of claims to be convinced of the existence of the gas chambers. Since no doubts can be expressed, no doubts can be refuted, and discussion is shut down. Everyone has to say the same thing, which inevitably imposes insincerity and subterfuge, reason enough to reject the Gayssot law or any other law of censorship.

It is, moreover, quite extraordinary that, less than a year after the fall of the Berlin Wall, at a time dominated by the denunciation of communism, the French Parliament should adopt a law restricting freedom of expression proposed by a Communist member of that parliament.

When it was adopted, the Gayssot law by no means met with unanimous approval. Since the Left was in power at the time, many right-wing politicians opposed it, including Jacques Chirac, future President of the Republic, Pierre Mazeaud, future President of the Constitutional Council, Jean-Louis Debré, future President of the National Assembly and the Constitutional Council, François Fillon, future Prime Minister, and Dominique Perben, future Minister of Justice, as well as Simone Veil, an Auschwitz survivor. Jacques Toubon, also future Minister of Justice, even retorted to Communist deputy Claude Lefort during a debate in the National Assembly: "There's a guy named Stalin in 1936: he did exactly the job you just did! It was

---

19 *Code pénal*, 2006, p. 2059.

called the trials! » However, when the Right came back to power, it was very careful not to abolish the Gayssot law.

If the law weren't bad enough in itself, it enabled certain "antiracist" organizations to abuse the law against their political enemies. A spectacular example of such abuses was provided by the lawsuits against Bruno Gollnisch, professor of international law and Japanese civilization at the University of Lyons and, at that time, a prominent member of the National Front.

During a press conference in Lyon on 11 October 2004, devoted to other issues, he was questioned about the gas chambers. His answers were considered to amount to "Holocaust denial" by some associations, and, because of that, he was suspended from teaching by his university for five years and was sentenced by the courts to three months' imprisonment (suspended), heavy fines and payment of damages to the associations that were prosecuting him for those remarks.

It would be too long to discuss in detail what Gollnisch said in this press conference but basically his answer was that historians should be free to investigate the subject of the gas chambers without being under the threat of the Gayssot law. Everyone knows that criticizing a law is not the same thing as violating it, except apparently in this case.

This sentence was finally overturned by the highest Court in France (the Court of Cassation), which ruled that "in the above-mentioned remarks that are attributed to him, Bruno Gollnisch says that he does not deny the homicidal gas chambers, but that the discussion among historians must remain free; that such a proposition in no way constitutes the crime of contesting a crime against humanity." In general, the Court of Cassation refers the case back to another court of appeal, but here it quashed the case without referral, which is very rare.

The Gollnisch case is a perfect illustration of the slippery slope that inevitably accompanies censorship laws - not only those who make explicitly forbidden statements should be censored, but also those who are interpreted as expressing them "indirectly". Indeed, throughout history people wishing to circumvent censorship have expressed themselves in all sorts of indirect ways, occasionally enriching literature by such evasions. But if we want to prohibit this, where does one stop?

Although spectacularly exonerated by the Court of Cassation, Bruno Gollnisch suffered years of legal troubles and suspension of teaching with loss of salary, which the Court of Cassation's ruling did not erase (it was an internal sanction at the university), before being subjected to "anti-fascist" demonstrations upon his return to the University of Lyons.

Follow-up

There have been many cases of censorships after the Faurisson, Chomsky and Gollnisch affairs, and for similar reasons:

- Abbé Pierre. Henri Groués (1912--2007) was a catholic priest known as the Abbé Pierre. He was involved in the Resistance during the war and helped hide Jewish children. After the war, he was elected at the French National Assembly as a left-wing Cristian and led several pacifist movements. He also founded the Emmaüs movement that tries to combat social exclusion. For all these reasons, he was probably the most popular figure in France.

But he was also a long-time friend of Roger Garaudy (1913--2012) a Marxist philosopher and high-level member of the Communist Party until his exclusion in 1970. Garaudy eventually converted to Islam and later wrote a book "*Les mythes fondateurs de la politique israélienne*" (The Founding Myths of Modern Israel), for which he was sued and condemned on the basis of the Gayssot law. The Abbé Pierre expressed his sympathy for Garaudy in a open letter, mixing up theological considerations on the "promised land" with a defense of free speech for Garaudy and about the Holocaust in general.

This provoked another storm of protest in France, including from the Catholic Church, and the good Abbé had to apologize and was essentially forced to retire from public life.

But having Roger Garaudy convicted and obtaining an apology from Abbé Pierre, a personality who was extremely popular in the eyes of the French (and who remained so after this case) was a kind of Pyrrhic victory. Indeed, Roger Garaudy had converted to Islam in 1982, and this allowed his theses, and with them those of the Holocaust deniers, to break into the Muslim world. There it was easy to present him as a victim of the "Zionist lobby" which "controls France". This was a collateral damage of the censorship, which was both entirely predictable and totally unforeseen by the censors.

But the "Garaudy-Abbé Pierre" scandal was nothing compared to the one that was going to be provoked by a very talented humorist, with an African father and a French mother who started as an anti-racist and anti-National Front militant: Dieudonné M'bala M'Bala.

- The problems of Dieudonné started with a sketch in Marc-Olivier Fogiel's show "*On ne peut pas plaire à tout le monde*" (one cannot please everyone) on December 1, 2003. Disguised as an Israeli religious extremist, Dieudonné first exhorted suburban youth to join the American-Zionist "axis of good", thereby visibly mocking George Bush's "axis of evil", which included Iraq, Iran and North Korea, and ended with a salute with one arm outstretched, exclaiming: Isra-heil.

This may be considered bad taste, but it has to be put in the perspective of French humor: Pierre Desproges, one of the most famous French standup comedians could make a joke about someone claiming that "the reason why so many Jews went to Auschwitz is because it was free." And the singer and comedian Carlos could tell the following joke: "What separates man from animal? Answer: the Mediterranean."

After that sketch, attempts were made to ban Dieudonné from performing his show, as a way of punishing him for this sketch, not for antisemitism.

But Dieudonné did not give in, and his following show, "My apologies", in which he asked forgiveness from the "chosen people", was a way to raise the ante. The dynamics of repression/resistance took over. You sue me, I respond with an additional provocation, then you sue me again, etc. Next we were treated to the baptism of Dieudonné's daughter, with Jean-Marie Le Pen as godfather, then to a show at the Zenith in Paris (a very big performance hall) on 26 December 2008, where Robert Faurisson took the stage and was awarded "the prize for infrequentability" by Dieudonné's assistant, Jacky Sigaux, disguised as a deportee. Difficult to be more provocative!

After that, there were numerous attempts, sometimes successful, sometimes not, to ban his shows wherever he went, along with a police raid with dogs at 6 a.m. at his home (he has many small children) in search of inexistent drugs and weapons. The result is that he became and remained extremely popular among large segments of the youth.

- Pressure within universities. Many people are familiar with the intimidation caused by the "social justice warriors" in various academic institutions. However, the intimidation tactics can also come from the top. On 26 April 2018, the Free University of Brussels (*Université Libre de Bruxelles* - ULB) awarded an honorary doctorate to the famous British director Ken Loach, as well as other personalities. However, before giving this award, the university had to face a wave of indignation from civil society and even from former ULB law student Charles Michel, who was then the Prime Minister of Belgium. A petition demanding that Ken Loach not be so honored was signed by a Nobel Prize winner in physics and 650 Belgian and foreign intellectuals and personalities, particularly French.

Loach was denounced for having made "ambiguous" remarks about the Second World War and the creation of the State of Israel, and for contradicting accusations of antisemitism in the British Labour Party. The university asked him to make a public statement acknowledging the existence of the Holocaust, which he did, noting that he never denied it, adding, with respect to the allegations of Holocaust denial made against him: "The paper that made these false allegations refused to print my full response. As a consequence, the poison was allowed to spread unchallenged. No doubt this was the intention. It was malicious and unprincipled.[20]"

Following this statement, the university maintained its decision to award him an honorary doctorate, while stressing that Loach's political positions were binding only on him and not on the university (which is implicitly obvious, regardless of who the recipient of such a doctorate might be). But Loach nevertheless said he found it "shocking and deeply offensive" that he was called upon to make that statement. He said he agreed with the Jewish Socialist Group, whose opposition to antisemitism is absolute and total, that "accusations of antisemitism are being weaponised to attack the Jeremy Corbyn-led Labour party. Those who try to smear me in this way know that I have always fought all racism, including antisemitism. I doubt everyone can say the same."

Ken Loach did not let the Belgian Prime Minister off easily for his attempt to influence his former law school. Charles Michel gave a speech at a rally celebrating the 70th anniversary of the founding of Israel. Noting that Mr. Michel is a lawyer, Loach asked:

> "Did he ask about Israel's violations of international law? Did he ask about the illegal occupation of the Palestinian territories? Has he raised the issue of the killing of unarmed Palestinian civilians? Did he talk about Israel's refusal to allow the UN to investigate its territory?[21]"
>
> If not: "Were the [ULB law] courses that bad? Or did he fail his exams?"

Although the ULB is to be congratulated for having resisted the pressure it was put under, one can understand Ken Loach's irritation at being forced to make the declaration imposed on him and one can also wonder which Belgian university will in future take the risk of honoring such a "controversial" personality. The strategy of intimidation can have effects even when it does not succeed directly.

To turn to another example, in 2017, University College London organized a conference to celebrate the fiftieth anniversary of Noam Chomsky's publication of *The Responsibility of Intellectuals*. The conference proceedings were published in a book to be launched on 29 October 2019. But in preparation for this event, the university issued guidelines to prevent the expression of five unacceptable anti-Semitic ideas, including: "Suggestions (overt or implied) that Jews as a group or particular sections of the British Jewish community invent, exaggerate or 'weaponise' incidents of anti-semitism for political or other benefit.[22]"

---

20 https://www.rtbf.be/info/regions/detail_ken-loach-a-l-ulb-accuse-par-des-organisations-juives-l e-cineaste-doit-clarifier-sa-position?id=9900009.

21 Here I had to translate back into English Loach's comments that I have only in French: https:// www.rtbf.be/info/societe/detail_ken-loach-tacle-charles-michel-sur-son-cursus-de-droit-a-l-ulb -a-t-il-reussi-ses-examens?id=9903059

22 https://www.thecanary.co/exclusive/2019/10/22/a-uk-university-is-trying-to-censor-jewish-crit ics-of-israel/.

As Chomsky noted, this is tantamount to "stating that it would be antisemitic for anyone to say or imply that any Jewish group has ever exaggerated incidents of anti-semitism in the Labour Party or elsewhere. I'm frankly at a loss for words.[23]"

Of course, the university defends itself against limiting freedom of expression and aims only to ensure that "opinions and ideas put forward do not give rise to an environment in which people will be subjected to – or could reasonably fear being subjected to – harassment, intimidation, abuse or verbal violence, particularly with regard to the characteristics protected by the 2010 Equality Act, including religion and belief." One only has to think for a moment about what such a vague recommendation (what does "could reasonably fear" mean?) would imply for freedom of expression if it were applied equally to all groups and beliefs, to understand the hypocrisy of placing this restriction while claiming to defend that freedom.

- Étienne Chouard, a professor of economics, became known in 2005 for his work in denouncing the European Constitutional Treaty, which was finally rejected by a comfortable majority of French (and Dutch) people, but adopted in another form (the Lisbon Treaty) by the French parliament in 2008.

Chouard came back into the news during the Yellow Vest movement, because his idea of radical, direct democracy, based on the citizens' initiative referendum, is very popular among them.

But Chouard also has a big flaw in the eyes of some self-styled "antifascists": he talks to everyone, including people considered to be on the "far right". In June 2019, two journalists from the *Media*, a WebTV close to *La France insoumise* (the party of Jean-Luc Mélenchon), Denis Robert and Mathias Enthoven, invited Chouard to a special program intended (in principle) to "clarify" his controversial positions.

After a long discussion in which Chouard explained why democracy requires readiness to discuss with people on all sides, and why there is a need for skepticism concerning history, which is usually written by the victors, journalists abruptly asked him if he had any doubts about the existence of the gas chambers.

Chouard, taken aback, asked what kind of question was that? He adds that it was not his subject and that he had not studied it. True to the rational skepticism he had just defended, Chouard said that he was willing to say that the gas chambers existed, but that there was something absurd in demanding such an answer from someone who had never studied the question and who would be a "thought criminal" if he denied it.

As was to be expected, the journalists waxed indignant in face of such a reply and, after this show, the sky fell on the head of the unfortunate Chouard, who could at most be guilty of a certain awkwardness linked to his sincerity. The LICRA announced that it would sue him, he apologized on his blog and had to submit to a hu-

---

23 https://www.jewishvoiceforlabour.org.uk/article/ucl-attack-on-academic-freedom/.

miliating session of *mea culpa* in a TV show confronted by Elisabeth Lévy, a well-known journalist and polemicist. He was taken off his weekly discussion program on the TV network Sud Radio.

Conclusions

Without the lawsuits against him, Faurisson would have remained an obscure researcher on the Holocaust. However, the hysteria surrounding his writings, the attacks against him, but even more against Chomsky, Garaudy, Abbé Pierre, Gollnisch, Chouard, and many less well-known people, have given maximum publicity to his theses and have made them popular among populations that are not enthusiastic about Israel (given that the main purpose of the constant focus on the Holocaust is to legitimize the actions of that State, even though there is no logical link between the two). This in turn is used as a weapon to demonize those populations (often of Muslim origin) when they refuse to listen to lectures about the Holocaust.

But that is not all. I myself have been censored or boycotted numerous times, including for a physics seminar in May 2019 that was cancelled because of my views on free speech. More spectacularly, after that cancellation, a letter of protest was written by my colleague Alan Sokal and signed by various prestigious personalities including Noam Chomsky, Richard Dawkins, Steven Pinker, and the Nobel Physics Prize Steven Weinberg. Its publication was refused by *Le Monde*, *Le Figaro*, *Le Point*, *Marianne* and *Mediapart*.

This does not affect me very much, since I can still do other things to keep myself busy.

What is interesting in this censorship is that I am a nobody. I have no political ambitions, no organization, and no party would want me. But suppose that, instead of being a retired physicist, I were a journalist, an ambitious politician or a young researcher in the ideological disciplines: philosophy, history, social sciences. I am sure that I would not dare to say a fraction of what I say.

And this is why censoring me, but also thousands of other people with heterodox opinions but in no position of influence, matters: if you can crush nobodies, what will happen to people who want to make a career in journalism, politics or the universities? It is the principle of "making an example".

This explains why so few people dare challenge our absurd foreign policies: the constant flow of money from the United States to Israel, our endless wars in the Middle East, the fact that we have been arming the same jihadists who kill us in Paris, London or Brussels, the support of Juan Guaido who is nobody anymore even in Venezuela, our hostility towards the Russians, the Chinese, the Iranians, etc., who do not threatens us in any way.

That is probably the real decline of the West: the disappearance of the critical spirit, due to all the direct and indirect censorship of which a tiny fraction has been discussed here. It is this critical spirit that has been our strength in the past, for better or for worse, and we will not come out of our decline if we do not resurrect it.

Bibliography

Ayad Christophe/*Guiral*, Antoine, 2008: Sarkozy comme chez lui en Israël. In: Libération, June 23

Chomsky, Noam, 1981: His right to say it. In: The Nation, February 28.

Chomsky, Noam, 1984: Réponses inédites à mes détracteurs parisiens, Paris.

De Gaulle, Philippe, 2004: De Gaulle, mon père. Entretiens avec Michel Tauriac, Paris, Plon, volume 2, p. 323.

Morin, Edgar/*Naïr*, Sami/*Sallenave*, Danielle, 2002: Israël-Palestine: Le cancer. In: Le Monde, June 4.

Robespierre, Maximilien, 1791: Discours sur la liberté de la presse, par, 11 may. Available on : The Project Gutenberg EBook of Discours par Maximilien Robespierre.

Robinson, Paul, 1979: The Chomsky Problem, In: The New York Times, February 25.

State Power and Resistance

Georg Meggle

Chomsky on Terrorism

For Günther
in memoriam of my mom

Why not just tell the truth?[1]
Noam Chomsky

Especially since 9/11, there are entire libraries that are overflowing with works related to the horrendous topic of terrorism. Within these libraries, Noam Chomsky's contributions occupy a bookshelf for themselves. But there are some radical differences between his and nearly all the other works on terrorism. This article will focus on only one of these differences. It is, I suppose, the one most relevant for our own thinking and talking about and maybe also reacting to terrorism and the alleged 'War on Terrorism'.

Let me start with a personal confession: Even before reading again – but this time a bit more systematically – Chomsky's numerous books and papers on terrorism, I knew, of course, that he is one of our very few great masters in clear thinking. But now, I am overwhelmed in finally seeing the shockingly clear and evident premises on which his perspective on terrorism is based. As repeatedly remarked by Chomsky himself, this perspective can be logically checked "in two minutes by a literate teenager".[2] Thus, why is it that this Chomskyian perspective is hardly shared or noticed?

1 Basics

1.1 Point of View

Though Chomsky himself denies that there is any intrinsic connection between his linguistic research and his political writings, I take it for granted that in both cases – with respect to language as well as to historical events – his point of view is the same: In the end, Chomsky's main interests are focused not on phenomena in isolation, but on the structures behind them. Obviously, this focus does not imply a disin-

---

1 Cf. Chomsky 1992: 18, and passim in nearly all of Chomsky's publications.
2 Chomsky 2002a: 56.

terest in the phenomena. Quite to the contrary: I know of no other single person in history who has presented us with more – and more detailed – reports for the annals of humanity and inhumanity. But on each of these many thousands of pages it is evident for me that its author is craving for some deeper understanding – to be found by identifying some structure behind the myriad of events, many of them consisting in bloodbaths and atrocities.

In order to detect structures, one needs to take one's stance from a distance. And to take such a distanced point of view is exactly what was explicitly recommended by Chomsky when answering the question of "How the 'War on Terror' Should be Reported" in his 2002-lecture "The Journalist from Mars".[3] It is Chomsky himself who *is* this very journalist.

"A good Martian reporter would … want to clarify a couple of basic ideas" – ideas which in these paragraphs I'll try to give a rough introduction into. "First of all, he'd like to know what exactly is terrorism".[4]

1.2 Universal T-Concept

What is Terrorism (T, for short)? Or, to be more specific, when is an action a terroristic one (a T-Act)? This question could be – and has been – answered quite easily:[5]

UT   *T-Acts are acts of (attempts of) achieving one's ends by means of violence-induced strong intimidation.*

This explication is a most general one, leaving open (a) who the actor is (a particular individual or a collective, an institution, a state or a group of states) [question of agency] (b) against whom the violence is directed [question of victimhood], (c) who the intended intimidation-addressees are, (d) what kind of (physical or psychological) means the intimidating violence is making use of (ranging from knives, anthrax-letters, misinformation, cyber-warfare and economic blockades to biological, chemi-

---

3   This 2002-lecture (part of Chomsky 2002a) is, to put it simply, the best introduction into Chomsky's position on Terrorism of which I know – along with his 2004 Lecture at the London Royal Institute of Philosophy with the title "Simple Truths, Hard Problems" (= Chomsky 2005a), and chapter 8, "Terrorism and Justice: Some Useful Truisms", of his book Hegemony or Survival (= Chomsky 2004). As additional basic summary texts on Terrorism I would recommend: Chomsky/Herman 1979b [§ 3.1: The Semantics of Terror and Violence, 85 – 95], Chomsky 2003d, and both chapter 5 of Chomsky 1988 and chapter 8 of Chomsky 2004.
4   Chomsky 2002a: 76.
5   This "easiness" refers only to this rough version of T, of course. But it is this version only that is relevant in the following. As soon as one enters into the details, problems abound, of course. And this is normally the level where we philosophers or logicians are – and obviously very often are expected (and maybe even educated) to be – losing contact with the reality. Not so with Chomsky. For some of my own explication endeavors see Meggle 2006.

cal or nuclear weapons) [question of T-instruments], (e) of what degree of strength the intended and/or effectuated intimidation (including awe and horror) is, (f) what the direct reactions of the respective T-addressees are intended to be, (g) of what type one's (final) ends are (political, religious, ideological or merely criminal, personal ones etc.), (h) whether – and in what respects – the T-act in question is a successful one (reaching its multiple aims in the way intended) or not [question of success], and (i) whether the T-act itself has been already performed or its performance only being threatened.

Most of these distinctions are independent of each other and so may overlap. And thus, obviously, the spectrum of T-phenomena is a very wide one.

The twofold instrumentalist structure of this T-concept was explicated very clearly by the historian David Fromkin already in 1975:[6]

> Terrorism is violence used in order to create fear; but it is aimed at creating fear in order that the fear, in turn, will lead somebody else – not the terrorist – to embark on some quite different program of action that will accomplish whatever it is that the terrorist really desires.

And notice, that, as stressed by Chomsky himself again and again, UT is presenting roughly the same concept as had been defined in the official U.S. Code and Army Manuals in the early 1980s when, against insurrectionary forces in South and Central America, the 1st War on Terror had been declared by the Reagan administration, this way:

> T = The calculated use of violence or the threat of violence to attain goals that are political, religious or ideological in nature ... through intimidation, coercion or instilling fear.[7]

And it is the same concept as expressed also – disregarding some too narrow specifications – in a quite similar definition of the British government:

> T = The use, or threat, of action which is violent ... and is intended to influence the government or intimidate the public and is for the purpose of advancing a political, religious, or ideological cause.

These "seem to be satisfactory definitions—not perfect, but at least as good as others regarded as unproblematic".[8]

It is this simple T-Concept, which is used by Chomsky in his thinking about Terrorism. Let me add that UT is spelling out what one could call the *descriptive aspect* of T, i.e. the necessary and jointly sufficient factual conditions for an action to be correctly referred to as a terroristic one (= a T-Act).

---

6 Fromkin 1973: 693.
7 This quotation is to be found in many papers of Chomsky – as e.g. in Chomsky 2002a: 79.
8 Chomsky 2005a: 18.

1.3 Minima Moralia

But there is also an *evaluative aspect* of T[9]. To be dubbed as an agent of T is, to be sure, one of the strongest and most deadly condemnations available in our times. Namely, (it is generally thought today that) it implies that

MT *T-Acts* are to be morally condemned.

Though MT follows already from the much more general principle of condemnation of Violence,

MV Acts of *Violence* are to be morally condemned.

it should be obvious that the strength of condemnation as expressed in MT is comparable only to the extreme cases of violence that would correspond to war-crimes.[10]

MWC *War Crimes* are to be morally condemned.

1.3.1 Universality

Now, though Chomsky does not pretend to take part in doing moral philosophy, there is one "truism" which he is always and absolutely sticking to:

U Any sound moral reasoning has to be universal, i.e., "we [have to] apply to ourselves the same standards we apply to others, if not more stringent ones".[11]

For Chomsky, this principle of universality, equivalent with double standards or special pleadings being strictly forbidden, is "the most-elementary of moral principles".[12] It is the very cornerstone of Chomsky's own personal and, in his case, amounting to the same thing, political stance, and thus of his critique of our whole Western T-discourse (= our *Culture of Terrorism*[13]) in particular.

This U-principle can also be easily discovered by our Journalist from Mars, "at least as understood by the leaders of the self-declared war on terrorism, because they

---

9   This usual distinction between descriptive versus evaluative aspects (of a certain term or concept as, e.g., T) is part of my own explication. I could not find it in Chomsky's own writings. Why this is not the case is one of the many questions that has been left unsettled by me up to now. Suggestions are welcome, of course.

10 Alex Schmid has defined T as (or better: simply compared T with) the non-war-time-equivalent to War-Crimes. Cf. Schmid 1983. In his otherwise very useful overviews, the whole field of U.S.-Terrorism just does not exist.

11 Chomsky 2004: 187.

12 Chomsky 2006: 36.

13 = Chomsky 1988a.

tell us, they tell us constantly, that they are very pious Christians, who therefore revere the Gospels, and have certainly memorized the definition of 'hypocrite' given prominently in the Gospels – namely, the hypocrites are those who apply to others the standards that they refuse to accept for themselves".[14]

1.3.2 Other Truisms

In addition to U, there are some additional "truisms" mentioned by Chomsky which – as truisms – should be taken into account in any "sound" argument about Morality in general and in any Ethics of Terrorism in particular:

C.1 Facts matter.[15]
C.2 Acts are to be evaluated in terms of the range of likely consequences.[16]
C.3 People are primarily responsible for the likely consequences of their own action, or inaction.[17]
C.4 Responsibilities mount with greater opportunity and more clearly anticipated effects.[18]
C.5 First, do no harm.[19]
C.6 There is an obligation to help suffering people as best we can.[20]

These principles are – in addition to U (the Principle of Universality) – "truisms" for Chomsky. And rightly so, I would say. But, obviously, Chomsky's truisms are not truisms for everyone.

1.4 Main Moral Argument

In its essentials, Chomsky's critique of terrorism (and of other sorts of calculated violence) – with thousands of pages referring to an incredibly huge amount of historical as well as present day 'horrible' facts – boil down to nothing else than a simple but uncompromisingly rigorous application of

• the Universal Terrorism-Definition (UT),
• the presupposed Moral Evaluation of Terrorism (MT) and
• the most elementary Moral Principle of Universality (U)

---

14 Chomsky 2002a: 77.
15 Chomsky 2005a: 27.
16 Chomsky 2004: 187.
17 Chomsky 2003d: 619.
18 Chomsky 2003d: 619.
19 Chomsky 2001b: 43.
20 Chomsky 2003d: 619.

to (our way of talking and thinking about and reacting to or even bringing about) these very facts.

Thus, the logical form of Chomsky's central argument (as being explicated here) is this one: Let $F_1,...,F_n$ be some facts about an action of agent X. And let UV be any adequate definition of Violence in general (including UT as a special sort).[21] Then, given that these facts are fulfilling all the conditions of UV (or of UT, in particular), this very action of X *is* an act of violence (or a T-Act) – and therefore, via MV (or MT) (if these principles are accepted), this action of X has to be condemned. Thus, according to U, the same condemnation should hold for anybody else's (for any agent's Y ≠ X) action fulfilling $F_1,...,F_n$ as well.

In short: Moral evaluation (including condemnation) – of violence and of terrorism, too – must not depend on agency, i.e., not on *who* the respective T-Agent is. This is the standard as applied in criminal law. And it is the reason also for which *Justice*, when personalized in statues, is presented as a blindfolded person. To be really impartial, she must not know *who* the defendant is, but only what the relevant *deeds*, which s/he is accused for, have been.

2 Moral Verdict

2.1 The Verdict

Chomsky is extremely shy in uttering moral verdicts. However, there is one salient exception: when and as far as the logic (inconsistencies included) of our own usual political-moral verdicts is concerned. In this case, Chomsky's verdict is a crystal-clear one: Most of our common condemnations of terrorism are blatant offences against the Principle of Universality – though hardly ever acknowledged or even just recognized as such. To put it blankly: We – or at least most of us – are deeply permeated by hypocrisy. With regards to violence & terrorism, insincerity is the vice most typical for our culture. It is this reason for which it is called by Chomsky to be a *Culture of Terrorism*.[22]

2.2 Exemplification

In his 2004 Royal Institute Lecture[23], Chomsky dared to apply his central moral argument even to what has been taken to be one of the foundations for our "post-

---

21 For one of the best works on that topic see Messelken 2012.
22 See Chomsky 1988a.
23 = Chomsky 2005a.

World War II international justice": the War Crime Trial at Nuremberg. To back his verdict on this trial, he only had to quote the tribunal's chief counsel:[24]

> *Since both sides in World War II had played the terrible game of urban destruction*—the Allies far more successfully—*there was no basis for criminal charges* against Germans or Japanese, and in fact no such charges were brought ... Aerial bombardment had been used so extensively and ruthlessly on the Allied side as well as the Axis side that neither at Nuremberg nor Tokyo was the issue made a part of the trials.[25]

Chomsky's verdict: The Nuremberg-Laws on (= their definitions of) War-Crimes were *not* universal. They do *not* satisfy the Principle of Universality. "Nazi war criminals were absolved if the defence could show that their US counterparts carried out the same crimes".[26] "The proper conclusion at Nuremberg and since would have been to punish the victors as well as the vanquished foe. Neither at the postwar trials [of Nuremberg and Tokyo] nor subsequently [such as in the Yugoslavia vs. NATO-Tribunal] have the powerful been subjected to the rules, not because they have not carried out crimes—of course they have—but because they are *immune under prevailing standards of morality*".[27]

According to Chomsky, under a really universal application of the Nuremberg laws, "every post-war American president would have been hanged".[28]

2.3 Double Standard

This Chomskyian dissenting truth-telling by "of course they have" is the centre of his entire – and would be of any other sound – moral reasoning both on war crimes and on terrorism. This last quote from above – via its reference to our *"prevailing standards of morality"* – is the key to any deeper understanding of all his many works on political and very often state backed violence in general and on our T-topic in particular.

So, just keep in mind – and please do really never forget: With respect to (our talking and thinking about) war crimes and terrorism, there are two radically different standards (definitions) to be distinguished. The *universal* one (UT, a standard in

---

24 See Taylor 1970.
25 Quotation as in Chomsky 2005a: 7; my italics.
26 Ibid.; my italics.
27 Ibid.: 8; my italics.
28 As quoted in https://chomsky.info/1990____-2/ , reporting on a speech delivered at 1990; download at Oct 04, 2020.

accordance with principle U) on the one side, and a "prevailing" or an "*operative*" one on the other.[29]

"The operative definition of '[war] crime' is: 'Crime that *you* carried out but *we* did not.'"[30] In other words: The basic adequacy criterion for any *operative definition* of War Crime or Terrorism is simply this one:

OP   War Crimes / T-Acts cannot be Acts performed by US.

This gives US the privileged status of immunity. It guarantees US a principled exemption from any criminal court investigations. OP implies directly: "Tribunals [on war crimes or T-Acts] must be restricted to the crimes of *others*".[31]

But evidently, this criterion OP entails the direct negation of the Principle of Universality U. The two standards are not only different, they are logically incompatible. Thus, U versus OP is a paradigm case of *Double Standards* (as forbidden by U).

For additional remarks on OP's (general and Chomsky's main) reference of US, see the notes in 5.1 below.

3 The Terrorism-Industry

Let's take stock: Our Martian Journalist (= Chomsky) has identified a contradiction in Earth's present way of handling – and waging war on – Terrorism. There *is* a universal definitional criterion of Terrorism (= UT); but its application would lead to the conclusion that even WE may be or in fact are T-Agents. ("US is a leading terrorist state".[32]) But, for US, that is totally unacceptable. We definitely want to stick to our WE ARE THE GOOD ONES self-image – as expressed and continually corroborated by following OP. Thus we have a classical dilemma. We just can't have it both ways. We cannot stick to the Principle U and adhere to our OP-directed self-image at the same time.

3.1 Collective Cognitive Dissonance

Psycho-Sociologists would speak here of a situation of Cognitive Dissonance. The typical reaction of an individual in such a dilemma is just to deny one side of the

---

29 This distinction corresponds to Chomsky's distinction between the two meanings "the terms of political discourse typical have … . One is the *dictionary meaning*, and the other is a meaning that is useful for serving power – the *doctrinal meaning*" (Chomsky 2002c: 86; my italics).
30 Chomsky 2000c: 8; my italics.
31 Chomsky 2005a: 8; my italics.
32 Chomsky 2004: 189; and Chomsky 2016: § 17; and passim.

two horns constituting it. The same holds, according to Chomsky's diagnosis, with regards to our (thinking and talking about our) own aggression, war crimes and Terrorism. While officially sticking to our ideals – to U, e.g. – , we tend to do all that is necessary to maintain, by following OP, the image of US as the GOOD ones, thereby actually denying U.

Humans are social animals. Thus, in the collective version of Cognitive Dissonance the denial tendencies might be even much stronger than in the individual case – including "the overriding need to reject the principle of universality".[33]

3.2 Necessary Illusions & Manufacturing Consent

For this collective denial to be kept stable, some *Necessary Illusions*[34] – as, for example, the just mentioned one of "WE are the Good Guys" – need to be fixed and enhanced systematically, ideally by means of specialized ideological institutions, i.e. by our Mass Media and our academic scholarship.

It is exactly this context where Chomsky's (and his friend Edward Herman's) *Manufacturing Consent*,[35] the joint study on *The Political Economy of the Mass Media*, gets its paradigmatic (and rightly much praised) relevance. That Terrorism itself is relying on the media's cooperation for getting its work done, that is – correctly or not – taken to be a commonplace. But in *Manufacturing Consent* this idea is getting a much deeper meaning. Our consent is not only relying on at least some cooperation between the T-Agents and their intimidation-addressees-related Media, but it is also created by US.

The "propaganda model" proposed by Chomsky/Herman as a general explanation-device for how our Media are functioning, "suggests that the 'societal purpose' of the media is to inculcate and defend the economic, social and political *agenda of privileged groups* that dominate domestic society and the state. The media serve this purpose in many ways: through selection of topics, distribution of concerns, framing the issues, filtering of information, emphasis and tone, and by *keeping debate within the bounds of acceptable premises*".[36] The propaganda model "focuses on [the] inequality of wealth and power and its multilevel effects on mass-media interests and choices. It traces the routes by which money and power are able to filter out the news for print, marginalize dissent, and allow *the government* and *dominant private interests* to get their message across to *the public*. ... The raw material of news must pass through successive filters, leaving only the cleansed residue fit to print. They

---

33 Chomsky 2005a: 13.
34 = title of Chomsky 2003a.
35 Chomsky/Herman 1988.
36 Ibid.: 298; my italics.

fix the premises of discourse and interpretation, and the definition of what is news-worthy in the first place".[37]

This model has been applied to T by Chomsky in many volumes and with respect to many places. Mainly in relation to the U.S.'s direct and indirect T-wars in Asia (Vietnam, Laos, Cambodia, Indonesia, East Timor, East Pakistan, Afghanistan), South and Central Amerika (Cuba, Brazil, Chile, Uruguay, Honduras, Guatemala, El Salvador, Nicaragua, Venezuela), Africa (Sudan, Libya) and the Middle East (Palestine, Lebanon, Iraq, Syria, Iran) – and, not to forget, Southern and Eastern Europe (Italy, Greece, Yugoslavia / Kosovo) and Southern Arabia (Yemen). All the respective T-reports of Chomsky's are also reports on US: on how WE – in following and even supporting the propaganda of OUR Media – are taking part in these T-wars.

3.3 Operative Semantics

No matter whether you see the main function of language in representing one's thoughts (as Chomsky does) or in interpersonal communication (as some other philosophers do, including myself), it is common knowledge that thoughts and linguistic meanings are intrinsically connected. So the most effective way of regulating one's thoughts is to regulate the regular meaning (= the prevailing usage) of our words. Word-Meanings are, at least in part, regulated by conventions. Thus, in order either to upheld or to change these meanings, you should try to uphold or change the respective conventions.[38] Arguably, this is the very domain wherein the Media's power on the Public Mind is at its strongest.

And this holds even more with respect to our political concepts, the class of our most contested concepts: Democracy, Freedom, Peace, Security, Human Rights etc. Every single use of such a contested word, both in fixing, spreading and receiving the News, is a non-neglectable move in the daily struggle to get the meanings of our words to be enhanced and/or moulded anew.

---

37 Chomsky/Herman 1988: 2; my italics
38 Notice, that this paragraph may be impregnated by my own Social Meaning Theory as developed in Action Theoretical Semantics = Meggle 2010. I am not sure how this perspective could be correlated with Chomsky's own Semantics. For this and many other linguistic questions I would rely nearly blindly on my friend Günther's experience. See Grewendorf 1995 und 2006.

3.3.1 The Media

As far as the political-semantic battle between the two standards UT versus OP is concerned, it does not take much research to see what alternative the media are taking sides with. A billion times each day with the latter one alone. To use Chomsky's words: "Don't take my word for it; try the experiment".[39] Well, just check it yourself, please – including your own verbal behavior.

Now (and to realize this point is of the utmost importance): Normally, already by applying the universal simple definition UT to a single terrorism-case of US, you would be stepping beyond "the bounds of acceptable premises". The Universality Principle is "understood to be an extremely dangerous *heresy*, and therefore it's necessary to erect impregnable barriers against it, even before anybody exhibits it, even though it's so rare".[40] Just by using the definition UT you are diverging from the "*moral orthodoxy*".[41] And so the truth, that WE may be T-Agents as well, becomes "a thought virtually inexpressible in enlightened Western commentary, or dismissed with horror as 'anti-Americanism', 'conspiracy theory', 'radical and extremist' or some other intellectual equivalent of four-letter words among the vulgar".[42]

So, here you have a short explanation by Chomsky himself of why these vulgar words are being so often applied to him – and why, when taking sides with him in starting to talk and think beyond these narrow "bounds of acceptable premises" by yourself, you too would be treated in the same way. Again, as Chomsky would say here: Well, "try the experiment"!

But the ideological warfare about the usage of the term "Terrorism" is not being fought only in the Media.[43] In the Terrorism-Industry there is also a special academic branch.

---

39 Chomsky 2002a: 77.
40 Chomsky 2002a: 78; my italics.
41 Chomsky 2004: 207; my italics.
42 Chomsky 2005a: 13.
43 I can testify to this Chomskyian diagnosis by myself. Some years ago I got an invitation by the organizers of a big international Terrorism-Conference, that I gladly accepted. I handed in the requested Abstract (see below) and was immediately disinvited. Should I confess that I am almost proud about that?

3.3.2 Academic Scholarship

Already beginning with the Reagan administration – "largely a figment of the public relations industry"[44] – , but much more so since 9/11, the so called "Terrorism Industry"[45], a huge net of institutions (Governments, strong private Interest Groups, Think Tanks, Media, the Academy – including Historians, Political Scientists and Philosophers – and, in the end, even the UN) is one of the most expanding business branches in the world. The number of T-Experts or "terrorologists"[46] – rather conformist 'intellectuals' working in this Industry – has been rocketing up. Many of them are working in or cooperating with flourishing and very well subsidized Think Tanks. And one of the main jobs in this industry has been just to fix the meaning/usage of the term "Terrorism" according to OP, thereby giving in to the "overriding need to reject the principle of universality".[47]

Starting that semantic policy was quite rational. The T-Industry knows:

> *Defining Terrorism is not merely a theoretical issue, but an operative concern of the first order.* ICT (International Policy Institute for Counter Terrorism)

Georg Meggle
Logics of Terrorism

ABSTRACT

Going against usual practice in our discourse on terrorism, the term 'logics' in this title is really not meant metaphorically. What I am after are the basics of a proper logics of terrorism. Starting with David Fromkin's instrumentalist intuition, a Terrorism-Act is defined as violence used (i) in order to create fear; but aiming at creating fear (ii) in order that the fear in turn will lead somebody else to embark on a different course of action that will ultimately accomplish whatever it is the terrorist really desires. This double instrumentality of T-Acts – and the essential connectedness of (i) and (ii) in T-Acts - will be explicated in this lecture. To this end, I will employ the diverse logics of instrumental actions. What we end up with is then a strictly axiomatized semantics of T-Acts. Having such semantics of T-Acts will put a stop to our thinking (and talking) about terrorism as a topic beyond any possible precise conceptual clarification. But be forewarned – as it is occasionally the case with philosophical clarifications, having to admit to the validity of some of the theorems of the T-logics may for some of us turn out to be rather shocking. And a prime example for such a T-theorem is …

The metatheorem announced, but left unknown to my intended audience, would have been: With the exception of a single negation shift, the logic (= the basic concept) of Terrorism is exactly the same as that of Deterrence. And my added question would have been: Why is it then that Deterrence (including the strategy of MAD / Mutual Assured Destruction) has been praised in the West as a sort of Rationality at the highest level, whereas "Terrorism" (of the Others) is being regularly condemned by us as a manifestation of pure irrationality?

44 Chomsky 1992: 47.
45 See Herman/O'Sullivan 1990.
46 Chomsky 2003a: 114.
47 Chomsky 2005a: 13.

And it was also rational for the Academy to get and stay involved in this semantic war on words. The propagated premise of this war is that defining Terrorism is a really hard challenge for intelligence. And this premise, though obviously false (just check UT in 1.1 above again), has been nearly universally accepted. And so, apart from very few 'non-commissar' intellectuals (including some Analytical Philosophers taking sides with Chomsky) who remain openly allied to the universal definition UT, the academic mainstream in the T-Industry has been subscribing to the proposition that finding a good T-definition must be a very hard intellectual problem. And so it would have been if and to the extent that one takes the question to be solved by delivering such a definition as this one: "How can we define it [= Terrorism] in such a way as to violate the principle of universality, exempting ourselves but applying to selected enemies? And these have to be selected with some precision".[48]

According to Alex P. Schmid, one of the leading figures in the more serious section of the T-Academy, there are more than 100 different T-definitions[49]; and there are even some dissertations whose main object had been to prove that explicit T-definitions are neither possible nor of any help.[50] As Chomsky's works on terrorism show: Most of the T-contributions of our academy are not something to be very proud of.

In addition: Much of this work plainly contradicts the propagated academic self-image that the academy is the one institution most dedicated to the systematic search for truth. Whereas in fact "a very important function of [those] ideological institutions – the media, the schools, and so on – is to prevent people from perceiving reality".[51] Following this indoctrination system, we are "protecting ourselves from understanding the world".[52]

3.3.3 T-Lists

Maybe you remember Carl Schmitt's famous remark: "The sovereign is he who decides on the state of exception".[53] Today, implementation of Terrorism – Terrorism from the other side, of course – seems to be treated as a kind of equivalent with such a state. And so, pace Schmitt, the saying goes: "The sovereign is he who decides on who is a T-Agent and who is not". And, arguably, as those in power do not like to wave their claim to it, they don't like to accept any definition that is not made up

---

48 Chomsky 2005a: 19.
49 Schmid 1983.
50 See, e.g., Malik 2001.
51 Chomsky 1992: 48.
52 Chomsky 1992: 17.
53 Schmitt 1922: (2005-edition) 12-13.

either by themselves or by some of their assistants. So, their own practical solution to the 'hard' T-definition problem is the one most easily to be handled by themselves: They create and actualize concrete T-Lists. Thus: X is (to be counted as) a T-Agent = X is a member of such a T-List.

Nowadays, there are many such lists, of course; and there are innumerable 'T-Agents' on such lists. Surely Chomsky and some of his friends have belonged to these "Terrorists lists" for a long time.

Normally, this procedure is accompanied by nominating special delegates who are responsible for making proposals for actualizing or revising such lists. And as there are no (universal) criteria accepted beyond these stipulated lists, they cannot be challenged by appeal to such criteria independently.

Again, without having to enter into deeper arguments, Chomsky's judgment on this point is very clear: Such a terrorism list is only representing the respective "arbitrary decision by the executive".[54] And: "The very idea that the state should have the authority to make such judgments unchecked is a serious offence against the Charter of Liberties, as is the fact that it is considered uncontentious".[55]

3.3.4 UN-made Definitions

The United Nations is the organization most obliged to find a solution transcending the enduring Double Standard situation with respect to T. I am certain – and Chomsky will be as well, I guess – that this problem could and would have been solved from the very beginning, if the UN, in following its obligations, would not have been barred by those parties who are, quite understandably, most interested in not losing their present state of immunity against any possible T-accusations.

In fact, the whole intellectual policy of searching for a universal definition has been quite unnecessary. We already had and have one – it is simply our (and the former Pentagon's) definition from 1.1. above, i.e.:

UT   *T-Acts are acts of (attempts of) achieving one's ends by means of violence-induced terror, i.e. by means of violent intimidation.*

So, when talking about the UN's mission to do its T-definitional job, the only real question would turn out to be: Why not just install this simple definition universally?

Writing the history of not-really universal UN-definition-proposals – or, to be more exact, of those nearly universal UN-definitions un-made by the opponents of

---

54 Chomsky 2016: 96.
55 Chomsky 2016: 97.

universality – is overdue. Here is only one example out of this long series, as commented on by Chomsky.[56]

In December 1987, the UN resolution 42/159 was adopted by the UN General Assembly. It was the year the officially recognized international terrorism (i.e., not that of US) had reached its so called peak – and President Reagan had spoken of "the evil scourge of terrorism". The main point of the resolution was to differentiate between international *terrorism* versus *resistance*, which had been the topic of a proceeding international congress. So the focus was on the legitimacy of actions to realize "the right to self-determination, freedom, and independence, as derived from the Charter of the United Nations, of people forcibly deprived of that right ... particularly peoples under colonial and racist regimes and foreign occupation".[57]

The vote was 153 to 2 (with a single abstention). The two countries that voted against the resolution were the U.S. and Israel. The reason given by them was related to the phrase "colonial and racist regimes" as it was understood to refer to their ally South Africa. Chomsky's comment: "Evidently the US and Israel could not condone resistance to the apartheid regime, particularly when it was led by Mandela's African National Congress, one of the world's 'more notorious terrorist groups', as Washington determined at the time. The other phrase 'foreign occupation' was understood to refer to Israel's military occupation ... Evidently, resistance could not be condoned in that case either. ... The public knows nothing about [this] major UN condemnation [of Terrorism] ... by virtue of the usual double veto".[58]

By the way: As a means of giving some perhaps interesting hint to a possible later author of this overdue background history of T-relevant UN-failures: It may be worth noticing that for Chomsky the whole terrorist/counterterrorist ideology – the Reagan administration's official kernel of its 'new' international policy – had one of its sources in Israel. "Israel is the source of the 1980s 'terrorism industry' (then transferred to the U.S. for further development), as an ideological weapon against Palestinians".[59] For more details on this transfer see Herman/ O'Sullivan's *The "Terrorism" Industry* from 1990,[60] where there is also a reference to one of the main influencers behind this transfer – a later on very well-known politician today to be nicknamed "Bibi".

And then, there is the Resolution 1566 (Oct 08, 2004) according to which even only starting or joining a philosophical (i.e., an absolutely open) debate about what are the reasons for T-Acts to be morally justified or not, could already count as sort of a T-Act. Thus, as Chomsky evidently has entered this discussion (as we do in

---

56 Chomsky 2004: chapter 8.
57 Chomsky 2004: 190.
58 Chomsky 2004: 190 f.
59 Chomsky 2002b: 135.
60 Herman/O'Sullivan 1990.

writing or reading this article), he (and we) could be labeled as "Terrorists". And that in the name of the UN![61]

3.4 Reasons behind the T-Industry

So there is a big and very efficient "Terrorism"-Industry working ultimately for one main purpose: to uphold and enhance the semantic conventions favoring OP.

In order to be kept stable, conventions have to be based on shared interests. What are these interests in the case of Western and especially of the U.S.'s backing of OP? Chomsky's straight answer: The Quest for Regional and Global *Dominance* and its main motivation: the so called "Fifth Freedom" = *Greed*.[62]

Both interests are given broad and systematic consideration in many of Chomsky's books. The widest historical perspective is that of *Year 501*,[63] the title of the book (written in 1992) referring to "the 500-year Reich", i.e., "the Colombian era of world history"[64], starting with 1492 and "given different names: imperialism, neo-colonialism, the North-South conflict, core versus periphery, G-7 (the 7 leading state capitalist industrial societies) and their satellites versus the rest. Or, more simply, Europe's conquest of the world."

This Chomskyian history of the West is correlated with a revisionist interpretation of Adam Smith (one of the sources most relevant for Chomsky's own look at the world), distinguishing explicitly between "*the interests of consumers and working people* on the one side and the interests *most particularly attended to* by the system"[65], i.e., the class of "*merchants and manufacturers*" as "*by far the principal architects*" on the other side. As to the summary of this Adam Smithian perspective:[66] "Two of the enduring features of the European conquest" are (a) "*Centralized state power* dedicated to *private privilege and authority*", (b) "the rational and organized use of *savage violence*", (c) "the *domestic colonization* by which the poor subsidize the rich" – "The costs were socialized, the profits poured into the coffers of

---

61 See Meggle 2020.
62 See Chapter 2 "The Fifth Freedom" of *Turning the Tide* (= Chomsky 1985) for more explanation of this freedom going beyond the Four Freedoms as announced by President Roosevelt in January 1941, i.e., "freedom of speech, freedom of worship, freedom from want, and freedom from fear" (op. cit.: 45) – "US rhetoric … noble and often inspiring" (44). But, comments Chomsky, it is this Fifth Freedom – "the freedom to rob and to exploit" (47) – which is the most important. It is the "operative policy in the real world", following "its own quite different course, readily discernible in the actual history and rooted in institutional structures that change very slowly, if at all" (44).
63 = Chomsky 1993.
64 Chomsky 1993: 3f.
65 The quotations marked by * are those from Adam Smith as quoted in Chomsky's own quotations.
66 Chomsky 1993: 26; my italics.

the *principal architects*", (d) "the *contempt for democracy and freedom*", and (e) "Yet another enduring theme is the *self-righteousness* in which plunder, slaughter, and oppression are clothed". (And here I'd like to ask the reader to go through this central Chomskyian passage slowly again and again!)

4 Therapy

Here you are: You know, at least theoretically, that there is a contradiction between the Principle of Universality U and the "self-righteous" WE-Exemption Postulate OP; and you have been told or maybe even had some experience occasionally by yourself, that all the diverse T-Industry-Institutions backed by our deeply entrenched Western hegemonic/economic interests are rationally doing their best to achieve just one thing in the end: to keep you ignorant about this U versus OP contradiction in all concrete (former, present and future) cases – and in most cases surely very success-fully so just by presenting the world from their/our own OP-Perspective.[67] What to do about your situation?

Chomsky's therapy consists in recommending to start a two-level Self-Diagnosis. Just look into the mirror! First, check your Background; and then: Check your own Face – your own Self. Or, in Chomsky's own words: First, look at the facts (C.1 again)! And second: Just start a simple thought-experiment! In other words: First, take reality into account! Then, just start to think (à la Kant) by yourself.

4.1 Reality Check

For every T-Act there is an agent and (an intended and/or factual) victim. The per-spective of the Operative Postulate OP is biased with respect to both. With respect to the agency this postulate focuses on THEM (thus exempting US); and vice versa with the victimhood: WE are the victims, THEY are the agents. OP is "a principle of [our] intellectual culture". It guarantees, "that although you investigate enemy crimes with laserlike intensity, you never look at your own".[68] "The crimes of ene-mies take place; our own do not".[69]

Thus, my translation of Chomsky's message is contrary to the deeply entrenched usual practice: Do oppose this very bias! I.e.: Do not only look at THEIR deeds, but

---

67 "A review of the scholarly literature on terror, the media, and intellectual journals will show that this usage [using "Terrorismus" as restricted by OP] is close to exceptionless, and that any departure from it elicits impressive tantrums. … If there is an exception, I haven't found it" (Chomsky 2003c: 323).

68 Chomsky 2002: 76.

69 Chomsky 2005a: 16.

also at OURs! And: Do not only look at THEIR victims (those on OUR side), but also at the victims of our OUR deeds (the victims on THEIR side). And in doing this, just check whether OUR deeds do fulfill the T-Act-defining conditions (of UT) or not. And if they do, just dare to call them so. That's very simple. Isn't it?

This Chomskyian anti-hypocrisy-advice sounds very easy. But it seems to be true that the easier an advice is, the harder it is to be followed. One has to practice – and to exercise again and again – following it in order to get used to doing it. Otherwise you will be damned to fail. Anyway, It would be of no use for you to just to read dozens of books of Chomsky's, but not to try to follow his simple advice by yourself. And if you have tried, you will, I am sure, necessarily have noticed how hard even such (easily to be advised) attempts normally turn out to be.

That is just the way conventions work in general and, as "Terrorism" is one of our worst human options, understandably much more so for the conceptually T-reductive OP-convention in particular. Just imagine – or just propose or even do it by yourself – what would happen if these kind of counter-conventional exercises would be installed somewhere in one of our educational institutions. I know it: You may lose your job. Or, even much more effective: You may not get one in the first place.

For the war-crime-aspect of OP, a concrete example of this honesty-test (as exemplified by Chomsky himself) has been already given. See the Nuremberg Trial case in 2.2 above. And surely the British "Terror"-Bombings of German cities were large scale T-Acts as well. And then, do not forget about the atomic bombing of Hiroshima and Nagasaki. Both kinds of bombings were clear T-acts – but hardly ever recognized by us with this label, of course; and both of them were certainly on a much larger scale than 9/11. Etc. etc.

p.s.: Did you really never come across the idea, that, if 'the other side' would be even approximately of the same sort as we are (and would have had the same technology as we have), that we would have stopped existing long ago?

4.2 Thought-Experiment

The second strategy of Chomsky to get us to switch our usual perspective from OP to U – or, to be more to the point, to test whether we really do want to sincerely adhere to the Principle of Universality that, by referring unendingly to "our values", we at least rhetorically pretend to revere – is to engage us in a simple thought experiment. It's the usual ceteris paribus role-switching test: How would you react if, what you have done to another person, s/he would do to you?[70] Or, and that is the one essential point to be examined by this test: If someone else would do the same to

---

70 I think it would be an interesting project to check, why so many things which we (think we) are acquainted with on the interpersonal level seem to be nearly lunatic to us when applied to

you as you have done to him, would you really be willing to apply the same standard to his/her deed as you had applied already to what you had done to her/him?

There is not very much imagination needed by this test. (Nowadays it is, as I have heard, even practiced in kindergarten.) The only thing that is needed is something that obviously seems to be much harder – and so is mostly missing: A minimal *willingness* to get this test really started. (As an adult, you have to start it by yourself!)

Just to take one example out of the thousands of others to be found in Chomsky's political volumes about the Western Wars of/on Terrorism. Obviously, the US sees itself as "unquestionably authorized to bomb another country to compel its leaders to turn over someone whom it suspects of involvement in a terrorist act".[71] Thus, "a fortiori, [by applying the Principle of Universality] Cuba, Nicaragua, and a host of others are entitled to bomb the US because there is no doubt of its involvement in very serious terrorist attacks against them. ... This conclusion surely follows if we accept the principle of universality".[72]

But: "The conclusion of course is utterly outrageous, and advocated by no one ... another instructive comment on the reigning intellectual and moral culture, with its principled [= OP-backed] rejection of unacceptable platitudes [as U]".[73] The Chomskyian verdict is crystal clear – and thus for most Western humans and many near friends of mine very painful. It is true, i.e., it is a fact, that this result of simply applying the Principle of Universality to this symmetrical (counterfactually imagined) case of Cuba's bombing the U.S. is "advocated by no one". So this is plain proof that *no one is successful in this test*. No one – not one – of US.

When being asked to undergo this test, the normal reaction, as experienced by myself in many public debates and academic seminars, is just to try to avoid the logic of this test. And that is most easily done by denying that the presupposed *ceteris paribus condition* is fulfilled. But by this type of reaction one would totally miss the very point of this test. Maybe in reality the situation *is* in fact a ceteris *non* paribus case. But as this second type of Chomskyian strategy is – contrary to the first one – meant to be not a *reality* check, but really a pure *thought* (or imagination) experiment, the very question of whether the real situation *is* a ceteris paribus or a ceteris non paribus one, does not matter at all. The only question to be answered is: *If* the situation – maybe counterfactually – *would* be ceteris paribus, then what? Would you then be ready to apply the same standard?

That's the test for honesty versus hypocrisy you will come across again in §§ 5.3.1 and 6.

---

the collective level. If you have some suggestions, just inform me, please. I myself presently am at a loss.
71 Chomsky 2005a: 27.
72 Chomsky 2005a: 27.
73 Ibid.

5 Comments & Questions

In order to simplify the above reconstruction as much as possible, I decided to keep part of my comments separate. They are primarily addressed to a philosophical audience; and so I would not mind, if some of the less sophisticated people might just prefer to skip this final paragraph and leave our joint anti-T-trip at § 6.

5.1 Who is US?

The central antidote to the Principle of Universality U is, as first explained already in 2.3 above, the prevailingly adapted principle OP,

OP   War Crimes / T-Acts cannot be Acts performed by US.

by means of which the installation of a corresponding "Terrorism" double standard will be guaranteed.

What is the possible reference of US? What has it been in Chomsky's papers?

5.1.1 WE-Collectives

Well, though it is true that in Chomsky's work this US-particle mostly, if not even nearly exclusively, refers to the United States (U.S.) and its respective friends and clients, it should be absolutely clear that for Chomsky this is a focus of choice, not one of conceptual necessity.

The discrimination of THEM (= not US) implied by OP is an attitude to be found in any WE-Group, at least in any human and humanoid one, and also in many other animal WE-Collectives beyond our own species. And the boundaries that determine who is one of US and who is not, even if having started with socio-biological backings, have become, in the course of our long cultural evolution, more and more flexible. Today, any discrimination in the wide sense (any conceptually possible distinction with respect to living beings) may turn into the basis of a discrimination in the narrow, evaluatively negative, sense. So, nowadays and from now onwards, we can never be sure that having overcome the traditional discriminations (like Parental Lines, Families, Tribes, Sexes, Nations, Religions, Wealth, Education etc.) there will not arise some new ones. Thus, the anti-discrimination-business seems to be a safe bet, I would say. Therefore, maybe the morally necessary struggle against double standards may also never come to an end.

Chomsky has made it explicitly clear, that OP, this strong negative discrimination source, has been used by many different collectives – especially when justifying their own counter-terroristic measures against the "Terrorists" from the OTHER's side. By the Nazis against the "Terrorists" engaged in the insurgency in the Ghetto of Warsaw, by the Russians against the "terrorist" rebels in Chechnya, ... , and by US against – well, just check the many parts of the world listed in the last paragraph of 3.2 above.

5.1.2 U.S.

Why does Chomsky's T-critique focus on T-Acts performed by the U.S. and its clients? First, we all have only "finite energies" rationally to be distributed "most efficaciously. ... A serious person will try to concentrate [its] efforts where they are most likely to ameliorate conditions". (Here you see some application for Chomsky's "truisms" C.2 and C.5.1.) And so "The emphasis should, in general, be close to home." And "This consideration is particularly relevant in a democracy." Thus, "for privileged Western intellectuals, the proper focus for their protest is at home"-[74] Second, remember his moral truisms (C.3) and (C.4) from 1.3.2 above:

C.3   People are primarily responsible for the likely consequences of their own action, or inaction.
C.4   Responsibilities mount with greater opportunity and more clearly anticipated effects.

And, third, because his country, the U.S.A. itself (and often in cooperation with its 'friends'), is quite obviously responsible for most of the large scale T-Acts in Human History.

The two responsibility-principles explain also why the early socialist Zionist Chomsky hoping for an Israelian/Palestinian Confederation turned into one of the sharpest critics of the T-Acts performed in the name of Israel. Neither is his first critique a manifestation of "Anti-Americanism", nor is his second critique a sign of "Anti-Zionism" or, as some propagandists would have it, even of "Antisemitism". To the contrary: In both cases his critical engagement is the result of a lifelong strong caring. "I strongly oppose discriminatory, repressive and aggressive politics of Israel, not 'although' I am 'of Jewish origin' ... , but in part *because I am Jewish*, and have been deeply concerned with these issues since childhood".[75]

For the U.S. as being part of the Western US, see 3.4 above.

---

74 Chomsky 1979a: 38.
75 Chomsky 2003c: 14; my italics.

5.2 Checking the Argument

Chomsky's argument as reconstructed in 1.4 above is the basis of all his statements about and of his verdicts on Terrorism, mainly on that of the U.S.A. Now, if one would like to deny the conclusion of this argument, one trivially would have to deny (á) the logical validity of that argument itself or (â) the truth of at least one of its premises and/or (ã) the adequacy of at least one of the presupposed definitions UV (or UT) or principles MV (MT) or U. So, in order to demonstrate that Chomsky's central verdict is correct, we would have to show that none of these objections could be sustained.

Now, going through these various verdict-denying objections step by step would be a project for a full-fledged dissertation. So, my subsequent comments are only very much restricted ones. I will focus on those few (ã)-aspects about which Chomsky and I may disagree.

5.2.1 The Universal T-Definition

We surely do not disagree with regards to the Universal Definition UT itself. But there may be some disagreement with respect to the need to become more specific about exactly what necessary conditions postulated in this definition are the ones responsible for backing the usual moral condemnation of T-Acts as expressed in MT (as a special case of MV, the Moral condemnation of Violence).[76]

The aspect most discussed in the philosophical T-Ethics (as a special branch of a more general Violence-Ethics) relates to the question of whether – and in what sense – the victims of the respective (Terrorist) Violence are what Just War Theory would call "innocent victims" (civilians, e.g.) or not. It is this "innocent" vs. "not innocent victims" distinction which, in my own writings, made me come to distinguish between T-Acts in the strong sense (innocent victims as intended or at least not sufficiently avoided targets) versus T-Acts in the weak (= not strong) sense. And my suggestion has been that – contrary to the Moral Evaluation Principles

MT   *T-Acts* are to be morally condemned.
MV   Acts of *Violence* are to be morally condemned.

---

76   I take it to be obvious that MV is too strong from the very start. Everybody who is in favor for maintaining some police-forces must deny it.

as presupposed by Chomsky – there may be situations where T-Acts in the latter sense may be in fact morally justified;[77] but, I suggest, never T-Acts in the strongest sense (innocent victims being the direct targets).[78]

Chomsky does not enter this discussion in detail. Though his sympathy is very openly with the resistance movements even when they are applying violence as used in weaker T-Acts.

But this moral reservation of Chomsky's is no fault in his moral judgment. All the large scale T-act-cases referred to in his reports about our own Western crimes against humanity are state-directed T-Acts of the most extreme sort. And so, for them the question of whether condemnation is in order or not just does not arise. But, as a professional (= more commissar-like) Moral Philosopher Chomsky could not have afforded this abstention. (This is one of the many reasons Chomsky has been always a bit envied by me. And from many others, I suppose.)

5.2.2 The Universality Principle

The Principle of Universality, as stated in

U   Any sound moral reasoning has to be universal, i.e., "we [have to] apply to ourselves the same standards we apply to others".

is, to repeat, the very hub – the most essential part – of Chomsky's thinking about Violence and Terrorism. It is *the* touchstone of all his moral verdicts.

For Chomsky, U is one of his "truisms". With regards to it he really is a "literalist",[79] i.e., someone who takes this principle seriously without exception (letter by letter, page by page, book by book, and interview by interview) – contrary to an "interpretationist" who, willingly or not, tends to decline from U by giving in to some special pleading, enabled by adhering to the 'principle' OP.

But what if there are some reasons for calling into question even this basic principle U itself? That is a question any critical philosopher cannot – and so also should not – avoid. But, though Chomsky is the most critical living intellectual I have met, he does avoid it. Or, to be fair: He has not (yet) discussed it, as far as I know. Though, as a former student of the philosopher Nelson Goodman, he surely will be very well acquainted with the kind of problem that is at stake here: the so called Goodman Induction Paradox.

---

77 For a specification of such a case see Meggle 2004b.
78 Yet see Steinhoff 2011. But notice that this is only mentioned here not to decide this question but just to make the point that in order to keep the ethical discussion open the question should not be treated as already settled from its very beginning. I.e., contrary to the handling of this question by the UN-Resolution mentioned in § 3.3.4 above.
79 Chomsky 2005a: 21.

Roughly: There are no both universal and precise criteria by means of which normal (universalizable) predicates (as *blue* or *green*) can be distinguished from non-normal (non-universalizable) ones (as *grue*, for example). Though these non-normal predicates could be defined in a universal logical form, they nevertheless imply a reference to exactly one individual only. So, by this Goodmanian Pathologisation, the very meaning of "Universalization" is being put into question. This would not be a problem for Chomsky's Principle of Universality, if the same problem would not arise – as noticed and discussed by my own former teacher Franz von Kutschera – for normative Universalizability as well.[80]

Now, although it would certainly not be good advice to stop any further explications, if the reason for stopping them would be to avoid getting into additional problems, I nevertheless think that the following position is roughly o.k., at least for all practical applications: "I see no reason for demanding a kind of precision in the formulation of moral principles which we know to be impossible in formulating the meanings of the bulk of the predicates in our language; indeed, since the moral principles would have to be formulated in terms of these same inexact predicates, the task would be Sisyphean"[81]. And so we can continue to make our "decision in the light of certain salient features of the situation as we see it, without bothering about how we would use the predicate, or apply the moral principle, in certain hypothetical, borderline, obscure or improbable cases".[82]

But, to conclude this digression, let's nevertheless just keep in mind that there is some need for a deeper and more general discussion about the question of how the perspectives of a critical thinker engaged also as a political activist on the one hand and of a critical 'pure' Analytical Philosopher on the other hand justifiably may diverge. And as Chomsky obviously is one of the best thinkers on both sides, his work should be given more philosophical scrutiny in this respect also.

5.3 What Sort of Ethics ?

Though Chomsky's thoughts about our T-crimes (Western or not-Western-ones) are not part of professional exercises in traditional moral philosophy, his verdicts *are* clearly moral ones. But "moral" in what sense?

---

80 For the essentials of these analogical problems see von Kutschera 1982, § 1.6, and Meggle 2003.
81 Hare 1972, 24.
82 Hare 1972: 25.

5.3.1 Meta-Ethics

My thesis answering this question has been kind of a big surprise even for myself: Chomsky's Ethics is Applied Meta-Ethics – just as propagated most convincingly by the leading Utilitarian of the 20th century: Richard M. Hare.[83] With one difference: For Hare , "Ethics … is the logical study of the language of morals";[84] and so, for him, Ethics proper could and should be identified with Applied Metaethics. But this extremely strong and much disputed position is nothing Chomsky is necessarily committed to also. For him (Chomsky), Ethics proper – whatever it may be – need not be reducible to "the logical study of the language of morals".

This is not the place to start a closer check of Chomsky's ideas about what the necessary presuppositions for a working Ethics would be like. But to back my thesis it may suffice to focus on the status that Chomsky's Universality Principle has been attributed to in and by his verdicts. "Those who cannot accept this principle should have the decency to keep silent about matters of right and wrong".[85] Hare, as we (Günther and me) had the pleasure to get to know him, would be surely extremely happy to see Chomsky to be (knowingly or – most probably, I guess – not) one of his most rigorous followers. For Hare, "all *moral* valuations are of type U"[86], and so anyone denying U would therewith testify that s/he just does not know what "moral" means.

Some of the other "truisms" of Chomsky's (see 1.3.2) would best be interpreted as metaethical principles as well – i.e. as principles which must hold for any workable Ethics irrespective of its substantial moral content. I do classify the principles (C.1) – (C.4) this way.

Serious denial of (C.1) – *Facts Matter!* – would be the end of any Ethics. If, what happens, would not matter, then there would be no point at all in thinking about what one ought to do in the world as it is[87] Ethical assessments do depend on facts. And that entails: Ethics should rely on facts, not on Fake Facts or Propaganda. (But notice that by this conclusion I do not even want to deny that Fake News themselves can and do matter very much.)

---

83 R. M. Hare was Günther's, the editor of this volume, and my own supervisor at Oxford in the academic year of 1970/71.
84 Hare 1952: v.
85 Chomsky 2004: 202.
86 Hare 1972: 21. Though "U" in this article of Hare's is referring to Gellner's "U-type evaluations". But that comes to the same thing as both Gellner and Hare take "the impartial judgements of a judge" (op. cit., 13) as the paradigm case of evaluations of that type. And this would be also the perspective of our Martian Judge (= Chomsky).
87 So, if I would be a fanatic anti-Human Terrorist from Beteigeuze craving to annihilate human life on earth, then I would know how to destroy any social life on that planet most effectively: Just by making the Earthlings to believe that there are no facts, i.e., no truths, but only Fake News. I.e., by making them deny Chomsky's C.1 "Facts Matter!"-Maxim.

And the consequentialist principle (C.2) – It is the likely consequences of our acts that counts – is (or is at least meant to be by Chomsky) a universal postulate for any sound Ethics as well. Next, the two principles (C.3) and (C.4) are just trying to spell out what the concept of "responsibility" is all about; they do not tell us, what our responsibilities – i.e., our obligations – are demanding from us in real life. With respect to each of these metaethical principles there is of course a big philosophical debate.

It would be a real challenge to try to axiomatize at least part of these Chomskyian metaethics (C.1 to C.4). Hopefully some students will take up this job at some point.

5.3.2 Radical Meta-Ethics

Chomsky's Principle of Universality – or, for that matter, Hare's Postulate of Universalizability – should not be mixed up with the Golden Rule to be found in nearly all religions. This rule – both in its positive and in its negative version ("Do to others as you would have them to do to you", Luke 6:31; versus "That which is hateful to you, do not do to your fellow. That is the whole Torah") – is, starting with what you do in fact want (or don't want) to be done to you (or not), already prescribing what you ought (or ought not) to do to your fellow. And such an Ethics of Reciprocity, if taken literally, would be already a sort of Substantial Ethics, rightly criticized for its counter-intuitive consequences. (The rule implies that for a masochist it is o.k. to make some fellow suffer; and it allows you to kiss a person just if you would be happy to get kissed by her/him.[88])

The Universality-Principle on the other hand, in contrast to the Golden Rule, is situated at a much more abstract level. It does not postulate some imagined reciprocity of wants or even deeds, but only one of standards. And as the unrestricted acceptance of the identity (entailing equality and reciprocity) of the standards applied is the criterion of one's sincerity, the Universality Principle, one might say, is just defining the rules of the moral game. The Golden Rule belongs to a substantial Ethics. The Universality-Principle is the central maxim of Chomsky's Meta-Ethics.

Another comparison that is worthy, I guess, of being explicated in some more detail by the generation to follow – could be Discourse-Ethics as developed by K.O. Apel and Jürgen Habermas. Hare's Meta-Ethics, Chomsky's U-Principle and the

---

88 It should be clear that these short remarks on the Golden Rule are much too rough and speedy. The rule is in need of much more serious discussion, of course. See Lenzen 2013, e.g., where there is the proposal to restrict this reciprocity to the era of legitimate interests. That would lead to a version of a neminem laedere Ethics as Chomsky is subscribing to by his "don't harm"-maxim C.1. The strongest enhancement for a neminem-laedere-Ethics I know of is that of Lenzen.

Discourse-Ethics of the Frankfurt School share some common ground. All three recur to semantics at their very start.

By the way, it is this very meta-ethical starting point that turns Chomsky's moral verdicts into such extremely (and even for many colleagues nearly unbearably) radical ones. The reason behind this should be clear: It's U's simplicity, stupid! All the special pleadings and self-exemptions based on the Operative Principle OP are classified by these U-based verdicts just and simply as cases of Foul Play. And what makes these verdicts more dangerous is the fact that there is not just one referee in the game, but possibly infinitely many. Any "teenager" (see my first quote of Chomsky's in the first paragraph of this paper), who understands the dictionary version of the term "Terrorism" and sees what's happening again and again, would be able to detect this foul play – and start to cry "Stop it".

Though I am a student of Dick Hare, I had never thought that such a tiny part of Meta-Ethics could have such a radical potential. And not only in Animal Ethics and in many other fields of Applied Ethics, where this potential has been best exploited by another student of Hare's: Peter Singer. But also in the world of "Terrorism". However, now it should be clear: For the T-Industry a small piece of seriously Applied Semantics, done without any recourse to violence, can become more dangerous than a series of deadly bombs. Or, at least, it could be. And it may be, if ... (See § 6.)

5.3.3 Substantial Moral Principles

On the other hand, the additional two principles, i.e.,

C.5   First, do no harm.
C.6   There is an obligation to help suffering people as best we can.

clearly have substantial import. The negative maxim C.5 is, as every substantial moral maxim, in need of further contextual relativization (specification); and it is much stronger than one might suppose *prima facie*. And maybe it is this maxim by means of which (together with the metaethical maxim C.3 that people are primarily responsible for the likely *consequences of their own action, or inaction*) one can explain why Chomsky, when being asked about what we can do against terrorism by ourselves, is giving always the same simple advice: "Just stop to participate in it" (passim). And don't forget that sticking to the operative usage of OP *is* already kind of taking part.

And as far as C.6 is concerned, this maxim is stronger than the usual Mutual Assistance Principle which suggests that there is an obligation to help only if assistance

(i) is needed and (ii) its *risks and costs* are *relatively low*. In this sense, Chomsky's moral stance is a supererogatory one. His life and works are proof of that.

"Moral principles are no axioms"[89]: This is both true and false. It is true for the last two substantial moral principles C.5 and C.6, but false for the other four metaethical principles. Their metaethical "truism" is an analytical one. And the Principle of Universality itself is evidently (treated by Chomsky as) an axiom as well. His most radical and explosive one, as noted in 5.3.2 above.

5.4 Everything in Vain?

There are not many positions about which I'd like to disagree with Chomsky. But his negative evaluation – or even rejection – of the so called Just War Theory (JWT, for short) would be one of them. (Notice, that in JWT the term "just" is used only as an abbreviation for "morally justifiable".) There are many variants of JWT – no surprise with regards to its long history and its backgrounds in different cultures and religions; and notice that by defending JWT one need not subscribe to all the various details of these various versions.

Michael Walzer's *Just and Unjust Wars* (1977)[90] is the *locus classicus* of modern JWT. And this work would be, I think, a good starting point for a debate about what parts of JWT are worthy of being kept and which are not. So, following this start, let's just forget about the traditional conditions of "the right intentions" and that the war "must be openly declared or otherwise authorized by a legitimate authority"[91] – but this last one, I'd say, not without some hesitation: Giving it up could weaken the obligation to undergo some lawful checks by the World Court or some other legitimate institutions – there are not many left.

It is in the § "Truisms and Just War Theory" in Chapter 8 of *Hegemony or Survival*[92], that Chomsky has formulated his most explicit critique of JWT – with reference to the U.S.-guided war on Afghanistan started nearly immediately after 9/11 (2001). This war had been declared by some extreme JWT-apologists as "a paradigm example of just war".[93] These apologists even included my favorite JWT-proponent Michael Walzer, a shameful fact not explicitly mentioned by Chomsky. And, unfortunately, Walzer was also one of the leading figures behind the "What we are fighting for" declaration from Oct 2001 favoring to wage war against Afghanistan.

---

89 This remark of Chomsky's is quoted (in his - Günther's - German translation) and, obviously approvingly, stressed by Grewendorf 2006: 226.
90 Walzer 1977.
91 Chomsky 2004: 203.
92 Chomsky 2004: 198 – 207.
93 Chomsky 2004: 199.

Now, I do subscribe to all of Chomsky's objections against both this war itself and its diverse alleged JWT-justifications. But I do not take his arguments to be stringent objections against the JWT-device itself. These alleged justifications did, so I would insist, constitute a clear *misuse* of JWT. But the misuse of an instrument is no proof for its general un-usefulness.

There were some JWT-adherents (like myself) who – correctly, I think – used this very JWT-device, in clear opposition to Walzer et. al., *expressis verbis* for arguing *against* this war.[94] We insisted on the fact that several necessary conditions for a just war were *not* fulfilled in this case, and that this war therefore could *not* be a case of just war, let alone a paradigm case. JWT cuts both ways; it can be used both as an instrument for justifying and for condemning wars. It's the facts that matter.

Thus, Chomsky is right in remarking that "the former director of Human Rights Watch Africa ... spoke for many others around the world when he ... [was] saying that I am unable to appreciate any moral, political of legal difference between the *jihad* by the United States against those it deems to be its enemies and the *jihad* by Islamic groups against those they deem to be their enemies".[95] However, this laudable speech, given in full accordance with the Universality-Principle, is no objection against JWT itself, only against its misapplication.

But maybe Chomsky's main argument against JWT is not its misapplication in the Afghanistan war or in some other cases, but the very fact that at present it would be "unthinkable"[96] that JWT is being really *universally* applied – i.e., applied not only against Islamic "aggressors ... with a moral orthodoxy divergent from the West" or against socialist "Cuba and Nicaragua", but also "applied to the US or Britain" as well. And in fact, it is unthinkable it could have been. But unthinkable only within "the prevailing moral and intellectual culture", i.e., the culture dominated by its prevailing – non-universalist, but self-exemptionist – maxim OP!

Hopefully, in the end, not all people living in our T-Culture are necessarily *un*able to think beyond this culture's narrow bounds. Even not so with regards to terrorism, including that produced by US. The "many others around the world" that the (above quoted) "former director of Human Rights Watch Africa" had spoken for, could and did obviously think a bit more freely. So, today's unthinkability does and should not exclude the chance of some more free thinking in the days to come. Otherwise, following the same argument of Chomsky's, today's corresponding unthinkability of his Universality Principle as being not only preached but also practiced universally, would turn out to be an argument against this principle itself as well. But then, with regards to the likely consequences (see the axiom C.2), all of the endless Chom-

---

94 Form my part, see Meggle 2003b.
95 Chomsky 2004: 201.
96 Chomsky 2004: 205.

skyian endeavors to stir up our closed human minds would be damned to be in vain.[97]

6 Your Choice

Summary: There are two ways for you to speak and think about Terrorism: either literally (following the simple universal definition UT) or non-literally (following the operative exemption device OP).[98]

UT *T-Acts are acts of (attempts of) achieving one's ends by means of violence-in-duced strong intimidation.*

OP *T-Acts cannot be Acts performed by US.*

It is only UT which is in accordance with the Principle of Universality

U *Any sound moral reasoning has to be universal, i.e., "we [have to] apply to ourselves the same standards we apply to others".*

Abiding by this Universality Principle is the criterion deciding about honesty or hypocrisy. So, in order to honestly think and talk about Terrorism, your words must follow UT.

Now, what side are you on? "That's your Choice!"[99]

There is a gigantic "Terrorism"-Industry that has been active for some decades, the main job of which is just to slur, obliterate and openly deny these simple logical

---

97 I am not sure whether this attempt of mine to refute Chomsky's JWT-rejection is missing some point of his argument. If so, then again I'd like to ask for some little help from my friends, Noam himself included. But if not, how then to combine his rejection with his analysis that "universality" "is the most elementary principle of just war theory" (Chomsky 2004)?
By the way, I'd like to take this quotation to be an additional argument for my classification of the Universality Principle as a metaethical axiom (see 5.3.1 above). Up to now I know of no single version of JWT in which this principle is explicitly referred to. So I take it that Chomsky is just postulating that any sound use of JWT would have to follow his Universality axiom. And with respect to this postulate I would agree.
As to my possible misunderstanding of Chomsky's JWT-rejection: Maybe, I fell victim to missing some irony in Chomsky's argument. Sometimes, when speaking about some state of affairs being "unthinkable", what he (ironically) means is only "unthinkable from the prevailing (narrow) point of view, but very much thinkable from the perspective of a really open mind". And often even his use of "universal principle" is impregnated by the same high-level irony. So, let me advise you that, when reading Chomsky, you should translate his Unthinkability and Universality into either "real" or "only alleged Unthinkability / Universality", with only the former being "really universal itself".

98 Notice that there is a good deal of variance in the denominations of this distinction in Chomsky's texts. The literal (dictionary) usage of "Terrorism" (and other contested concepts) is connected with truth and seriousness, the non-literal (operative, propagandist, doctrinal, technical, interpretationist) usage with open or hidden deceit.

99 Chomsky 1992: 355.

connections. The Terrorism-Ideology constructed by this Corporate-Military-State-Media-Academic Complex is trying to entangle us "in webs of endless deceit, often self-deceit" (First sentence of the Introduction of *Turning The Tide*[100]=). "But with a little honest effort, it is possible to extricate ourselves from them".[101]

One tenet of Operative Semantics as developed in this T-Industry claims that with UT alone there is no possible way for clear thinking about Terrorism (see 3.3.2). This is simply false. Counterexample: NOAM CHOMSKY.[102]

Bibliography

Notice that in the Literature-list below all the texts containing special longer T-related parts are marked at the end of the respective entries by references to these parts within square brackets.

By the way, many of Chomsky's publications are available also in the net. See http://chomsky.info and http://ChomskyList.com. But best, I think, you meet him 'personally': by means of some of his innumerable interviews, most of them long monologs of a beautiful mind.

Barsky, Robert F., 1997: Noam Chomsky. A Life of Dissent, Toronto, ECW Press.
Baumann, Marcel, 2013: Schlechthin Böse? Tötungslogik und moralische Legitimität von Terrorismus. Wiesbaden, Springer.
Chomsky, Noam,

1969:   At War with Asia. London, Fontana / Collins.
1979a: & *Herman*, Edward: The Washington Connection and Third World Fascism. The Political Economy of Human Rights – Volume . Nottingham, Spokesman.
1979b: & *Herman*, Edward: After the Cataclysm. Postwar Indochina and the Reconstruction of Imperial Ideology. The Political Economy of Human Rights – Volume II. Boston, South End Press; new edition: Haymarket Books, 2014.
1985:   Turning the Tide. US Intervention in Central America and the Struggle for Peace. Boston, Pluto Press. [1.7: The Planning of State Terror. 3.4: Contemporary State Terrorism: The System Established. 3.5.6: Reaction at Home:Succcessful Terror and its Rewards.]
1988a: The Culture of Terrorism. London, Pluto Press.
1988:   & *Herman*, Edward: Manufacturing Consen. Toronto, Pantheon, [2]1994.

---

100 Chomsky 1985: 1.
101 Ibid, same sentence.
102 Though, when referring to himself, the words "with a little honest effort" would be just another typical Chomskyian self-understatement. There is nothing on Earth which could compete with his "unthinkably" great efforts.

1991/92:	Deterring Democracy. London, Verso / Vintage.
1992:	Chronicles of Dissent. Interviews with David Barsamian. Monroe/Maine, Common Courage Press. [Terrorism: The Politics of Language, 47-60.]
1993:	Year 501. The Conquest Continues. New Edition: London, Pluto Press, 2015.
1994:	World Orders, Old and New. London, Pluto Press.
1999a:	The New Military Humanism. Lessons from Kosovo. London, Pluto Press.
1999b:	Sprache und Politik. Ed. by Schiffmann, Michael, Berlin / Bodenheim, Philo.
1999c:	Profit over People. Neoliberalism and Global Order. New York, Seven Stories Press.
2001a:	9-11. New York, Seven Stories Press.
2001b:	Propaganda and the Public Mind. Interviews by David Barsamian. London, Pluto Press.
2002a:	Media Control. The Spectacular Achievements of Propaganda. New York, Seven Stories Press, ^{2}2002.
2002b:	Pirates and Emperors, Old and New. International Terrorism in the Real World. New Edition: London, Pluto Press. [2: Middle East Terrorism and the American Ideological System. 5: International Terrorism: Image and Reality=IT.]
2002c:	What Uncle Sam Really Wants. Tuscon, Odonian Press, ^{13}2002.
2003a:	Necessary Illusions. Thought Control in Democratic Societies. CBC Massey Lectures, New Edition: Anansi Press. [Appendix V.3: "The Evil Scourge of Terrorism\".]
2003b:	Understanding Power. The Indispensable Chomsky. Ed. By Mitchell, Peter/ Schoeffel, John, Vintage, 2003. [1: 4-6:The U.S.Network of Terrorist Mercenary States. 3: 77-84: Libyan and American Terrorism. 5: 144-145: Supporting Terrorism.]
2003c:	Radical Priorities. *Ed.* by Otero, C. P.; expanded 3rd ed., Oakland, AK Press, ^{3}2003.
2003d:	Commentary: Moral Truisms, Empirical Evidence, and Foreign Policy. In: Review of International Studies, 29, 605 – 620.
2004:	Hegemony or Survival. America's Quest for Global Dominance, New York, Metropolitan Books, (Penguin Books, 2004). [8. Terrorism and Justice:Some Useful Truisms.=TJ.]
2005a:	Simple Truths, Hard Problems: Some thoughts on terror, justice, and selfdefence. In: Philosophy, 80, 5 – 28.
2005b:	Imperial Ambitions. Conversations on the Post-9/11 World. Interviews with David Barsamian, New York, Metropolitan Books.
2006:	Failed States. The Abuse of Power and the Assault on Democracy. London, Metropolitan Books.
2007a:	Interventions. San Francisco, Open Media Series. [p.1-5: Lessons Unlearned. 35-39: 9/11 and the "Age of Terror". 67-71: The United States; Terrorist Sanctuary. 125-128: Dr. Strangelove Meets the Age of Terror. 137-140: The Legacy of Hiroshima and the Present Terror. 141-145: 9/11 and the Doctrine of Good Intentions.]
2007b:	& *Achcar*, Gilbert: Perilous Power. The Middle East & U.S. Foreign Policy. Dialogues on Terror, Democracy, War, and Justice. Edited by Shalom, Stephen R., Boulder & London, Paradigm Publishers. [1: Terrorism and Conspiracies.]

2010:   Hopes and Prospects. Chicago, Haymarket Books.

2016:   Who Rules the World? New York, Metropolitan Books. [2: Terrorists Wanted the World Over. 17: The US is a Leading Terrorist State.]

2017:   & *Vltcheck*, Andre: On Western Terrorism. From Hiroshima to Drone Warfare. New Edition, London, Pluto Press.

2020:   Internationalism or Extinction. Ed. by Derber, Derber et. al., New York / London, Routledge.

Fromkin, David, 1975: The Strategy of Terrorism. In: Foreign Affairs, 53:4, 683 – 698.

Grewendorf, Günther, 1995: Sprache als Organ – Sprache als Lebensform. Frankfurt, Suhrkamp.

Grewendorf, Günther, 2006: Noam Chomsky. München, Beck.

Hare, Richard M., 1952: The Language of Morals. Oxford, Clarendon Press.

Hare, Richard M., 1972: Universalisability. In: Hare, R. M.: Essays on the Moral Concepts, London, Macmillan, Chapter 2, 13 – 28.

Herman, Edward, 1982: The Real Terror Network. Terrorism in Fact and Propaganda. Boston, South End Press.

Hermann, Edward/*O'Sullivan*, Garry, 1990: The "Terrorism" Industry, The Experts and the Institutions that Shape our View of Terror.

Lenzen, Wolfgang, 2013: Sex, Leben, Tod und Gewalt. Eine Einführung in die Angewandte Ethik / Bioethik. Berlin, LIT.

Kutschera, Franz von, 1982: Grundlagen der Ethik. Berlin / New York, de Gruyter.

Macfarquhar, Larissa/*Haupt*, Michael, 2003: Wer ist Noam Chomsky? Hamburg, Europa.

Malik, Omar, 2001: Enough of the Definition of Terrorism, London, Royal Institute for International Affairs – Chatham House.

Meggle, Georg, 2003a: The Universalizability Problem in Moral Philosophy. In: Egidi, Rosaria et. al. (Eds.), Normativita, Fatti, Valori. Roma, Quodlibet, 71 – 84.

Meggle, Georg, 2003b: Is this War Good? An Ethical Commentary. In: Jokic, Aleksander (Ed.): Lessons of Kosovo. The Dangers of Humanitarian Intervention, Broadview Press, 17 – 30.

Meggle, Georg, 2004a: Gerechte Kriege – Die Philosophie und die Ideologie. In: Giesen, Klaus-Gerd (Ed.): Ideologien in der Weltpolitik, Wiesbaden, Verlag für Sozialwissenschaften, 129 – 146.

Meggle, Georg, 2004b: Gerechter Terror. In: Der blaue Reiter. Journal für Philosophie 19 (1/2004), 27- 31.

Meggle, Georg (Ed.), 2005a: Ethics of Terrorism & Counterterrorism. Frankfurt, Ontos.

Meggle, Georg, 2005b: Terror & Counter-Terror: Initial Ethical Reflections. In: Meggle 2005a: 161 – 175.

Meggle, Georg, 2005c: Is This War [in Kosovo] Good? An Ethical Commentar., in: May, Larry et. al. (Eds.): The Morality of War: Classical and Contemporary Readings. New Jersey, Prentice Hall, 2005, 385 – 396.

Meggle, Georg, 2006: What Is Terrorism? In: Babic, Jovan (Ed.):Terrorism: Moral, Legal, and Political Issues. Filozofski Godisnjak 19, Beograd, 11-24.

Meggle, Georg, 2010: Handlungstheoretische Semantik, Berlin/New York, de Gruyter.

Meggle, Georg, 2020: Zum "Terrorismus " im Sicherheitsrat. In: Bublitz, Jan et. al. (Eds.), Recht – Philosophie – Literatur. Festschrift für Reinhard Merkel zum 70. Geburtstag. Berlin, Duncker & Humblot, 1453 – 1459.

Meßelken, Daniel, 2012: Gerechte Gewalt? Zum Begriff interpersonaler Gewalt und ihrer moralischen Bewertung. Paderborn, Mentis.

Primoratz, Igor, 1990: What is Terrorism? In: Journal of Applied Philosophy, 7.

Talbott, Strobe & *Chanda*, Nayan (eds.), 2002, The Age of Terror. New York, Basic Books.

Taylor, Telfort, 1970: Nuremberg and Vietnam: an American Tragedy. Times Book.

Walzer, Michael, 1977: Just and Unjust Wars. New York, Basic Books.

Schmid, Alex P., 1983: Political Terrorism. A Research Guide to Concepts, Theories, Data Bases and Literature. Amsterdam.

Schmitt, Carl, 1922: Political Theology. Four Chapters on the Concept of Sovereignty (1922), trans. by G. Schwab, Chicago, University of Chicago Press, 2005.

Singer, Peter, 1979: Practical Ethics. Cambridge University Press. [3]2011.

Steinhoff, Uwe, 2011: Zur Ethik des Krieges und des Terrorismus. Stuttgart, Kohlhammer.

Robert F. Barsky

The Chomsky Approach: Considering the Limits on State Action

I'm writing this essay inside of my home in Atlanta, a city we moved to from Ottawa, Canada a few weeks ago. Outside is the sound of helicopters, some of which might be on patrol in the skies above the protests against police brutality (including the killing of Rayshard Brooks, nearby), while others shuttle urgent care cases of covid-19 to the Emory University Hospital. Most residents on my street sit in their homes, or on their porches or patios, conflicted about whether to partake in the marches, sit-ins, and protests. Should they take the risk involved with being in a crowd during a pandemic, in order to voice their support for #blacklives matter and in opposition to police violence? Should they stay inside, and write a cheque to help support victims of police brutality that is, unsurprisingly, happening around the country as people protest against – police brutality? Or should they put their resources into defeating the current administration, and therefore focus on canvassing for votes in favor of the Democratic Party? Hundreds of thousands of people have sought answers to questions like these from a reliable voice of the anarchist left, a voice that has been reckoning with some of the most challenging questions that humans can formulate for much of his long and productive lifetime: the 92-year-old Noam Chomsky. For the concept of the State these issues are crucial, because they guide us on the one hand into an examination of what constitutes state power, and on the other, to inquire about legitimate and illegitimate action when authorities abuse of that power.

If the question is important, and topical, Chomsky can be looked to for valuable but oft-overlooked information and, moreover, a perspective rooted in attitudes that have been honed in regards to ideas and actions articulated by philosophers, scientists, linguists, historians and writers from as far back as the written record provides. Unlike most commentators, however, Chomsky doesn't provide the kinds of guidance that people expect; to the contrary, he insists upon the power of inquiry, questioning, and, less obviously for many readers, he makes constant implicit reference to works from a canon as vast and comprehensive as the questions themselves. The result is a complex approach to contemporary questions that points not only to the issues in question at a particular moment, but also gesture towards longer-term objectives that are far more radical than simply reforming the current system. You should vote, he says, but only "against" horrible candidates, rather than "for" (say) the Democratic candidate, because we won't find anyone who upholds a platform that is compatible with the kinds of ideals Chomsky espouses in his work. And at the end of the day, despite the obvious differences between candidates like Trump and Biden, the two Parties they represent are in fact almost indistinguishable in regards to crucial issues relating to corporate power, or the contemporary distribution of wealth. You should participate in popular defiance and dissent, but only if its non-violent, because otherwise you play right into the hands of those you are challenging. You should support progressive causes, but you need also to be aware of arguments on all sides, and embrace those that are true rather than just to your liking. And most importantly, you should seek out instruments of oppression, arbitrary authority, and illegitimate prestige, recognizing that even the so-called 'experts' who might seem to be in accord with your views may be espousing ideas that aren't compatible with the long-term survival of the human species.

Behind Chomsky's views is another massive corpus of work, from his own pen and from diverse sources connected to language studies, philosophy, political theory, history, anthropology, and cognitive studies, connected, in short, to whichever field helps to shed light on the many complex and important questions with which he engages. It's not unusual for well-known social commentators to have connections to a variety of disciplines, but the level of Chomsky's engagement in the sciences, including, for example, cognitive sciences, linguistics, the history of science, is extraordinary. From Chomsky's perspective, if we want to understand how people can or should live in society, we need to know something about the history of social groupings, the ways that power has evolved in particular settings, the multitude of efforts that have been made to shift peoples' attitudes, the way that we learn and acquire information, and the many different pedagogical experiments that have been tested over time. So of course, confronting racism and its deleterious effects is an urgent policy matter that can be addressed by reconsidering policing, challenging contemporary laws relating to issues of race, and advocating for equality and human rights irrespective of race or country of origin; but at a deeper level, the current challenges facing all of us are connected to profound and perhaps unanswerable questions about human motivation, deviance, and human nature. To engage with the broad corpus of Chomsky's work is to encounter topical questions posed by diverse populations in search of some enlightenment and guidance, alongside profound questions that date back to the very origin of our species. In this chapter, I'll set out some perspectives to Chomsky approach, and link it to the foundational ideas and motivations that underwrite both his scientific and his political work, ideas that are connected to creativity, questioning, and radical query.

This is a crucial moment to be considering this approach, because many activists are describing this moment in American history as dramatic, perhaps even revolutionary. Is it? On what grounds could we make these claims? Is there an opening to advance a truly radical reform of political and social institutions in the US? If so, do we need to assemble a vanguard of brilliant social theorists to chart a new approach to the State? Or should we let the marketplace of ideas take the lead, and hope for broad-ranging reforms that bubble up from the crowds of people risking their and others' health to challenge the status quo? These are all ginormous questions, but Chomsky and others are providing some inkling as to ways forward, and we will overview their public statements briefly in regards to this particular moment in time. We will then turn to two characteristics of Chomsky's approach: his devotion to profound and radical questioning, and his interest in a completely different approach to society, which challenges the vast array of arbitrary authority in the current world and favors ways of instead promoting creative inquiry.

To think about Chomsky's interest in questions and questioning, I'll introduce the work of a contemporary philosopher named Michel Meyer, the architect of work on "le questionnement" (the history of questioning in philosophy) and "la problématologie" (a means whereby questions are posed but are always maintained, rather than falling-away in the face of assertions and answers). Meyer is working entirely from the perspective of philosophical inquiry, but many of his insights help us to connect Chomsky's insistence on radical questioning to a vast tradition of work that has undermined inquiry in favor of authoritative declarations and assertions. To think about how different Chomsky's long-term objectives are from most social commentators, we'll look to some of his recent statements about the nature of a society that would favor creative engagement with crucial concerns, statements that connect his work to a wide array of thinkers who have sought to consider how to reconcile universal rights with individuals' abilities to think and act creatively in appropriately rich and diverse anti-authoritarian settings.

Is this Moment Different from Previous ones?

Whatever its long-term implications, the current uprisings have galvanized some communities of resistance, and we've heard some surprisingly uplifting statements from activists, scholars, and historians, many of whom have deep familiarity and direct engagement with the issues at hand. A short foray into their views is instructive, and it helps set the stage for an investigation into the distinctiveness of Chomsky's Approach. We can begin with Ta-Nehisi Coates, an American journalist and author who has written widely on political, cultural and social issues affecting African Americans. His approach is historically-informed, and surprisingly optimistic: "The idea that black folks in their struggle against the way the law is enforced in their neighborhoods would resonate with white folks in Des Moines, Iowa, in Salt Lake City, in Berlin, in London — that was unfathomable to him in '68, when it was mostly black folks in their own communities registering their great anger and great pain. I don't want to overstate this, but there are significant swaths of people and communities that are not black, that to some extent have some perception of what that pain and that suffering is. I think that's different."[1] There is something to this view, apparent in predominantly White neighborhoods in which people proudly brandish placards and banners in support of #blacklivesmatter, and it's very clear from reports emerging out of the marches that there is significant White support for this movement. I might add that on their corporate banners and websites, companies like Uber[2], Amazon[3], Google, Apple[4], Walmart[5], McDonalds[6] and Starbucks have (hypocritically,[7] or with very vague commitments[8]) voiced public support for the movement. These outward signs of support may not translate into true commitment, and they may in some cases be rather cynical attempts to ward off criticism, or to ensure that corporations don't lose market share to those in favor of current reforms.

Indeed, it's safe to say that the stakes for White people who claim to be engaged with introspection about their own racism are rather low, relative to the inequalities and violence to which the movement refers. But even if corporations are taking stances guaranteed to assure their market dominance, and protection against looting or profiling, it's nonetheless refreshing to hear privileged people considering the backs of those upon whom their own successes have been erected. Or is it? And is it enough? It's always instructive in such issues to read the works of Cornel West, who takes a more radical stance, challenges the norms deemed to be acceptable in our society, and advocates on behalf of more significant social reforms: "The fundamental question at this moment is: can this failed social experiment be reformed? The political duopoly of an escalating neofascist Donald Trump-led Republican party and a fatigued Joe Biden-led neoliberal Democratic party – in no way equivalent, yet both beholden to Wall Street and the Pentagon – are symptoms of a decadent leadership class."[9] To make his assessment, West always looks to history, and in this case bemoans the demise of those institutions to which reformers would have turned, and supported, in moments of upheaval, including unions: "The weakness of the labor

---

1   https://www.vox.com/2020/6/5/21279530/ta-nehisi-coates-ezra-klein-show-george-floyd-police
    -brutality-trump-biden.
2   https://www.gartner.com/en/marketing/insights/daily-insights/uber-delivers-on-black-lives-matt
    er.
3   https://www.businessinsider.com/amazon-tweeted-a-statement-in-support-of-george-floyd-prote
    stors-2020-5.
4   https://www.washingtonpost.com/technology/2020/06/10/big-tech-black-lives-matter/.
5   https://corporate.walmart.com/equity.
6   https://musebycl.io/diversity-inclusion/mcdonalds-names-7-victims-racial-violence-black-lives-
    matter-ads.
7   https://www.theguardian.com/technology/2020/jun/09/amazon-black-lives-matter-police-ring-je
    ff-bezos.
8   https://www.eater.com/2020/6/12/21288501/mcdonalds-starbucks-respond-to-black-lives-matter
    -george-floyd-protests; https://www.vogue.com/article/starbucks-black-lives-matter-t-shirt.
9   https://www.theguardian.com/commentisfree/2020/jun/01/george-floyd-protests-cornel-west-
    american-democracy

movement and the present difficulty of the radical left to unite around a nonviolent revolutionary project of democratic sharing and redistribution of power, wealth and respect are signs of a society unable to regenerate the best of its past and present. Any society that refuses to eliminate or attenuate dilapidated housing, decrepit school systems, mass incarceration, massive unemployment and underemployment, inadequate healthcare and its violations of rights and liberties is undesirable and unsustainable." Even so, West is surprisingly upbeat, invoking the approach and tenor of the protests, and referring, like Coates, to the broad-ranging support from historically disengaged sectors: "Yet the magnificent moral courage and spiritual sensitivity of the multiracial response to the police killing of George Floyd that now spills over into a political resistance to the legalized looting of Wall Street greed, the plundering of the planet and the degradation of women and LGBTQ+ peoples means we are still fighting regardless of the odds. If radical democracy dies in America, let it be said of us that we gave our all-and-all as the boots of American fascism tried to crush our necks."[10]

Is there grounds for such optimism? Did "we" indeed give it our all? And if so, who exactly was involved in these efforts? And how do these efforts relate to historical uprisings? West's assessment is radical, in that he implicitly advocates for a society that challenges the assumptions of neoliberalism and capitalism. He is the honorary chair of the Democratic Socialists of America, which he has described as "the first multiracial, socialist organization close enough to my politics that I could join." Chomsky has never joined a particular party, one way in which he differs from most social commentators, and neither does he claim affiliation to any organized religion or faith, despite his strong Jewish roots. So, while many of West's critiques resonate with Chomsky's, their ultimate aims and objectives remain distinct one from the other.

In regards to the distinctiveness of the current protests, it's instructive to read the work of Heather Ann Thompson, a scholar of 1960s and 1970s protest movements, because she looks to past uprisings in order to ground her observations about current events:

> So, not only is the wanton murder of black men by racist whites similar to what has happened before in history, but so is today's collective uprising. It's a mix of protest in terms of carrying signs and slogans, but also rage and tears and lashing out. And, like in the 1960s, there has been some looting, because the glaring injustice of racial inequality is time and again accompanied by the injustice of economic inequality. That is why in these moments people also lash out at the rich and property. So in that sense we've been here before.[11]

---

10 https://www.theguardian.com/commentisfree/2020/jun/01/george-floyd-protests-cornel-west-american-democracy.
11 https://www.vox.com/identities/2020/6/2/21277253/george-floyd-protest-1960s-civil-rights.

Cornel West, like many others who look back to history for some guidance on present movements, has insisted upon the originality of this movement. This makes sense, given the widespread participation of multiple constituencies, the role of the internet as an organizing tool, and the real challenges that have been made to such ensconced institutions as police departments. On this point, Thompson is less optimistic than most: "There's much that's different too though, and it's all pretty scary. We have a president who has no regard for the First Amendment, the press, for calming dissent, for doing concrete things that could make this a better situation rather than worse. We don't know our way forward from this moment. In the past there were at least calmer heads at the top trying to figure out what to do to bring peace. Some people wanted more cops, but others were saying we actually need to make substantive changes and fix what got us into this mess."[12] The question of a "way forward" is crucial, and we'll take a look at it later on in regards to Chomsky's longstanding engagement with what is known as the "New Left", and his own abhorrence for those (such as intellectuals and politicians) who would wish to use their prestige or authority in order to claim the role of "vanguard" in the course of popular uprisings. He warns us against self-professed "experts" who would seek to take control over a movement, and he has generally been in favor of popular uprisings. But here too, there are some important distinctions. In regards to the current protests, he told the *Guardian* that: "Marches are a tactic. Not much has emerged about strategy, or even specific articulated goals, beyond major reform of police practices and responsibilities." So, he sees a need for greater strategic direction, and wonders whether popular movements will emerge "that seek to deal with the brutal legacy of 400 years of vicious racism, that extends far beyond police violence". This is an important component of the Chomsky approach, a forward-looking perspective that contemplates a world free of the power structures that inevitably lead to exclusion and repression, rather than a focus upon short-term promises or achievements.

Imagining such a "good society" is a tall task, since it requires addressing the many connected issues that define the "mess" to which Thompson refers in her assessment of the current movement in regards to history. One of the most powerful figures from historical and cultural perspectives, Henry Louis Gates, provides a sense of the many layers involved with any such effort: "Racism has been part of America's cultural DNA since before the ink dried on the Constitution. Dominant in some and recessive in others, it's a gene that has mutated over time yet remains part of the inheritance weighing us down, one generation to the next. The damage it has done is systemic and goes all the way down to the cellular level." Efforts to recognize, treat, or even eradicate this "gene" go back to the earliest days of the US, and it's most likely in the micro-resistance that people have heroically confronted their

---

12   ibid.

oppressors, as Gates himself has made so clear in his assiduous work in the archives of Black history in America. Reactions against the advances have been swift, powerful, and have had horrendous consequences: "As a country, we've been here before, first following the collapse of Reconstruction and the rise of Jim Crow, and then again in a less well-known series of events that unfolded in 1919. Following the Influenza Epidemic of 1918, and the return of black soldiers from World War I, and at the apex of the legitimization of Jim Crow, white vigilantes engaged in an appalling series of lynchings of innocent black victims, so brutal that it was soon dubbed 'the red summer' of 1919." Anyone familiar with Chomsky's work knows that in spite of how hideous is the current juncture in terms of a progressive agenda, we are still light years' ahead of where we were, even just a few decades ago. Gates also refers to "great progress" in race relations, and then emphasizes the work that remains: "Those of us who love freedom and justice and believe in an America that stands for racial equality and community across the color line must join arms and fight white supremacy wherever and however it rears its heinous head."[13] In my own opinion, part of this great progress is due to literary work, notably that which Gates himself has spearheaded, and the wide diffusion of novels by the likes of James Baldwin, Richard Wright, Alice Walker, or Toni Morrison, who provide narratives that allow readers to enter the very bodies of characters wrought be racism and oppression.

As we contemplate the great progress that has been made through activist efforts, we turn to the words of Angela Davis, who has spent much of her life fighting against white supremacy, and for social justice. Surprisingly, hers is one of the most optimistic voices in the fray: "This is an extraordinary moment which has brought together a whole number of issues," she says, although it could just be a reckoning related to the pandemic, rather than a newfound thirst for social justice in America. "I don't know whether it would have unfolded as it did if not for the terrible COVID-19 pandemic, which gave us the opportunity to collectively witness one of the most brutal examples of state violence." This is an interesting comment, since it suggests that not only is there a pent-up frustration and anger, but there's also a "posture of self-criticism" assumed by people who are trapped in their homes, and thus compelled by inactivity to stare at such images as the murder of George Floyd. There's nothing new about the violence, or the desire of Black people to liberate themselves from the yoke of racism, but there's now a captive audience who is being forced to examine itself and others with respect to blaring images of police repression: "For hundreds of years, Black people have passed down this collective yearning for freedom from one generation to the next," she says. "We are doing now what should have been done in the aftermath of slavery."[14]

---

13   https://www.gwinnettdailypost.com/opinion/columnists/thomas-racism-rioting-and-redemption/article_26cbd6e6-4c2f-5427-a6af-a215122592ac.html.
14   https://www.wbur.org/hereandnow/2020/06/19/angela-davis-protests-anti-racism.

Davis follows Cornell West by connecting racism and oppression to the economic organization of society, in part by invoking the term "racial capitalism". She employs this term in order to "encourage people to think about the ways in which capitalism and racism are interlinked," an idea that resonates through many observers to the current situation, including Chomsky. "There is no capitalism without racism," and institutions such as Police departments and the prison industrial complex are "the most dramatic expression of structural racism", a point she has been making since the 1970s, when such efforts led to her and others being "treated as if we were absolutely out of our minds." It's only with such efforts that we can "reimagine the meaning of public safety" and "think about funding agencies and individuals and organizations that will help address issues of health — physical health, mental health." Davis's insistence upon systemic and systematic oppression, and her belief in the power of non-violent resistance, tie her approach to what Chomsky advocates, as we'll see: "I think that bringing people together in movements, creating solidarity [means] representing ourselves not primarily as individuals, but as members of communities of struggle."[15]

Chomsky's Perspective

Invoking one of Chomsky's own mantras, Angela Davis has noted in her remarks that "activists who are truly committed to changing the world should recognize that the work that we often do that receives no public recognition can eventually matter."[16] Chomsky wholeheartedly agrees, and focuses a considerable portion of his work on the unsung heroes of progressive politics, whose names will never make it into history books. For him, this great work happens in realms that are quite distinct from contemporary policy debates. It's certainly worthy of our attention that a candidate like Bernie Sanders has political convictions that are grounded in socialism, New Deal policies, or in great efforts undertaken by the labor movement. But most of what matters outstrips what is being discussed in today's news reports, so Chomsky's approach goes beyond the headlines and into the hard work of sustained activism. Angela Davis suggests that activists' efforts are especially important under Trump because he "is totally ignorant of U.S. history." In this respect, Davis's views are quite different from those expressed by Chomsky, who sees so-called missteps in regards to broader systems of institutional power. Unlike the unimaginably callous, hateful, spiteful, self-centered moron that many people see when they watch Trump carry on publicly, Chomsky also sees a canny politician, who knows exactly how to rally his own base. He traces in Trump's actions, even those which are supposedly

---

15 Ibid.
16 Ibid.

ill-conceived, the connection between individuals and the vast power apparatus they represent. Rational people imagine that Trump's scheduling of a rally on Juneteenth (the June 19 celebration of the end of slavery in Texas) in Tulsa, Oklahoma, was a gross oversight. On the contrary, Chomsky would suggest. Trump's choice of speaking to his followers on the site of one of the worst acts of racist violence against Black people in American history was calculated to appease what he (rightly) perceives to be a fundamentally racist voting base. That Trump moved the rally to the next day wasn't a victory for activism, as Davis described it, but rather further evidence of Trump's use of racism, violence and hatred, for his re-election.

And yet, there seems amidst all of the gloom and doom to be reasons for real optimism. Angela Davis concludes her own remarks by saying that she is "just so happy that I have lived long enough to witness this moment. And I think that I see myself as witnessing this moment for all of those who lost their lives in the struggle over the decades."[17] Even Chomsky joins this chorus of sanguinity. "The popular reaction to the gruesome Floyd murder has been astonishing in its national scope, fervent commitment and interracial solidarity. The malignancy that infects the White House has been exposed in all its ugliness." Where will all this lead? Will Chomsky be celebrating in November, if the GOP is driven from its madcap quest to undermine progressive social movements, to impose out-of-step judicial appointees, and drive the world into environmental catastrophe? Could Biden, alongside his long-awaited vice-president, and the Democratic Party, help promote the kinds of values that Chomsky supports? Hardly. On the election, Chomsky's views have deep roots:

> There is a left perspective on this, which has apparently been long forgotten: you don't vote for people, you vote against people. If you're a left activist, politics doesn't mean concentrating laser lights on elections. Elections are an event, they take place, they should take 15 minutes of your time, away from real politics, which is constant activism. You take the 15 minutes, you decide if there's someone so rotten that you wish to protect the world against him. If there is, then you vote against him, which technically means voting for the opposition.[18]

The reference to "fifteen minutes" is one of those comical quips in Chomsky's writing, which is designed to waken readers up from their slumber. Voting, sure, it's important. But the really important work isn't to elect Democrats, it's to take a longer view, towards saving the planet, and radically improving the existence of the poor, oppressed and marginalized. This longer-term perspective is evident in Chomsky's discussion of the protest movement:

> It's very easy and right to sympathize with the protestors, especially Blacks, who are victims of 400 years of vicious repression, so yes, we ought to sympathize with them. You

---

17 Ibid.
18 https://www.reddit.com/r/chomsky/comments/gvk3vv/noam_chomsky_on_george_floyd_protests_and_2020/.

could also ask, is it wise? And that extends to the other protestors. Maybe what you are doing is understandable. But is it wise? Here you have to ask the question that should be foremost in the mind of any activist: there's a difference between feel-good politics and do good politics. So you have to ask yourself: is this something that simply makes me feel good? If so, then it's just self-indulgence, forget it. Is it something that is going to advance the cause that I'm interested in? then you get serious questions. On this, we have a ton of evidence. The overwhelming evidence is that violent protests are a gift to the right. Constantly, they reinforce the Trump types. It's a gift to them, they love it. Non-violent protests are much harder, they take a lot more courage, but they succeed. They do have the effect of increasing support for the cause you are pursuing. The evidence on this is pretty strong. It's difficult. You can understand that people are so angry that they'll smash a store window or something. Understandable, but not wise.[19]

What would make Chomsky celebrate? What is a longer-term objective worthy of our efforts? A crucial one is shifting attitudes, an effort in which Chomsky's teacher Zellig Harris, and many others in his milieu, have struggled with for decades. The first step is to create awareness, and this is one of the ways in which the current protests differs from similar reactions in the past.

The public support both for Black Lives Matter and the protests is well beyond what it was, say, for Martin Luther King at the peak of his popularity, at the time of the "I Have a Dream" speech. It's also far beyond the level of public reaction to earlier police killings. It may be the most similar to the reaction to the beating of Rodney King in Los Angeles. They beat him almost to death. Most of the attackers were freed in the courts without charge. There was a week of protest; sixty people were killed, and they had to call in federal troops to quell the protests. But that was in Los Angeles. Now it's everywhere. And it's not just the police killing — it's background issues. It's beginning to move into concern, inquiries, and protests about the facts that lead to events like this occurring. This rise in consciousness is aided by the rise in consciousness of four hundred years of vicious repression.[20]

That is a remarkable observation, and it returns us to Chomsky's belief that "many years of intensive activism" are bearing fruit. Once again, though, fruit is not the defeat of the GOP in November, even if this would be a positive development. Instead, Chomsky talks about "creating the structures of mutual support and cooperation that extricate people from the governmental structures, which have been shown to be completely inadequate in dealing with particular problems, like getting water to people — more fundamental problems of why we were so desperately unprepared for the crisis."[21]

---

19 Ibid.
20 https://jacobinmag.com/2020/06/noam-chomsky-donald-trump-coronavirus-george-floyd-prote sts?fbclid=IwAR33gSj_QEzzS_WHnIcY53j5C_-6lBnwehHwQ-qxhRHitUIK_9u2O1gpaKA.
21 https://www.reddit.com/r/chomsky/comments/gvk3vv/noam_chom-sky_on_george_floyd_protests_and_2020/.

The idea of mutual support, and taking control over our own lives instead of deferring to "masters" like government authorities and corporate stooges, comes from heroic efforts undertaken in the course of important struggles by, for example, Republicans fighting fascism in the lead-up to, and course of, the Spanish Civil War, or the Wobblies demanding proper working conditions for workers in America. Sometimes activists rise up to power, as Chomsky describes in regards to President Lula in Brazil, whose presidency "initiated a new era in Brazilian history." The reaction to such events is often disheartening in the longer term, alas. In this case, Lula was jailed on trumped-up charges, and this was followed by the election of the "ultra-right fanatic [Jair Bolsonaro] who's destroying the country." The reaction to Obama's 8 years, hardly a "new era" in US history but comparatively somewhat decent compared to the murderous ways of George W. Bush, was the election of Donald Trump, who Chomsky describes as "the worst criminal in history, undeniably. There has never been a figure in political history who was so passionately dedicated to destroying the projects for organized human life on earth in the near future." Here, the real human cost of this government come to the fore, and dramatically exceed the pandemic and police violence:

> The ice sheets are melting; they're not going to recover. That leads to exponential increase in global warming. Arctic glaciers, for example, could flood the world. Recent studies indicate that on the present course, in about fifty years, much of the habitable part of the world will be unlivable. You won't be able to live in parts of South Asia, parts of the Middle East, parts of the United States. We're approaching the point of 125,000 years ago, when sea levels were about twenty-five feet higher than they are now. And it's worse than that. The Scripps Oceanographic Institute just came out with a study that estimated that we are coming ominously close to a point [similar to] 3 million years ago, when sea levels were fifty to eighty feet higher than they are today.[22]

So yes, we are in a moment of massive upheaval, and Trump, "the worst criminal in human history," needs to be overthrown, because "his minor crimes are to destroy American democracy and to amplify a pandemic killing over a hundred thousand people. But those are minor crimes by his standards."[23] But the Chomsky Approach sets sites much higher, not by looking to alternative political parties or pragmatic approaches to policy. A foray into the broader corpus of his work reveals a deep-seated interest in questions, wonder, mystery, and being surprised.

---

22 Ibid.
23 Ibid.

Most of the issues discussed in this chapter would require us to explore thousands of pages of work, from many realms and historical periods. But we can at least perceive Chomsky's approach by recalling some of the many conversations he has had over the years with curious questioners. One such conversation is in a film called *Is the Man Who is Tall Happy?*,[24] which is worth our attention in this regard because the filmmaker, Michel Gondry, asks probing questions and then follows-up on crucial issues with rather innocent replies and questions, sometimes days or weeks later. This method of interviewing over a prolonged period pushes Chomsky to make some fascinating remarks about his life, his work, and, moreover, about the creative process. I'm interested in bringing this interview to bear here because throughout the film Chomsky offers some really interesting glimpses into what motivates his thinking, and because he insists upon the value of challenging dogma and assumptions that generally are thought to be beyond question. He invokes his early childhood, and the Deweyite progressive school he attended before high school, which was "not unstructured," but which nevertheless "emphasized initiative, creativity, and working with others." Students were encouraged to pursue their own interests, and to work with others, and the result was a satisfying, stimulating and productive training which, incidentally, he remembers very well, in contrast to his high school years which he "barely remembers". Citing René Descartes, Chomsky suggests that students "should be taught to challenge and question", rather than obey and conform. Education shouldn't be "like pouring water into a vessel," but should instead be akin to "traveling upon a stream, and that's how modern science started." Most notable in this conversation is Chomsky's idea that learning occurs when we are "asking questions, and being surprised," qualities that are often repressed in religious, pedagogical, and political settings. Why is this so important? In one of those breathtakingly elegant utterances that are for me the hallmark of Chomsky's approach, he states that "the world is a very puzzling place, and if you are willing to be puzzled, you'll learn."

These kinds of statements, and they run throughout the entire Chomsky corpus, provide some sense of the value of questioning over making assumptions, or accepting the known version of things. The importance of Chomsky's biography in this sense is that it's filled with moments when he himself followed this tack. He resisted pre-packaged ideas or credos, and asked himself, early on, what the anarchists' positions were, as they resisted Franco's fascism in Spain. Or what the Kibbutz Artzi movement was in Israel, and why it was being undercut in favor of more doctrinaire approaches to political organization amongst the Kibbutzim. Or if his own teacher,

---

24   Michel Gondry, *Is the Man Who Is Tall Happy?: An Animated Conversation with Noam Chomsky*. 1h 28min., 25 November 2013 (USA).

Zellig Harris, was indeed correct to favor a structuralist approach to linguistics, given the behaviorist model of the brain that was implied by such work. He emphasizes that when he completed his PhD, he wasn't trained in any existing discipline, because his assumptions were at such variance with dominant ideas in the contemporary realm of linguistics. He speaks highly of his experiences at MIT, because the administration and faculty "didn't care" about anything other than interesting work, carried on with integrity and curiosity, rather than on the basis of pre-ordained notions. He also emphasizes the very simple questions that led him to profound insights, such as: Why do children learn language so quickly, even in the absence of huge amounts of verbal stimulus? Is it possible that children "learn" language, through practice, repetition, reward and punishment? Or might there be some biological processes involved that draw from existing species-specific mental capacity? He also looks backwards in time, to Galileo, Descartes, Humboldt and others, and finds questions posed that have for some reason been forgotten, or redirected, with unsatisfactory implications for true understanding. For him, Galileo was a revolutionary thinker, because of his willingness to be puzzled, and ultimately because he was willing to defy the authority of the Church, with all the risks that this entailed, rather than simply backing down. Newton was revolutionary because he challenged the notion that the world works like a machine, and thereby found the occult forces of attraction and repulsion. In short, says Chomsky, let's be puzzled about what seems to be obvious. And if we find something interesting in our investigations, let's pursue them, make them known, and diffuse whatever valuable knowledge we accrue along the way.

Puzzles, mysteries, courageous inquiries, and irreverent questions are all from this perspective exciting and valuable, because they can inspire creative thinking. In the film, Chomsky says that "inspiration is a mystery, from children to carpenters." He gives the example of carpenters who reached an insoluble problem, went away, and then came back and solved it. How? "We smoked some pot, and the answer came to us." He gives similar examples in his own work, when talking about taking a break from linguistics research and doing something else, like the muckraking work for which he is so well-known. He then describes returning to the problem with fresh eyes, a new perspective, and another approach. Education should teach these skills, rather than rote learning, punishment-reward, or obedience to what is most often the exercise of arbitrary authority. In other words, it's too often the case that education, and the exercise of power associated therewith, get in the way of the kinds of creativity and inspiration that truly advances knowledge. In the American context, there is also the growing overlap between education and religion (reinforced by a Supreme Court decision today, allowing states to fund religious schools[25]), in

---

25 https://www.scotusblog.com/2020/06/opinion-analysis-court-rules-that-religious-schools-cannot-be-excluded-from-state-funding-for-private-schools.

which questioning is frowned upon in favor of "faith" and obedience. The many Christian billboards that litter US highways are but a sign of that insistence upon power over inquiry, with their fearmongering and dial-an-answer mentality that has become so pervasive in US culture: ""Discover the bread of life or you're toast." "Turn or burn." "Stop, drop, and roll doesn't work in hell." "There's no air conditioning in hell." "Are you against Jesus? There will be hell to pay." "If you think it's hot in the summer, imagine hell."[26] These types of adages, easy-to-remember and devoid-of-content, are, like unproven and unprovable conspiracy theories spewed in the absence of any evidence, quite literally mind-numbing.

Authoritarianism, in all of its forms, is an attack not just on individual rights, it's also a way to undermine inquiry. Chomsky is adamant in this regard, and therefore challenges any kind of effort made to shut down inquiry. I encountered a memorable example of this in my very earliest correspondence with him, 30 years ago. I can recall the very first letter I addressed to him, in which I struggled to find the right words to address him. How should a curious young student introduce himself to Noam Chomsky? Dr.? Professor? Named Chair? All of the above? I was working on my PhD at the time, and a few months after our first exchange, I celebrated my thesis defense by adding my newly-minted title. He responded in the first line of his next letter to me: "Dear Mr. Barsky (Dr. now, I see; but titles are a pain, please drop mine)."[27] What does this mean? As he had pointed our repeatedly, the so-called 'talking-heads' that news programs use to provide expert advice on such matters as blowing up cities are usually pawns of power, and the public is inclined to accept their views simply because they often are "experts", as shown by their fancy titles and affiliations. I connected this once to a conversation I heard between two students, discussing a painful experience they had in class. One of them commented that her professor was incomprehensible, his logic was faulty, and his language garbled, "but he must be really smart, since he has a PhD". At its best, education must go beyond blind faith and acceptance of dogma on the basis of uniforms, titles, affiliations, and other superficial badges of authenticity. Chomsky made this point again, in the same letter to me, in regards to "intellectuals":

> As for political science theory, it is mostly trivialities or nonsense, as far as I know, dressed up in big words for careerist purposes. Historical studies are another matter. One can learn a lot from history, as from life, as long as it avoids the pretentious tomfoolery required by intellectuals for career and power reason. Take Foucault, whom you mention. With enough effort, one can extract from his writings some interesting insights and observations, peeling away the framework of obfuscation that is required for respectability in the strange world of intellectuals, which takes on extreme forms in the weird culture of

---

26 https://relevantmagazine.com/god/church/the-problem-with-aggressive-billboard-evangelism/.
27 Letter from Noam Chomsky to Robert Barsky, December 15, 1992.

postwar Paris. Foucault is unusual among Paris intellectuals in that at least something is left when one peels this away.[28]

These are powerful words, particularly when addressed to a graduate student in the social sciences or the humanities, given the incredibly privileged space that Foucault occupies therein. He then goes on to utter another crucial part of his approach, which is to weigh all arguments, no matter what their source, to evaluate their value:

> [My] opinion is that right-wing ideologists should be listened to carefully, and if their arguments hold up to scrutiny should be respected; I don't regard this as even a matter of dispute. I do that all the time, and often find arguments of "the right" much more impressive than those of "the left". The idea that some kinds of knowledge should be "played down because of negative implications" is one that I find a bit frightening. Who makes the decision to "play down the truth?" Who determines the "implications"? Where does that power lie, and what are its sources or its justification? I see here the road to fascism and Stalinism, ideas that have great appeal to the intellectual class – including those who call themselves anti-Stalinist, anti-fascist, liberal, etc., something I've attempted to document. True, individuals have to make their own decisions about what to "play down" and what to "play up." The marginal fringe of intellectuals who are more or less honest – the kind of "statistical error" that even the best-run system cannot avoid – the decision will be made on moral judgments as to human consequences; on that, I think, we agree. For the general run of commissars, the decision will be made on the basis of career and power interests.[29]

This was one of a plethora of insights that shook my own approach to the very core. Years later, I was struggling to complete the biography of Zellig Harris, and as I reviewed the many discussions therein of his relation to a little-known Zionist student organization called Avukah, I realized that I'd consciously resisted contacting a crucial figure associated therewith: Nathan Glazer. Almost everyone I'd interviewed about Avukah had mentioned "Nat", bemoaning how he had become such a traitor to the cause through his move to the ideological Right. And so, I avoided him, and contacted everyone else, even though they all mentioned how important he had been. So why then should I resist contacting him? When I finally did, I was treated to unparalleled insights about the era, about his role in Avukah, and about the attitudes he held so dear, all those years ago (the late 1930s and early 1940s). It had been easy to neglect his views on the basis of pre-ordained conceptions about his ideological orientation, and until I overcame that desire, to "play down" his role and ideas, the story of Avukah and Zellig Harris would remain incomplete. He was warm, generous, and truly brilliant. When I spoke with him, it was as though he was flung back in time, to the late 1930s and early 1940s, a bright-eyed kid excited by the ideas of this

---

28 Ibid.
29 Ibid.

radical organization, ideas which he later came to jettison, but which were nonetheless still vivid in his mind.

This leads us once again to the idea of questions, questioning, and deciding that some ideas, approaches or individuals are "beyond question", which is exactly what Chomsky challenges. Some questions are uncomfortable and difficult, and some ideas fly in the face of what we want to believe. Furthermore, there are some really unsavory people who espouse ideas that are in disaccord with our own beliefs, and it's really tempting to simply avoid confronting or challenging them. Chomsky's approach is to confront them head-on, particularly if they pose serious challenges, lest we land up in the religious billboard version of reality, where doubt or mystery or questions are confronted with images of pain, suffering, and burning. Chomsky makes this point once again in his correspondence with me, this time in regards to the question of how we "frame" knowledge:

> The idea of "framing of knowledge" in accord with our social goals is, again, a frightening one, fit only for totalitarians, in my opinion. Sorry to sound harsh, but I am sure you prefer honesty. The facts are what they are. An honest person will not shape them to be what he or she would prefer. To go back to an earlier discussion, the reason I find the intellectual environment of the sciences so much healthier than that of the social "sciences" and humanities is that there, these truisms are understood to be truisms.[30]

The effect of such words, uttered by someone like Chomsky, was for me a kind of liberation. Rather than being browbeaten into belief, Chomsky advocates for real questions, and irreverence in the face of arbitrary authority. His work is a catalyst for inquiry, in my opinion, because he inspires questioning, and refuses pre-packaged, pre-ordained ideas and untethered niceties. Returning to the aforementioned film *Is the Man Who Is Tall Happy*, released 25 years later, we find Chomsky expressing similar sentiments in regards to a future society: "We should be seeking out forms of authority and domination and challenging their legitimacy, needed for survival. Any form of coercion that requires justification. At various stages of civilization, it has been possible to challenge the forms of authority and domination that don't have legitimacy and attack fundamental human rights."

In another letter to Chomsky that I wrote in 1992, I mentioned that Pierre Bourdieu's book called *Language and Symbolic Power*[31] had been important for me, since it helped me to recognize the ways in which subtle cues, like accent or personality, influence our sense of what is being said. I had thought that there was an interesting connection between Bourdieu and Chomsky, since they both had overt desires to challenge the kind of authority that suffocates, shoots, or bashes in the skulls of dissenters. He agreed, but without much enthusiasm at the time:

---

30 Ibid.
31 *Pierre Bourdieu, Language and Symbolic Power*. Translation and Introduction by John Thompson. Cambridge, Harvard University Press, 1992.

Doubtless there is a power structure in every speech situation; again, that is a truism that only an intellectual could find surprising, and seek to dress up in appropriate polysyllables. As honest people, our effort should be to unmask it and diminish it, as far as we can, and to do so in association with others, whom we can help and who can help us with this necessary liberator task. Will it ever end? I presume not.

I was disappointed that Chomsky didn't share my enthusiasm about Bourdieu, a powerful thinker whose work I found complementary to the Chomsky approach. Years later, I was gratified to read an endorsement of Bourdieu's book *Firing Back,* in which Chomsky wrote: "Bourdieu once again selects the right targets and, as always, has much to say that is incisive and enlightening."

Shortly after these life-changing exchanges with Noam Chomsky, I was awarded a postdoctoral fellowship for research at the Université libre de Bruxelles, with the contemporary Belgian philosopher Michel Meyer. It was in Brussels that I eventually wrote the first draft of my biography of Chomsky, while studying Meyer's work on Problematology and questioning. With all of these years of hindsight, I'm realizing now that there's an interesting overlap between the two projects, relating to this oft-repeated invocation of inquiry, investigation, and questioning. Meyer's work focuses on philosophy, and the way in which questions have been relegated to a secondary position relative to assertions. To advance this project, Meyer has created the realm of "Problematology" as a means of maintaining the philosopher's focus on the guiding question, even as she proposes some resolution to it. I will provide a brief foray into this area, because I think it might be a powerful complement to Chomsky's approach. I will then conclude with a final rumination on the kind of society or social compendium that could be propitious to the work that Chomsky, and also Meyer, are proposing.

An Approach to Questioning

Michel Meyer is best known for this work on *problematology*, the study of questioning, and for *Le Philosophe et les Passions,*[32] his overview of the interaction between reason and passion in the corpus of major philosophical works. His work in the domain problematology, fully articulated in *De La Problématologie,*[33] is, like his work on rhetorics and passions, well known in Europe, where sales of his books number in the tens of thousands. He proposes by this approach to literally re-view the tradi-

---

32 See Michel Meyer, *Philosophy and the Passions*, translation, preface and introduction by Robert F. Barsky. Penn State University Press, 2000.
33 *Of Problematology: Philosophy, Science and Language*, translated by David Jamison, with the collaboration of Alan Hart, Chicago UP, 1995. Some of the prose in the following three paragraphs is derived from an introduction I wrote to: Robert F. Barsky, translation, preface and introduction. Michel Meyer, *Philosophy and the Passions*, Penn State University Press, 2000.

tion of radical questioning, which dates back to the earliest philosophical texts, but which has been undermined or ignored as "philosophical attention has been directed to language and discourse".[34] The implications of this work as we consider Chomsky's approach to questioning and inquiry are fascinating, for "in so changing, philosophy has ended up renouncing itself, so to speak, in favour of superficial topics, exhibiting a lack of rigor which has made possible the most esoteric word games" (2). Chomsky too has bemoaned the "word games" of postmodern writings, and challenged the obfuscation of intellectuals' writings, particularly in the social sciences. Meyer's rigorous philosophical work seems in this regard and others as an interesting complement to that of Chomsky. And it is all the more viable today, it would seem, in a critical and philosophical scene which lacks not only a central set of questions, but even some common ground for debate and discovery. This is not helped by ongoing attacks on the liberal arts and humanistic inquiry, and, moreover, it reflects an ever-widening engagement with Artificial Intelligence which Chomsky, a pioneer of the field, considers deeply problematic.[35]

All of Meyer's writings have a strong basis in the history of ideas, which makes them useful for those interested in situating issues in question within an appropriate philosophical tradition (as Chomsky does in such a memorable fashion in his remarkable book called *Cartesian Linguistics*[36]). For example, Meyer traces the roots of Problematology and questioning to Ancient Greece, but then tracks the ways in which radical questioning has been repressed in favor of propositions, assertions and unproven solutions. This leads to a paradox, one of many indicated in Meyer's writings: "A swift survey of history should suffice to convince us that questioning has never been the central theme of philosophy. Yet philosophy would never have developed nor been able to survive without resorting to questioning in practice. This is how questioning, by failing to thematize itself, was displaced and directed towards objectives outside itself".[37]

Meyer thus suggests that we cast a new look upon the history of philosophical practices, and that we consider the debilitating effect that the autonomization of answers as propositions has had; notably, it has led to the subordination of the idea of resolution to what he calls the *propositional model* of reason. In this sense, his work is an ambitious project that emerges in the face of the "betrayal" of philosophy, and responds to "the need to restore to it a principle and remove its ontologization, realizing that its deepest reality is not only in questioning, but in *radical* questioning, if

---

34   Ibid. 1.
35   See the fascinating debate between Peter Norvig and Noam Chomsky, recalled at: https://www.tor.com/2011/06/21/norvig-vs-chomsky-and-the-fight-for-the-future-of-ai
36   Noam Chomsky, *Cartesian Linguistics: A Chapter in the History of Rationalist Thought*, Cambridge, Cambridge UP, 2009.
37   *Of Problematology* (n 34) op. cit. 16.

we want it not to be altered into some kind of occult answer".[38] David Jamison, an important intermediary for the American intellectual setting, gives some indication of the breadth of Meyer's project:

> Meyer has constructed a theory of problematology which focuses on the interrogativity of the mind. His abiding concern in all his major writings with the phenomenon of questioning is consistent, he feels, with the developing interest in this subject by students of logic, philosophy, psychology and anthropology. With some of these scholars he has come to believe that questioning is 'the fundamental reality of the human mind, to which all other intellectual powers are connected'. It is, in short, 'the basic principle of thought itself, the philosophical project *par excellence*'.[39]

The work that remains to be done is, according to Meyer, vast, because the philosophical project has been inappropriately cast for thousands of years, so that now, "by constantly posing questions in a non-problematological way, philosophy has not questioned questioning, but has instead turned elsewhere, placing itself in competition with science, which, by the way, it has nonetheless made possible"[40].

The solution that Meyer proposes is dramatic: he calls for a return to the idea, begun but not pursued since Socrates and Plato, that interrogativity is the highest value of thought. Indeed, says Jamison, Meyer believes that in the dialogues, Plato "gradually but perceptibly moved toward the belief that questions held a subordinate position to that of answers".[41] To prove such a thing, Meyer must in *Of Problematology* rehearse the history of philosophical work on dialectics, questioning, rationality, meaning, logos, and scientific knowledge, and then propose a new approach: "It is time we restored philosophy to its natural function, which is metaphysical, thanks to problematological conception, if we want to arrive at an understanding of how thought takes root and grows. It is high time to abandon the sterile philosophical arguments which have... been part of the Kantian heritage."[42] It's fascinating to consider the force of this objective from the perspective of the thought process that he describes. The quests to understand how thought "takes root", and how it "grows", are both connected to the most powerful questions that Chomsky poses, in terms of what defines humans as creative beings.

In "The Nature of Problematic Knowledge", Meyer evaluates the use of language as a means of understanding and resolving problems. He writes that "communication is meant to put forward solutions to given and shared problems, to arouse the interest in such problems, to avoid the problemalization of the propounded solutions, or more simply, to require the solution from the addressee to whom the problem is then

38 Ibid. 9.
39 James L. Golden and David L. Jamison, "Meyer's Theory of Problematology", *Questioning Exchange* 2.2 (1988): 149-163, p. 149.
40 Ibid. 12.
41 Ibid. 151.
42 Ibid. 19.

expressed." The problem for philosophy, and indeed for the society at large, is that "the stability of the world is, as Hume suggested, nothing other than the repetition of the answers. Such a repetition gives us the impression that nothing is really problematic, simply because we seem to already have the solution before the question arises."[43] Meyer traces the history of this approach back to the Greeks, who shaped human thought "in the propositional model, which ignores questioning and its constitutive difference between questions and answers," so that "problematicity, when coming to the fore, was seen as evil." Plato, writes Meyer, "focused on answerhood as the elimination of problems. This means that answerhood is considered in itself, and not in reference to questions." As a consequence, "answers have become propositions, questioning has disappeared as sophistic or eristic, at any rate as the opposite of knowledge. Propositionalism looked for the truth of propositions in their justifiability (through other propositions) or in their auto-justifiability (through evidence or intuition), not in their relationship to given problems."[44]

All of this gives the sense that inquiry proceeds on the basis of evaluating propositions, because all answers are known in advance, and need only be reiterated. Nothing could be further from the Chomsky Approach.

Promoting Chomsky's Approach

The very basis of Meyer's Problematology is that answers and assertions and propositions all have the effect of eradicating the impulse that led to the exploration in the first place. It seems to me that if a branch of philosophy was devoted entirely to questioning and Problematology, the very idea of inquiry and study would shift, and the arrogance of assertions uttered authoritatively but without proper evidence, in realms of complex debate, would be challenged. Meyer's approach to Problematology, and his inquiries into questioning, would be helpful in this regard because it produces a series of questions relating to the "process of research and language use, ranging from conversational dialogue to the interpretation of literature". The rigor of his work, and the radical nature of his inquiry, provides some fascinating insights into the questioning to which Chomsky refers throughout his work, the questioning that refuses the many ways in which complex problems and sometimes unresolvable questions can be willed away with unjustifiable propositions. How might this bear upon the challenges we now face, as Americans seek to reconcile themselves to its racist past, and chart a course forward on the basis of newfound widespread dissent?

---

43 Michel Meyer, "The Nature of Problematic Knowledge" in *Questions and Questioning.* De Gruyter, 2011, 3.
44 Ibid.

My desire to connect Chomsky's comments about current events to his resistance of arbitrary authority, and then to think about this connection in light of Meyer's promotion of radical questioning, is to think about a desirable weigh-station en route to a good society. I think that the question that brings this entire discussion together could be formulated as follows: What kind of social organization is best suited to the kind of inquiry and investigation that Chomsky found in his earliest days, at the Dewey-inspired school he attended as a child, and what can we learn by connecting it to Meyer's work on questioning and Problematology? And what can we learn to-day from descriptions of possible worlds that are described by the many historical works that both Chomsky and Meyer invoke in their respective research projects? One way to begin what would be a massive overview of historical works is to con-sider a fascinating rumination on anarchism, in the course of which Chomsky cites the work of Michael Bakunin:

> I am a fanatic lover of liberty, considering it as the unique condition under which intelli-gence, dignity and human happiness can develop and grow; not the purely formal liberty conceded, measured out and regulated by the State, an eternal lie which in reality repre-sents nothing more than the privilege of some founded on the slavery of the rest; not the individualistic, egoistic, shabby, and fictitious liberty extolled by the School of J.-J. Rousseau and other schools of bourgeois liberalism, which considers the would-be rights of all men, represented by the State which limits the rights of each—an idea that leads inevitably to the reduction of the rights of each to zero. No, I mean the only kind of liber-ty that is worthy of the name, liberty that consists in the full development of all the mate-rial, intellectual and moral powers that are latent in each person; liberty that recognizes no restrictions other than those determined by the laws of our own individual nature, which cannot properly be regarded as restrictions since these laws are not imposed by any outside legislator beside or above us, but are immanent and inherent, forming the very basis of our material, intellectual and moral being—they do not limit us but are the real and immediate conditions of our freedom.[45]

This wonderful description provides the many interconnected layers that contribute to a liberating whole. Bakunin's emphasis is upon growth, development, creativity and the realization of individual and collective potential. These are the kinds pro-cesses that are promoted when instruments of repression and illegitimate authority are lifted, because they are latent in each and every person. Integrating insights from Meyer at this point, we can see how Propositionalism could itself be a form of re-pression, in the sense that it represses questions in favor of assertions, thus crushing the power of questioning. This has important implications in the realm of pedagogy, at all levels. Citing Bakunin, Chomsky often suggests that education drives curiosity, questioning and creativity out of students by encouraging them to compete with one another for grades, rather than explore ideas and insights.

---

45 Noam Chomsky, *The Essential Chomsky*, edited by Anthony Arnove, New York/London, New Press, 2008, p. 96.

It is sadly often true that rather than acting as stimulators of creative exploration, teachers rely upon authority, coercion, molding, punishing and rewarding as tools to instruct their students. According to this approach, teachers are authority figures who must be obeyed, because they are purveyors of truth who are charged with infusing knowledge and information. The guiding assumption for such an approach is that we all begin our lives with "blank slates" for brains, and as such we are malleable, and we need to be guided by an authority figure who will mould our thinking appropriately. Bakunin's approach, like those of early Wilhelm von Humboldt or Rudolph Rocker, challenge this pervasive conception of teaching by celebrating instead the unleashing of potential, and the catalyzing of creative impulses latent in all of us. A first step in this process is radical questioning and the dismantling of forces that favor and reproduce arbitrary authority.

Conclusion

Radical questioning stimulated in a rich and diverse environment free of coercion and arbitrary authority produces an environment in which revelations, realizations, and creativity are more apt to grow. Each of those whose comments we've surveyed in regards to the current protests in the US provide powerful examples of how to resist, and how to articulate that resistance in the face of the belligerence, intractability, self-satisfaction and self-aggrandizement of the ruling class. Each of them favor of freedom from oppression in all forms, as a means of unleashing the potential that is being crushed by classism, racism, and ideas of White Supremacy.

Interestingly, in his work on questioning and problematological thinking Michel Meyer finds considerable enlightenment in fictional texts, particularly those of the modern era.[46] In fact, throughout his entire corpus of writings Meyer mentions the interrogative power of fiction as a means of moving beyond the confines of propositions and assertions. I've discussed literary knowledge with Chomsky as well, because literature has different stakes in particular debates, and isn't tied to particular claims in the way that we see in the social "sciences". Marc Angenot[47] has described literature as a kind of 'fool', like the fools in Shakespeare's plays, for example, who can fearlessly challenge knowledge claims based exclusively on power rather than knowledge.[48] With this image of authorized dissent in mind, it seems to me that there is much to be learned from brilliant fiction. For the realms we have been dis-

---

46 See Michel Meyer, *Meaning and Reading*. Amsterdam and Philadelphia, John Benjamins, 1983.
47 See *Marc Angenot and the Scandal of History*, *Yale Journal of Criticism* Volume 17, Number 2, Fall 2004; Special Issue: Guest Editor: Robert F. Barsky.
48 See Robert F. Barsky, *The Chomsky Effect: A Radical Works Beyond the Ivory Tower.* Cambidge, MA: The MIT Press, 2011.

cussing, it seems particularly valuable to look to works written by such writers as James Baldwin, Richard Wright, Alice Walker or Toni Morrison, for through their stories we can enter into the lived lives of African Americans as they struggle to make sense of and challenge an inhospitable America. But of course, this is only part of the complex story unfolding now on the streets of American cities, and here, the many commentators we've mentioned, provide invaluable assistance. As we've seen, Heather Anne Thompson and Ta-Nehisi Coates offer some powerful historical details regarding this moment in relation to similar times of struggle and resistance. Cornel West and Henry Louis Gates provide us with historical, philosophical and political insights that draw from lived experiences spread across generations, and swathes of American spaces. Angela Davis brings us into the streets, where she courageously rises up against instruments and systems of oppression, using power of insight and persuasion. Each of these great writers deserves our close attention as we seek ways of engaging, and moving the progressive agenda forward.

At the end of the day, I think it fair to suggest that Chomsky's Approach combines different elements of these writers and activists, adding insights derived from investigations rooted in the science of the mind, alongside of wide-ranging consideration of those who have creatively challenged repressive, status quo thinking. His giant corpus considers the impediments to processes of liberation, challenges the legitimacy of institutions and officials in power, and promotes work that frees the inherent potential for creative and progressive work that we all possess. His words are resolutely uncompromising, for these are not matters of passing importance, and he helps us to understand the value of wide-ranging inquiry into questions as complex as racial inequality and the exercise of arbitrary authority. As we descend back into the streets of the US in this moment, or to any areas of resistance in a world held fast in the grips of neoliberalism, capitalism, and the suicidal quest for ever-rising profit, Chomsky's approach would have us keep such objectives in mind. They help us to go beyond the immediacy of the current "mess", and into a more glorious future than the one whose track we are all following now, in which the final stations can only be class war, racial tension and, ultimately, catastrophic environmental destruction.

Bibliography

Angenot, Marc, 2004: *Marc Angenot and the Scandal of History, Yale Journal of Criticism* Volume 17, Number 2, Fall; Special Issue: Guest Editor: Robert F. Barsky.
Barsky, Robert F., 2000: Translation, preface and introduction of Michel Meyer, *Philosophy and the Passions*, Penn State University Press.
Barsky, Robert F. and Noam *Chomsky*, 1992: *Letter from Noam Chomsky to Robert Barsky*, December 15.

Barsky, Robert F., 2011: *The Chomsky Effect: A Radical Works Beyond the Ivory Tower.* Cambidge, MA: The MIT Press.

Bourdieu, Pierre, 1992: *Language and Symbolic Power.* Translation and Introduction by John Thompson. Cambridge, Harvard University Press.

Chomsky, Noam, 2009: *Cartesian Linguistics: A Chapter in the History of Rationalist Thought.* Cambridge, Cambridge UP.

--, 2008: *The Essential Chomsky*, edited by Anthony Arnove. New York/London, New Press.

Golden, James L. and David L. *Jamison*, 1988: "Meyer's Theory of Problematology", *Questioning Exchange* 2.2: 149-163.

Gondry, Michel, 2013: *Is the Man Who Is Tall Happy? An Animated Conversation with Noam Chomsky.* Documentary, 1h 28min. 25 November 2013, USA.

Meyer, Michel, 1983: *Meaning and Reading.* Amsterdam and Philadelphia, John Benjamins.

--, 1995: *Of Problematology: Philosophy, Science and Language*, translated by David Jamison, with the collaboration of Alan Hart, Chicago UP.

--, 2011: *Questions and Questioning.* De Gruyter.

The Authors

Robert Barsky is the author of numerous works about Noam Chomsky and his milieus, including a trilogy of books with the MIT Press called "Noam Chomsky: A Life of Dissent"; "The Chomsky Effect: A Radical Works Beyond the Ivory Tower", and "Zellig Harris: From American Linguistics to Socialist Zionism". Barsky is now working on a book and documentary film about the Zionist organization Avukah, which was an important influence within the milieus of Harris and Chomsky. He is a Professor at Vanderbilt University, and holds a Canada Research Chair (2019-20).

Željko Bošković is Professor of Linguistics and Faculty in the Cognitive Science Program at the University of Connecticut. His research interests include syntactic theory, comparative syntax and generative typology, and the relationship between language and broader cognitive mechanisms. He is the author of "The Syntax of Nonfinite Complementation: An Economy Approach" (1997, MIT Press), "On the Nature of the Syntax-Phonology Interface: Cliticization and Related Phenomena" (2001, Elsevier), and "Minimalist Syntax: The Essential Readings" (with H. Lasnik, 2006, Blackwell).

Jean Bricmont is a retired professor at the Physics Department, Université catholique de Louvain, Belgium. Research: mathematical and statistical physics, foundations of quantum mechanics. Titles: "Fashionable Nonsense", New York: Picador, 1998 (with Alan Sokal). "Humanitarian Imperialism: Using Human Rights to Sell War", Monthly Review Press, 2007, "Chomsky Notebook", edited with Julie Franck, Columbia University Press, 2010, "Making Sense of Quantum Mechanics", Springer, 2016.

Günther Grewendorf is a retired professor of linguistics at the Johann Wolfgang Goethe-University Frankfurt/Main. His research focuses on generative syntax, philosophy of language and forensic linguistics. His works include "Ergativity in German" (1989, Foris), "Sprache als Organ - Sprache als Lebensform", (1995, Suhrkamp, Greek translation: 1999), "Minimalistische Syntax" (2002, Francke: UTB), "Noam Chomsky" (2006, Beck), "Formal Linguistics and Law" (ed. with Monika Rathert) (Mouton de Gruyter, 2009), "Remnant Movement" (ed. 2015, Mouton de Gruyter).

Georg Meggle is Professor emeritus in Philosophy at the University of Leipzig. Since his retirement (2009) he teaches at the Al Azhar University and now at the AUC (American University) in Cairo, and in the summer term at the University of Salzburg. His main topics: Philosophy of Communication and Language ("Grundbegriffe der Kommunikation", 1981; "Handlungstheoretische Semantik", 2010); Logics and Ethics of Terrorism ("Ethics of Terrorism" & Counter-Terrorism, 2005); Deterrence, Deception and Collateral Damage. Presently he is also working on some other contested concepts (Antisemitism, Fake News etc.). He is founder and Honorary President of GAP (Society for Analytical Philosophy).

Milan Rai is an independent researcher, the editor of "Peace News", a radical nonviolence project based in London. His main research interests are British nuclear diplomacy in relation to the Global South, the Chomsky-Herman Propaganda Model, and revolutionary nonviolence. He is the author of "Chomsky's Politics" (1995, Verso), "War Plan Iraq" (2002, Verso) and "7/7: The London Bombings, Islam and the Iraq War" (2006, Pluto) among other titles.

Tom Roeper has worked for 45 years primarily in the areas of language acquisition and morphology. This work has extended into Applied areas of Communication Disorders and Second Language Acquisition. It includes a book "The Prism of Grammar" (MIT Press) aimed at parents and teachers, and a co-authored test for disorders (DELV-Diagnostic evaluation of language variation) aimed at African-American English. He has taught courses in Europe, South America, Africa and Asia on these topics. The Prism volume seeks to articulate a connection between linguistic theory and anarchism. He has also been active in progressive political movements from the Civil Rights movement to the Sanctuary movement in the US. He worked as a Civil Rights' worker in Mississippi in 1965 where he taught Freedom School.

Michael Schiffmann is a linguist, cultural scientist, translator, editor and author and teaches linguistics at the University of Heidelberg. He is working on a research project on the history of Noam Chomsky's generative grammar and is active in international campaigns to free political prisoners such as Mumia Abu-Jamal, Leonard Peltier, and Abdullah Öcalan. His translations into German include works by Mumia Abu-Jamal, Homi K. Bhabha, Noam Chomsky, Mahmoud Darwish, Angela Davis, and Edward Said. He is the editor and author of the book "absolute Noam Chomsky" (2004/2008) and has written a number of articles on Chomsky's political and linguistic work. His most recent translation is Chomsky's "Internationalism or Extinction" (2020) (in German as "Rebellion oder Untergang" (2021)).

Juan Uriagereka (University of Maryland) is a syntactician with a broad interest in biolinguistics and social change. His works include "Structure" (forthcoming, with H. Lasnik, MIT Press), "Biolinguistic Investigations and the Formal Language Hierarchy" (2018, Routledge), "Spell-out and the Minimalist Program" (2012, Oxford), and (as co-editor, with M. Piattelli-Palmarini & P. Salaburu) "Of Minds and Language: A Dialogue with Noam Chomsky in the Basque Country" (2009, MIT Press).

Bereits erschienen in der Reihe STAATSVERSTÄNDNISSE

Freund-Feind-Denken
Carl Schmitts Kategorie des Politischen
von Prof. em. Dr. Rüdiger Voigt, *2021, Bd. 144*

Staat und Zivilgesellschaft
Permanente Opposition oder konstruktives Wechselspiel?
hrsg. von Dr. Andreas Nix, *2020, Bd. 143*

Populismus, Diskurs, Staat
hrsg. von Dr. Seongcheol Kim und Aristotelis Agridopoulos, *2020, Bd. 141*

Staatskritik und Radikaldemokratie
Das Denken Jacques Rancières
hrsg. von von Dr. Mareike Gebhardt, *2020, Bd. 140*

Das Jahrhundert Voltaires
Vordenker der europäischen Aufklärung
hrsg. von Prof. Dr. Norbert Campagna und Prof. em. Dr. Rüdiger Voigt, *2020, Bd. 139*

Legitimität des Staates
hrsg. von Prof. Dr. Tobias Herbst und Dr. Sabrina Zucca-Soest, *2020, Bd. 138*

Staatsprojekt Europa
Eine staatstheoretische Perspektive auf die Europäische Union
hrsg. von Dr. Daniel Keil und Prof. Dr. Jens Wissel, *2019, Bd. 137*

Verfassung ohne Staat
Gunther Teubners Verständnis von Recht und Gesellschaft
hrsg. von Prof. Dr. Lars Viellechner, LL.M. (Yale), *2019, Bd. 136*

Politischer und wirtschaftlicher Liberalismus
Das Staatsverständnis von Adam Smith
hrsg. von Prof. Dr. Hendrik Hansen und Tim Kraski, Lic., M.A., *2019, Bd. 135*

Von Staat zu Staatlichkeit
Beiträge zu einer multidisziplinären Staatlichkeitswissenschaft
hrsg. von Prof. em. Dr. Gunnar Folke Schuppert, *2019, Bd. 134*

Theories of Modern Federalism
hrsg. von Dr. Skadi Siiri Krause, *2019, Bd. 133*

Die Sophisten
Ihr politisches Denken in antiker und zeitgenössischer Gestalt
hrsg. von Prof. Dr. Barbara Zehnpfennig, *2019, Bd. 132*

Die Verfassung der Jakobiner von 1793 und ihr historischer Kontext
Von Dr. Andreas Heyer, *2019, Bd. 131*

Überzeugungen, Wandlungen und Zuschreibungen
Das Staatsverständnis Otto von Bismarcks
hrsg. von Prof. Dr. Ulrich Lappenküper und Dr. Ulf Morgenstern, *2019, Bd. 130*

Repräsentation
Eine Schlüsselkategorie der Demokratie
hrsg. von Prof. Dr. Rüdiger Voigt, *2019, Bd. 129*

---

weitere Bände unter: www.nomos-shop.de